Louisiana Hayride

AMERICAN MUSICSPHERES

Series Editor
Mark Slobin

Fiddler on the Move
Exploring the Klezmer World
Mark Slobin

The Lord's Song in a Strange Land
Music and Identity in Contemporary Jewish Worship
Jeffrey A. Summit

Lydia Mendoza's Life in Music
Yolanda Broyles-González

Four Parts, No Waiting
A Social History of American Barbershop Harmony
Gage Averill

Louisiana Hayride
Radio and Roots Music Along the Red River
Tracey E. W. Laird

LOUISIANA HAYRIDE

Radio and Roots Music Along the Red River

Tracey E. W. Laird

OXFORD

UNIVERSITY PRESS

2005

OXFORD
UNIVERSITY PRESS

Oxford   New York
Auckland   Bangkok   Buenos Aires   Cape Town   Chennai
Dar es Salaam   Delhi   Hong Kong   Istanbul   Karachi   Kolkata
Kuala Lumpur   Madrid   Melbourne   Mexico City   Mumbai   Nairobi
São Paolo   Shanghai   Taipei   Tokyo   Toronto

Published by Oxford University Press, Inc.
198 Madison Avenue, New York, New York 10016

www.oup.com

Oxford is a registered trademark of Oxford University Press

Library of Congress Cataloging-in-Publication Data
Laird, Tracey E. W.
Louisiana hayride : radio and roots music along the red river /
Tracey E. W. Laird.
p. cm.—(American Musicspheres)
Includes bibliographical references.
Discography: p.
ISBN–13 978–0–19–516751–1
ISBN 0–19–516751–1
1. Country music—Louisiana—History and criticism.
2. Louisiana hayride (Radio program) I. Title.
ML3524.L29   2005
781.642'09763'99—dc22   2004014612

2   4   6   8   9   7   5   3

Printed in the United States of America
on acid-free paper

For Sir B, and a future great

Preface

This book is about music, race, media, commerce, and place. As the title suggests, the narrative comes to fruition with a discussion of the *Louisiana Hayride*, Shreveport's radio barn dance on station KWKH from 1948 to 1960—a forum for musical innovation that shaped the future of both country music and rock-and-roll. But the book covers more ground than that. In my consideration, the *Hayride* acts as a centerpiece for the larger ethnomusicological question of how intersecting forces of geography, history, demography, and economics shaped the character of the region and, thus, set the stage for this unique radio program of singular influence.

The seeds for this book first took root during my graduate study in Michigan. As a native Louisianan, I found the intangible differences of speech rhythms and body language in the Midwest unsettling. This sense of disquiet led me to questions of place: What molds the personality and culture of a particular locale? More specifically, what about my hometown of Shreveport informed my perspective on music in a regionally definitive way? Two answers came to mind: the Red River and the close proximity of Shreveport's black and white citizens.

The Red River midwifed Shreveport during the nineteenth century and remained the focus of business and pleasure there for several decades afterward. Although the river's role was slight for most of the 1900s, that role metamorphosed twice over at century's end. Casino riverboats arrived at Shreveport, permanently docked on the Red River, and gave rise to a new riverfront entertainment district. And the Army Corps of Engineers completed a decades-long lock and dam project, which reopened the river as a working commercial port. Whether active or not, the Red River indelibly marks the spirit of the region and its people's sense of place.

Place in the South inexorably invokes race. As a child of integration in a region where blacks and whites live in near equal numbers, I grew to realize that the two groups share much in common—most importantly, a twisted and tragic history apart, along with a hope for a better future together. I would not presume that a small exploration of one aspect of roots music might help to heal the social or political wounds that are slavery's legacy; but if my work were perceived in a spirit of healing, I would be pleased. In the same year I was born, Tony Russell wrote the following in *Blacks, Whites, and Blues:* "Indeed, the only way to understand fully the various folk musics of America is to see them as units in a whole; as traditions with, to be sure, a certain degree of independence, but possessing an overall unity.[1] Russell's words stayed with me as I wrote this story about a white country music barn dance in postwar northwest Louisiana, and they return every time I encounter music and musicians who refuse to stay neat and tidy in the black-and-white musical categories handed down from commerce to academic discourse. In the following exploration of roots music, I always try to call attention to places where the boundaries between white and black musical cultures have subtly, surely eroded.

In addition to place and race, this book addresses twentieth-century media, specifically the Shreveport radio station KWKH. When I returned to Shreveport in 1995 to begin studying the musical history of the river town in which I grew up, I knew the *Louisiana Hayride* would figure prominently. Therefore, I began tuning into the still-vital 50,000-watt "Voice of the Ark-La-Tex" KWKH, the station that broadcast the historic show. One day I won a call-in radio contest and joined the KWKH morning announcing team as "DJ for a Day." I emphasized my best microphone low tones, regaled the announcers with ideas about my project, and with great delight took a part-time job as a disc jockey, mostly weekends and fill-ins for regular deejays, and mostly on the AM side of the AM-FM station.

KWKH-AM broadcast the old-time country music, as well as regular local and farm news. Larry Scott, one of country music's best-known disc jockeys, still hosted his night-fly country show, keeping bleary-eyed truckers awake on Interstate 20. I recall him lugging in milk crates full of his personal album collection every night. Although I worked at the station only six months, I was thrilled by spinning old Floyd Tillman and Bob Wills wax and by feeling a part of history at the radio station whose importance in country music I was only beginning to understand. I grew up familiar with much of the music I played on KWKH, but had never given it much thought before then.

By the time I ended my brief disc jockey career, I newly appreciated the significance of KWKH, its unique geographic location in Shreveport, and the singularity of its postwar barn dance, the *Louisiana Hayride*. From this, my interest spread to the background of the area itself, the context in which the *Hayride* developed, the history of media of which KWKH was part, and the revolution in American culture that followed World War II. Only against this backdrop do the details of the *Louisiana Hayride*'s operation and the procession of key players across its stage take on their full meaning.

More than anything else, I hope that I have presented a model for a study of a southern river city, the way that the facts of its history relate to the musical products of its culture. In researching the history, listening to the music, and talking to the people who were there, I know how many more stories are left to tell in cities like Shreveport, Louisiana, outside of the established music meccas of Nashville, New York, and Los Angeles. Shreveport is just one of many maverick cities with a history of nurturing influential musicians who have, in turn, made enduring contributions to U.S. music and culture. Country music is the most obvious example of this but, again, it is only one of the complex creations born from the whole of southern culture. Like every other aspect of the South, country music on the *Louisiana Hayride* is not easily reduced to its geographic or cultural origins, its racial and social milieu, or its importance in U.S. society. My study here hopes to be faithful to the cultural gestalt of the South and, in so doing, cast a new die.

Many people have helped see this project through and I would like to mention some of them here. I wish to acknowledge my indebtedness to the writers and researchers cited in these pages, whose individual efforts informed my current understanding of country music and rock-and-roll. The scholars who more personally directed my education each strengthened and guided my work in immeasurable ways. They include University of Michigan professors Judith Becker, Rich Crawford, Steven Whiting, and Paul Anderson. I also thank my Ann Arbor colleagues and friends including Laird and Rose Pruiksma, Kit and Denise Taylor, Amy Beal and Ralf Dietrich, Kyra Gaunt, H. K. Chae, Susan Walton, and Jennifer DeLapp.

I am grateful to Mark Slobin for overseeing this project—it is a great honor to be associated with his work and the work of other contributors to the American Musicspheres series. I especially appreciate the patience, clarity of thought, and insightful feedback from Kim Robinson at Oxford University Press and the gracious assistance from Eve Bachrach as well. I thank the production team who saw the book through its final stages, and especially Bob Milks, who guided the process with a strong eye for detail. The professionalism and responsiveness of everyone I encountered at Oxford have made this undertaking a pleasure.

In addition, I am grateful to all the individuals who agreed to personal interviews, offering the insights one can only gain from being there: the late Stedman Gunning, Frank Page, Jerry Kennedy, D. J. Fontana, Stan Lewis, Sleepy Brown, Tillman Franks, Jean and Ruth Harkness, Homer Bailes, Sonny Harville, Billy Walker, Jimmy C. Newman, Joe Osborn, Ray Bartlett, Jim Ed, Maxine, and Bonnie Brown, Tony Douglas, Jimmy Lee Fautheree, Ernest Ferguson, Ray Hendricks, James O'Gwynn, Roy Sneed, Mallie Ann Stilley, Ann Stuckey, Margaret Lewis Warwick, Johnnie Wright, Kitty Wells, and Bob Sullivan.

I deeply appreciate Rachel Stone, who, at a critical early stage of my research, entrusted me with a box of tapes from her *Sunday Stage* radio show, including her own interviews with significant players in Shreveport's local music scene. Her conversations with Homer Bailes, Sleepy Brown, Jimmy Lee Fautheree and "Country" Johnny Mathis, Tillman Franks, Murrell Stansell, Felton "Preacher" Harkness and Jack Green, and Joe Osborn helped me to develop my thoughts and prepare some of my own interviews. I appreciate further help from KWKH deejay Barney Cannon. I thank Maggie and Alton Warwick for their gracious willingness to help out with information and photographs, and Joey Kent for his enthusiasm and knowledge of the *Hayride* and Shreveport's musical heritage.

The kindness, knowledge, and support of the staff of the Noel Memorial Library at Louisiana State University-Shreveport are extraordinary. I am especially indebted to Archives staff members Domenica Carriere, Laura Conerly, and Glenda Sharbonne, along with Gene Romaine in Interlibrary Loan and Carla Clark for help early on. I also thank the Shreve Memorial Library Louisiana Room staff, Northwestern State University in Natchitoches, Centenary College's music librarian, Ron Bukoff, and Shreve Memorial reference librarian Jennifer Head. At Nashville's Country Music Foundation, I encountered helpful guidance early on from Ronnie Pugh, as well as from Alan Stoker, John Rumble, and later, Dawn Oberg. The library staff at Agnes Scott College provided efficient Interlibrary Loan assistance, for which I am grateful; and I heartily thank Mary Beth Faccioli for her reference detective work. I extend appreciation to W. Clark Whitehorn for the map and to Harry Lewman.

I am grateful for the collegiality and friendship at Agnes Scott College, including fellow Music Department members and other faculty, and the support of the college, especially the pre-tenure leave program and the encouragement of Dean Rosemary Zumwalt. Thanks also to the Information Technology Services Department for the laptop loaner. Without my Georgia friends Roger and Jaxi Rothman, Wendy and Ward Sayre, Mike and Judy Lynn, Kim and Jay Lyle, among others, I probably wouldn't bother. I especially mention my gratitude for the generosity of my colleague, friend, and "co-mentor" Michael R. Lynn, who put aside his passion for eighteenth-century France to read the manuscript with a keen eye for fuzzy thinking, disorderly prose, and tangential self-indulgences.

The love, support, and plain fun shared with friends and family members over the years have been critical toward the completion of this project. Among them, I would like to thank Tricia Wallace, Carey Thomas Campbell, Grant Summers and Sarah Kirkpatrick, Rob and Gina Parker, Brad and Kim Eddings, Janice Laird, Cathy and Cody Widiger, Eric Widiger. Throughout this process my mother Anne Widiger has been a special friend, sometime landlord, and overall supporter whose depths of forbearance and good humor are hard to fathom. May the publication of this book herald good times for Lori, Earl, Megan, and Jessica Byrnes. This book is a memorial to loved ones departed during the course of its research and writing: Jimmy E. Widiger, Otho H. Winterrowd, Kenneth D. Laird, Irene E. Winterrowd, and Kevin M. Laird. This book is a testament to the light and laughter and truth brought into this world by Zoey Laird and Henry Laird. Finally, this book would have never seen the light of day without Brandon Laird, first-string editor, friend, confidante, one-man think tank, music lover, writer, father, husband, inspiration. To him, I owe more than I can say.

Contents

Louisiana Hayride

Introduction: A Cradle of the Stars

By Horace's watch, it's time.

The white of Saturday night stars illumines the bas-relief eagle watching over the building's dedication to "those who served in the world war." The lamp moons of Leadbelly's Fannin Street wax across the hood of a '53 Louisiana Ford as it slips into the last parking space between two Texas Chevys. The Municipal Auditorium lights up tonight—as it does nearly every Saturday—a monolith, warm and alive beside Shreveport's cold grey Confederate sepulchers and tombs of gentry long ago buried in Oakland Cemetery. From open second-floor windows, the building breathes out the hum of amplifier tubes, the whine of microphone feedback. Behind the drawn velveteen curtain inside, a snare drum snaps its sound test beats through the electric gab of a crowd just now easing into their wooden slat seats.

In the wings, Horace Logan adjusts his gun holster and fingers the slipknot of his planter's tie. He jabs his arm out straight, clearing the sleeve from his wristwatch face. Sure enough, it's 7:59—show time. The Hayride producer, program director, and emcee sidles onto the stage, up to the mike—a crowd conductor ready to kick off the weekly broadcast of the radio barn dance. He coughs into his fist to clear his throat. Mister Logan, as Elvis politely addresses him, winces into the spotlight and beams at the audience.

"How many folks are here tonight from our fine neighbor to the north, Arkansas?" His question draws a slim salvo of hand claps and hollers. Horace pauses, runs a forefinger casually across the felt brim of his cowboy hat. "How many of you all out there are from right here in Louisiana?" Louder applause and a few swill-bellied whoops rise from the settling throng. Horace inconspicuously pulls back the sleeve from his wrist and calmly glances down to see the second hand tick to 50. He looks up and out, grins wide, and, in a stentorian voice that intuitively cues an audience to cheer, bellows:

"And how many people are here from the great state of Texas?" The tiers and coliseum floor explode in revelry. Riding the raucous pitch, fiddles saw and steel guitars slide into the top-of-the-show theme. So it begins, just as it

Fig. I.1 Cast of the *Louisiana Hayride* on stage at Shreveport's Municipal Auditorium, 1953. Louisiana Hayride Archives—J. Kent.

does every Saturday night for thousands of listeners from Amarillo to Yazoo: three hours of live music blow through the wireless like a rush of new wind through an open window[1] (fig. I.1).

This and many scenes like it played out across the nation during the golden era of the radio barn dance. KWKH's *Louisiana Hayride* staked its territory in the ethereal radio universe, one among many shows funneling live dobros and fiddles into parlors from the Gulf to the Great Lakes. The history of this radio genre reached back into the earliest days of mass broadcasting. WBAP in Fort Worth, Texas, created the prototype on 4 January 1923, when it broadcast a variety program led by fiddler and Confederate veteran Captain M. J. Bonner.[2] The next year, Chicago's WLS christened its *National Barn Dance* and Nashville's WSM soon followed with the debut of the *Grand Ole Opry* in 1925. Soon after, a long line of radio barn dances poured into Saturday-night living rooms from Virginia to California, manifestations of a pop culture phenomenon lasting the next two-and-a-half decades.[3]

But of all the barn dance radio shows, the *Louisiana Hayride* rises to the fore in country music after World War II, assuming a uniquely powerful role second only to the *Grand Ole Opry*. For all its sway, however, the Shreveport broadcast earns only scattered mention in books that address the dramatic shifts in music during the era. Synoptic histories of country music generally allot the *Hayride* a paragraph or two, or at least briefly conjure a metaphor that situates the show in terms of comparative influence: for example, the "high minor leagues" of country music, as one of Hank Williams's earliest biographers dubbed it.[4] Bill C. Malone, country music's preeminent historian, writes that "few could equal Shreveport's Louisiana Hayride as a forum for musical exposure, nor as a launching ground for future stardom."[5] Yet, despite the quotidian nods, the *Hayride*'s significance (and the regional importance of other barn dance shows in the roster, for that matter) remains largely overshadowed by the music scene in Nashville.

The paragon in the early story of the *Louisiana Hayride* is Hank Williams, country music's legendary songwriter and singer, and one of the most influential musicians in all of U.S. popular music. Williams's *Hayride* association is certainly one of the show's greatest claims to fame; while there, he exploded into the national spotlight with "Lovesick Blues" and launched a whirlwind career of hit recordings cut short by his untimely death in 1952. Williams's son, Hank Jr., also a successful performer in his own right, writes about the *Louisiana Hayride* and its impact on his father's career:

> Between the late forties and the late fifties, [the *Louisiana Hayride*] became an innovative force that changed the style and sound of country music and its impact on the American listening public. . . .
>
> The Hayride also did a lot to refine and redefine what was then called "hillbilly" music and make it a respected part of America's musical culture. It helped make it possible for country artists like my daddy to break out of the narrow "hillbilly" category and cross over into the mainstream of popular music.[6]

Hank Williams's fame via the *Louisiana Hayride* sealed the radio show's status as a forum from which hopeful country musicians of the postwar era could gain exposure and success; and Williams's fortune alone might have garnered a mantle of historical significance for the *Hayride* and KWKH. But Williams's association with the show was just one of the most conspicuous factors among many that multiplied the influence of the *Louisiana Hayride* on country music and rockabilly. There were idiosyncratic and local matters like the personal pluck of *Hayride* management, and the chance circumstance and human connections that drew specific personalities to the station at key moments. And there were broader aspects: the nature of the radio medium, the location and milieu of Shreveport, and the convergence of media opportunity that contributed to the *Hayride*'s success and, in turn, secured it a lasting legacy.

The *Louisiana Hayride* matters much more than its occasional acknowledgments allow. The radio show played key roles in the rise to prominence of both country and rock-and-roll. The *Hayride*, in fact, presents a microcosm of the post–World War II dynamic in the southern United States. A generation of white musicians began to play sounds that merged all the musical impulses—black and white—that surrounded them growing up. No form of popular music remained untouched by this phenomenon. But while the decade following World War II clearly builds to a cultural watershed (what Greil Marcus called "the rockabilly moment"), the roots of this momentum extend far back into the troubled yet intimate history of contact between southern blacks and whites. For this reason, I will not detail the week-to-week minutiae of operations or recount every individual performer on the *Louisiana Hayride*. Instead, I hope to examine the context of the radio show within a complex web of historic, geographic, and commercial realities that began shaping the region's culture during the 1830s.

The story begins as early as Shreveport's founding as a commercial port of the Red River, binding land to water, South to West, black to white, with thick, sticky, and often dirty fibers of cotton. It traces Shreveport's changing identity as railroads killed river trade, and oil and gas became the region's lifeblood. The rise of media—both phonograph and radio—and of country music enters this story with a fresh relevance wrought from a simple shift in point of view, away from commercial centers of power in New York or even Nashville, and toward the peripheral position of Shreveport and its radio barn dance.

Many familiar popular culture tropes about the rise of media, about country music, about Elvis Presley, and about the emergence of rock-and-roll look different from this shift in perspective southward and westward. And the questions raised in this book point to other useful inquiries: How do social and cultural forces within a particular time and place shape the ways people make and appreciate music? In this case, what can be learned about a region's identity—and, therefore, about a collective national identity—through a show like the *Louisiana Hayride*? Perhaps less philosophical, but no less important: Why should we concern ourselves with the *Hayride* if it was, in the words of one writer, just "another, more Southern-fried, version of the Opry"?[7]

First and foremost, the *Hayride* operated with a style and attitude completely different from the *Opry*. *Hayride* producers, in contrast to those at the more established *Opry*, took risks more willingly. They kept an entrepreneurial eye out for new talent and an ear to the ground for changes in what people might like to hear and when they would like to hear it. For instance, about a month before the *Hayride* aired, on 1 March 1948, KWKH began an early morning country music variety program, the *Ark-La-Tex Jubilee*, broadcast Monday through Friday from 5:00 to 6:00 in the morning. Featured performers on the show were Johnnie and Jack and the Tennessee Mountain Boys, Al Robinson and his Red River Ramblers, and announcer Horace Logan with his puppet sidekick, Cosmo. The *Jubilee*, as well as *Hayride* precursors such as *The Saturday Night Roundup* and *Hillbilly Amateur Show*, prefigure the station's willingness to play with the schedule and tenor of its programs to showcase untried artists and new music.

While the show benefited from its start by fortuitous associations with some established country music names, *Hayride* producers were also more ready than most to take chances. Artists whose styles did not easily fit into increasingly discrete musical categories, artists who would have been rebuffed by the self-consciously traditional *Opry*, found a welcome at KWKH. Hank Williams, in fact, failed to secure a position on the *Opry* before he came to Shreveport; and it was only after he proved successful on the *Hayride* that WSM became interested. In fact, because of its conservatism, even established artists were sometimes constrained on the *Opry*. Western swing trumpeter Sleepy Brown recalls that, while touring with the country paragon and cowboy politico Jimmie Davis and his ten-piece band, he enjoyed a respite at gigs in the Ryman Auditorium in Nashville: "[E]very time we would go on tour or go through the Grand Ole Opry, I was a trumpet player. And no horn or drums were ever used on the Opry, so the drummer and I would have to sit backstage. They just didn't allow it."[8] A more famous anecdote recounts Bob Wills's standoff with *Opry* management over drums during his orchestra's sole guest appearance there.[9] (Wills refused to play without his entire band, rejecting a compromise offer to place the drums behind a curtain; his band became the first to use drums on the *Opry* stage.)

The inherent quality of radio broadcasting—that of a theater of the mind, which captures imagination with far less venture capital than other media (e.g., movies, television, phonograph records)—aided the *Hayride* producers in creating a show vital to country music a full day's drive from Nashville. Recollections of Williams's early performances of "Lovesick Blues" underscore the unique opportunity for creating reality when experienced through the ears only. Tillman Franks, a local musician and *Hayride* notable who played bass with Williams the first time he performed "Lovesick Blues," explains what the live audience saw, and what their radio counterparts could never have imagined, during Williams's performance: "Ray Bartlett was an announcer here on KWKH. Ray Bartlett would get right in the orchestra pit and he would turn a flip when Hank would start doing that yodel. And he would get everybody clapping. So Ray Bartlett deserves lots of the credit for getting the people kicked off on that 'Lovesick Blues.'"[10] At other times Bartlett might have incited the crowd by dancing a tango with the curtain.[11] Only the enthusiasm of the live audience came through the speakers to radio listeners, whose stirred imaginations then filled in the visual spaces.

The radio station enjoyed the dual benefit of a strong signal and a strategic location. KWKH's 50-kilowatt transmitter allowed the AM signal to cover a huge geographic area. It reached listeners in twenty-eight states, but much of its audience was in the lower South and Southwest, the direction toward which its potent transmitter pointed after sundown. This partially explains the program's ascendancy throughout communities across the rural expanses of Texas and why a *Hayride* tour could sell out as far from home as Phoenix, Arizona.[12] Not only did the live *Hayride* broadcast win a large radio audience, but it drew weekly crowds to the Municipal Auditorium as well. Shreveport was advantageously located in this respect, an easy trip from towns in southwest Arkansas, east Texas, and north Louisiana. A 1951 article in *Shreveport Magazine* estimated that 65 percent of the live *Hayride* audiences were from out of town, and most of these were from Texas.[13]

Even before the *Hayride*, Shreveport's central location gave KWKH a growing reputation as a place where country performers could make a successful living. During the 1930s, the station had drawn a handful of country performers with impressive credentials and national notoriety, starting with Jimmie Davis and the Sheltons (known as The Lone Star Cowboys when the duet played with guitarist Leon Chappelear).[14] The later move by industry notables Dean Upson and the Bailes Brothers to KWKH countenanced the regional popularity of the show and the influence of the station.

Other well-established performers came to Shreveport in their wake, including fiddler Tex Grimsley and guitarist Cliff Grimsley with their band, the Texas Showboys; harmonica wizard Wayne Raney; the Mercer Brothers; Curley Williams and the Georgia Peach Pickers. Several performers who came to Shreveport because of their connection to Upson and the Bailes had been part of the *Grand Ole Opry* before, including Curley Kinsey and the Tennessee Ridge Runners, the Four Deacons, the Delmore Brothers, and Johnnie Wright and Jack Anglin and the Tennessee Mountain Boys, featuring the singing of Johnnie's wife, the future "queen of country music," Kitty Wells.[15] If this list were not enough to affirm KWKH as a viable and influential radio signal for live country music performance, then Roy Acuff's personal appearance on KWKH in March 1948 shortly before the *Hayride* started was nothing short of approbation from the era's most notable country music icon.

Once the *Louisiana Hayride* began, its immediate popularity with audiences and advertisers furthered the reputation of KWKH as a significant center for country music and the area as a place where country musicians could earn a living. After Hank Williams became a star, hopefuls gravitated to Shreveport expecting to follow Williams's trajectory of joining the *Grand Ole Opry* and finding stardom. Many of them did, including Red Sovine, Slim Whitman, Leon Payne, Webb Pierce, Jimmie C. Newman, Johnny Cash, George Jones, Johnny Horton, Jim Reeves, Floyd Cramer, the Browns, and Faron Young. For this reason, *Hayride* producers later dubbed the show "The Cradle of the Stars."[16]

Four additional factors synergistically transformed the hokum of a hayfield wagon into a launching pad for country music fame: FCC regulations, the CBS radio network, the station KTHS, and the Armed Forces Radio Services. Perhaps the most critical factor in the drawing power of the early *Louisiana Hayride* was the absence of television. The FCC freeze on television licensing from 1948 to 1952 gave the Shreveport program a tremendous boost. Even a major city like Houston, Texas, had only one television station at the time; no television station operated in Shreveport until January 1953. In effect, the freeze created an entertainment void, filled in part by the *Hayride*'s live weekly broadcasts.[17] Around the same time Shreveport experienced its first glance at television, the extensive CBS radio network picked the *Louisiana Hayride* as part of its program called "Saturday Night, Country Style."[18] CBS broadcast six barn dance programs in rotation, airing two shows each Saturday night. Thus, a 25-minute segment of the *Hayride* broadcast live nationwide every third Saturday. The CBS interest and investment made it clear that country music was ensconced in U.S. popular culture, and the tradition of the Saturday night barn dance was indeed an institution. The late Johnny Cash, another of country music's most enduring performers, wrote about how this network promotion affected his career:

> The nationwide exposure I got on the *Hayride*, via the CBS Radio Network, was the key factor in making my early records successful. Within a year, my name and voice were familiar to country music fans from coast to coast. The *Hayride* gave me the boost every successful recording artist has to have, just as it had with Hank Williams, Kitty Wells, Webb Pierce, Faron Young, Slim Whitman, Jim Reeves, and Elvis Presley before me.[19]

The third factor that maximized the influence of the *Hayride* was KTHS, the Little Rock, Arkansas, station acquired by the Ewing family (who already owned KWKH and the Shreveport *Times* newspaper) in a trade following FCC restrictions on multiple ownership. By this time, KTHS was also a 50,000-watt powerhouse. It began broadcasting the *Louisiana Hayride* in its entirety every week, giving *Hayride* performers even greater exposure to the north and east. A final boon came on 26 June 1954, when the Far East Network of the Armed Forces Radio Services picked up the *Hayride* for a weekly 30-minute segment.[20] All these broadcasts further boosted the prestige of the *Hayride* and the influence of KWKH.

By the early to mid-1950s, the country music mélange on the *Louisiana Hayride* had reached a large national audience. The list of country musicians who either began their careers on the *Hayride* or were significantly associated with the show was already extensive. They traveled from as far away as Canada (in the case of singer-songwriter Hank Snow), California, and West Virginia, all drawn to Shreveport by the *Hayride*'s promise of a shot at fame; but a number of *Hayride* house band musicians, particularly those who played around the mid-1950s, came from the immediate northwest Louisiana area. Whereas *Hayride* headliners presented a wide range of regional sounds and idiosyncratic styles, the local musicians' attitudes and repertoire reflected an ongoing interaction of white and black music characteristic of the flatland region around Shreveport since the nineteenth century.

The *Hayride*, a white country music show with a mostly white audience, employed these young musicians who performed country on the stage every Saturday night, but went home and listened to rhythm-and-blues stars Wynonnie Harris and Al "Stomp" Russell. During the same period KWKH broadcast the *Louisiana Hayride*, the station also featured late afternoon rhythm-and-blues shows, announced by the disc jockey Ray "Groovie Boy" Bartlett, who impersonated an African-American disc jockey during his show, *In the Groove*.[21] In hindsight, Bartlett's shows could very well be seen as an adaptation of blackface minstrelsy that began a century earlier.

KWKH program listings in the Shreveport *Times* include an early morning show called *Jive Parade* on New Year's Day in 1948. By at least August of that year, Bartlett was broadcasting his 30-minute disc jockey program

from 4:30 to 5:00 every weekday afternoon. By 1950 the show had expanded to 45 minutes, and by the following year was a full hour.[22] The late
1940s, in general, saw the beginning of radio shows featuring what would
(after 1949) be called rhythm-and-blues in stations throughout the country, many of them featuring African-American disc jockeys, rather than
whites imitating black dialect.[23] These shows influenced white youth of the
period, whose searching for cultural expression has been the subject of reflection from commentators as divergent as Bill Malone and Norman
Mailer. Cultural analyst W. T. Lhamon found a continuous thread of "deliberately speeding" mid-1950s culture connecting the method acting of
James Dean and Marlon Brando to the writings of Jack Kerouac to the
paintings of Jackson Pollock to the rise of rock-and-roll.[24] Adding Shreveport to this discussion of post–World War II cultural shifts offers the
chance to add two elements often missed in analyses of the 1950s: real
names and faces of the generation of white southern players whose coming-
of-age after the war indelibly marked their careers and musical sensibilities; and a direct, specific example—the *Louisiana Hayride*—of rock-and-
roll's deep roots in both rhythm-and-blues and country.

Ray Bartlett's *In the Groove* takes on particular significance for the
Shreveport country music scene because many young, white *Hayride* musicians during the 1950s had been exposed to his predominantly black
playlist. These musicians include Jerry Kennedy, Joe Osborn, James Burton, D. J. Fontana—all of whom went on to find extensive success outside
of Shreveport. Not incidentally, it was this type of young musician—with
one ear to country music and the other to rhythm-and-blues—who created the white southern sound that would become rockabilly. Elvis Presley, the "Memphis Cat" who began headlining *Hayride* shows in late 1954,
was only the most renowned of their ilk. The image of Presley's earliest
performances of "That's All Right, Mama" and "Blue Moon of Kentucky"
parallels Hank Sr.'s first renditions of "Lovesick Blues" on the *Hayride*; and
Presley's signing of a KWKH contract on 6 November 1954 is the other half
of the twain that meets to secure the enduring legacy of both country and
rock-and-roll on Shreveport's Red River.

Clearly, there was a fortuitous convergence of circumstance, talent, and
opportunity that initiated and perpetuated momentum in Shreveport during the era of the *Louisiana Hayride*. The city's history itself, however, is a
study in how geography, race relations, commerce, and media shape a region's distinctive culture and grassroots music. These forces set the stage
for the success and innovations of the *Louisiana Hayride*. For that reason,
the book proceeds in three major sections. The first section covers the
historical background beginning with the founding of Shreveport as a
commercial river port during the 1830s. The second positions Shreveport
within the birth and expansion of modern mass media, both phonograph
and radio. The third section dwells on the *Louisiana Hayride* during its
peak years, exploring the show's significance in two genres of U.S. popular
music and searching for the broader implications of that significance.

In chapter 1, I outline Shreveport's establishment and growth, emphasizing the region as a site of contact, first between Europeans and Caddo Indians, then between blacks and whites, the South and the West, sin and religion, gentility and crudeness. In chapter 2, I connect Shreveport's growth as a river port and the range of entertainments that typified the era's daily life to early twentieth-century culture; a particular focus at the end of this chapter is the life and music of Leadbelly, who grew up in the region and experienced formative musical development in the brothels and bordellos of Shreveport's riverfront. Leadbelly bridges the nineteenth-century background with the twentieth-century growth of media and raises particular questions about the nature of musical interchange across the borders of race in the South as well as the extent to which phonograph and radio industries dictate how we conceptualize black and white music. Together, these two background chapters underscore the notion that people, their culture, and their music often remain tied to the land long after the economic or geographic circumstances that brought them there pass away. Thus, rich musical practices exist in places that the dictates of economic potency would have us overlook. Recounting Shreveport's nineteenth-century past and reconstructing its musical practices insofar as possible provides insight into creative energies and attitudes manifest in the *Louisiana Hayride* during the following century.

The next two chapters move the historical context in a new direction. In chapters 3 and 4, I situate the rise of phonograph and radio media, respectively, within the context of Shreveport. The city enters the history of the phonograph business only from the economic sidelines, but from there raises questions about the industry's framework for southern music and its long-term conceptual implications. In contrast to the circumscribed phonograph industry, radio presented the opportunity for Shreveport to carve out space to become a critical site for southern roots music. The details of that development unfold against the larger background of radio's edgy and freewheeling beginnings, seen in vivid local color via the story of W. K. Henderson. KWKH evolved into a regional voice in the context of the radio industry's expansion and movement toward greater standardization, its changes in relation to World War II, and other, less bloody legal battles over multiple station ownership, the broadcasting of phonograph records, and issues with national implications for country music and U.S. media. These issues take on greater meaning in the context of Shreveport and the stories of individuals associated in different ways with the region and its barn dance.

In the final chapters, I turn the attention exclusively to the *Hayride* with an emphasis on its presence in U.S. post–World War II culture. Chapter 5 recounts the beginnings of the *Louisiana Hayride*, the spirit of its operation, the catalyzing performances of Hank Williams and other country music stars who either emerged on the *Hayride* stage or spent significant time there. Chapter 6 focuses on the *Hayride*'s significance after a mid-1950s cultural shift. It begins looking at how Elvis Presley's emergence to stardom on the *Hayride* embodies tensions between black and white culture that resonate with deep meaning not only for popular music but for society as a whole. It then moves to highlight four Shreveport native sons whose musical development during the late 1940s and 1950s exemplifies the unique cultural salmagundi of the Red River region, a tradition born from the overlapping musics of blacks and whites. By ending here, I suggest that while the cavalcade of *Hayride* stars certainly attests the enduring fame of the show, the stories of these sidemen and producers point to even deeper cultural significance. In the conclusion, I summarize and clarify some broader implications of the *Louisiana Hayride* in our understanding of race relations, media history, and popular culture in the post–World War II era.

1

The Character of a Region

The Spirit of the frontier and the Civilization of the South.
—Albert Harris Leonard, characterizing
nineteenth-century Shreveport

KWKH and its *Louisiana Hayride* manifested the dynamism of a mid-century turning point in the culture of the South and nation after World War II. A direct connection exists between the spirit and energy of the *Louisiana Hayride* and the character of the place, Shreveport, whose tangled roots extend deep into the relationships that defined the region: between whites and blacks, agriculture and frontier, river and rail, sin and salvation. Shreveport's current economic importance is now trumped by nearby Dallas and its cultural complexity leveled by catch phrases like "Bible Belt." From a contemporary perspective, it is easy to forget that Shreveport once dominated a significant region of four states, occupied a position of strategic military importance, and drew people, their business, and their music to its red, muddy thoroughfares. These people interacted across borders of race and power at a mid-nineteenth-century cultural crossroads, and the inevitable tensions of contact, both positive and negative, lent a singular character to this southern region.

The earliest traveler's account of Shreveport, Louisiana, describes it as a "rathole."[1] The new town, christened in late May 1836, formed a simple latticework of north–south and east–west rutty dirt roads that cut wide paths through the thick piney woods. Though disheveled, Shreve Town thrived commercially as a well-positioned port on the banks of the Red River, a 1,300-mile artery that snaked from the West Texas panhandle to the Mississippi River above Baton Rouge. Navigation to this north-west Louisiana region had only recently become possible because of the government-funded extirpations of steamboat Captain Henry Miller Shreve, who cleared the Red of the logjam that had distended it for centuries. Shreve then cast his lot with eight investors, who named their civic development venture Shreve Town Company, after the captain (fig. 1.1).[2]

The gigantic logjam precluded large-scale immigration by farmers into the fertile Red River Valley region of northwest Louisiana before the 1830s. Known as the Great Raft, it obstructed the main channel of the Red

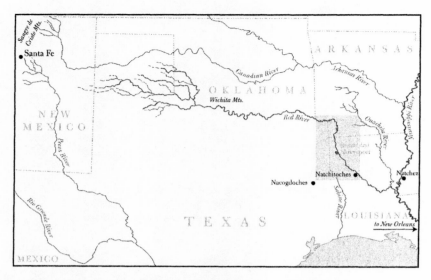

Fig. 1.1 Map of Red River. Courtesy of *Montana: The Magazine of Western History.*

River for approximately 200 miles.[3] Nineteenth-century government engineers estimated this blockage to be at least 400 years old, extending from the oldest Louisiana settlement, Natchitoches, to just above the future site of Shreveport. The Great Raft was not a solid formation, as the name suggests, but a series of smaller blocks, as deep as twenty feet in places. People and horses could walk across some of its sturdier sections. When heavy rains raised the river to overflow, the water created a protean matrix of bayous and lakes; these channels acted as the detour route for boats to bypass the choked Red.[4]

Hundreds of years before European contact, members of the prodigious Caddoan confederacy of Indian tribes thrived in the piney woods along these tortuous waters.[5] Three European explorers, the Spanish Hernando Desoto and Francisco Coronado in the mid-sixteenth century and the French Robert LaSalle in the late 1680s, all reported friendly encounters with the natives. The French explorer and trader Luis de Saint Denis built the first European fort and trading post in the territory in 1714. His settlement, located at the site of Natchitoches in north central Louisiana, predated New Orleans by four years. After nearly a century more of juggling between Spain and France, the land officially became a part of the United States via the Louisiana Purchase.

In April 1806, President Thomas Jefferson sent a surveyor named Thomas Freeman and the naturalist Peter Custis, along with a company of soldiers, to explore, map, and gather scientific data about the Red River, from basin to headwaters (incorrectly assumed to be in the Rocky Mountains). Three months and 615 miles later, the Freeman and Custis expedition encountered a detachment of Spanish troops sent from Nacogdoches, Texas, to stop the Americans. While Freeman and Custis did not see their entire mission through, they did establish diplomatic contact between the United States and the Alabama-Coushatta and Caddo Indian tribes, laying the groundwork for future American expropriations.[6] It was not until 1876, after the Spanish were long gone and Jefferson long dead, that United States Lieutenant Ernest Ruffner actually reached the source of the main river channel.[7]

By that time, white settlers had been in the area for some three decades. Driven west by overplanted, ruined farmland of the southeast, these farmers were running down new acreage. And with the people came music and culture: traditions like shape-note singing in church and hoofing to fiddle tunes in the farm house down the way made the same westward trek as settlers from the Piedmont region into Arkansas, Louisiana, and Texas.[8] These settlers also brought their knowledge of cotton and tobacco farming to the edge of a frontier.

Many of these migrants found the alluvial soil of the Red River fecund, but they faced a logistical problem unlike any they had known before. The earliest farmers in northwest Louisiana and southwest Arkansas found the reality of a clogged river channel and its swampy overflow hindered a critical part of their yearly agricultural cycle: They had no navigable waterway to deliver their harvest to market in New Orleans. And the journey over land to the great port city was prohibitive. By 1820, only a few riverboats ascended regularly from New Orleans to Alexandria, about 100 miles above the river's mouth; five years later, in 1825, a few small boats reached another 100 miles to Natchitoches.[9] To continue farther into the Red River Valley, these riverboats transferred their cargo to small keelboats or flatboats, bypassing the Raft through the system of lakes and bayous—Twelve-Mile Bayou, Soda Lake, Clear Lake, Black and Red Bayous—created by the river's backwater.

Some agricultural cargo, like tobacco and cotton, did make this arduous journey, as did typical frontier products like bear's grease, beeswax, deerskins, buffalo hides, and other furs.[10] But the financial cost and danger of this trip precluded large-scale development of the region. For years the early settlers petitioned Congress to clear the main river channel of the Great Raft and open the waterway for steam passage to New Orleans.[11] The government did not act on these requests until the early 1830s when the river became important for two military reasons. For one, the Red River could provide a swift entry into Texas, which the United States was interested in annexing. It would also be a supply route to Fort Towson located in Indian Territory, now Oklahoma.

Clearing the Great Raft posed a challenge distinct from other comparable waterway projects due to the type of soil that formed the Red River's banks. The same alluvium that made the Red River basin fertile allowed the river's current to sweep trees into the channel at such a rate that an 1873 Army chief of engineers reported that during peak flood season "the continuous falling of trees on some of the bends makes a noise resembling the distant roar of artillery."[12] The river's many twists and bends caused these floating trees to become trapped, piling one upon the other.

The task would eventually be accomplished under the direction of Shreve who, in the service of General Andrew Jackson after the Battle of New Orleans, first viewed the Raft in spring 1815 as pilot of the 75-ton capacity *Enterprise*. It took Shreve over six years and more than $200,000 to dislodge Mother Nature's pernicious boom. He finally finished the job on 15 February 1839, opening the Red River as a major tributary of the Mississippi River System.[13] Commerce now traveled from Shreveport and above, down to New Orleans, then out of the Gulf and around the coast to the rest of the country, and from the rest of the country back to Shreveport (fig. 1.2).

The gains of Shreve and his government were also the losses of the natives of the basin. In cozenage all too typical of stories about the expanding frontier, the U.S. swapped overvalued miscellany—allegedly amounting to some $80,000 with only $30,000 proffered in cash—for a tract of land estimated between 600,000 and one million acres, thus allowing for some half million acre margin of error.[14] As the Caddoes' hunting grounds were converted to cotton fields and their land overrun, they found themselves, as did so many American Indians, facing an impossible choice. Poised in the nebula between a past certainly changed and a future with no certainty at all, the Caddo leaders followed the logic of survival. The Red River, *mutatis mutandis*, became part of the Manifest Destiny. Such were the reasons Caddo chief Tarshar urged his confederation to cut their losses when the government agents came to make a deal in 1835:

My children, For what do you mourn? Are you not starving in the midst of this land? And do you not travel far from it in quest of food? The game we live on is going farther off, and the white man is coming near to us; and is not our condition getting worse daily? Then why lament for the loss of that which yields us nothing but misery? Let us be wise then, and get all we can for it, and not wait till the white man steals it away, little by little, and then gives us nothing.[15]

It offered little leverage to the Indians that the American Larkin Edwards, who had lived with them for thirty years and married a Caddo woman, served as their interpreter one last time. Nevertheless, gratitude was paid for his service. As part of the 1835 deal, Edwards retained a square mile of premium riverfront land, which would later form the heart of downtown Shreveport. In cruel irony, the Caddo left their home for a grueling migration to Oklahoma, the territory that sparked U.S. interest in controlling the Caddo homeland in the first place. Hunkered down on the banks alone, Edwards cashed in his chips the next year, selling his parcel to the Shreve Town Company for $5,000.[16] The developers promptly surveyed and cut a chunk of the land into blocks, which to this day constitutes the city's center (a prominent street is named for Edwards). The name changed to Shreveport in February of 1837.[17]

Shreveport's location was commercially profitable from the start. Situated on a bluff, it was readily visible and easily accessible from the river.

Fig. 1.2 Cotton grows along the eroding banks in this old photo of the
Red River. Noel Memorial Library Archives, LSU in Shreveport.

Traders from all directions—from Grand Ecore, Louisiana, to southern
Arkansas—quickly made the new steamboat port their main terminus.
This made Shreveport an increasingly important crossroads for the music
and culture the traders brought with them, not only via the newly open
waterway but across land as well. Many settlers arrived from the East via
the well-traveled Texas Trail. This historic route led from Georgia to Louisiana, through Cane and Bennett's bluff (a trading post established as early
as 1 July 1832 near the future site of Shreveport), and through Greenwood,
Louisiana, into Texas. Shreveport became an "aiming point" along this
land route, as many Texas Trail pioneers never moved past the city.[18] The
intersection of both land and water routes boosted Shreveport's ascendance as a regional commercial locus.

The promise and prospect of Shreveport realized a demography specific
to the commerce of agriculture. As cotton trade burgeoned so did the Shreveport population, both among white proprietors and farmers as well as
blacks, most of whom were slaves on larger-than-average plantations. In
1840, for example, the population in Caddo Parish (the equivalent of a
county, with Shreveport as parish seat) consisted of 2,416 whites and 2,837
slaves. It was, in fact, this region's large plantations, the intensive labor required to work them, and the relative preponderance of slaves to whites
that inspired Harriet Stowe to use northwest Louisiana as the setting for
the story of Simon LeGree in her famous novel.

A very small minority of blacks, however, did not languish under the
whip. Some 29 free blacks were counted in the census of 1840. Among
them was Norman C. Davis, a barber who bought ten acres of land flank-
ing Texas Avenue, Shreveport's main street, during the peak of slavery.[19]
Davis was also a member of the Shreveport Ethiopian Band, which in-

cluded both slaves and free men. This group gained exception to the local ordinances prohibiting African-Americans to assemble and make music, provided they notify a local constable beforehand and return home an hour before midnight. Records of Norman Davis's life and groups like the Shreveport Ethiopian Band are sparse, but they point to how local black residents carved out avenues for musical expression early in the town's formation. As a free black landowner, Norman Davis by necessity would have navigated between both black and white cultures. His life suggests a shadowy glimpse of possibilities for individuals to cross racial borders during the nineteenth century. By the same token, a broader consideration of nineteenth-century musical life in Shreveport, the subject of the next chapter, suggests more general settings in which blacks and whites might have interacted around music. Later recordings by artists like Huddie "Leadbelly" Ledbetter, also discussed in the next chapter, bear concrete testimony to the musical interchanges across racial boundaries only glimpsed in nineteenth-century accounts.

Amid conditions of glaring inequality and race-based oppression, these types of exchanges emerged in the context of close contact and proximity of the region's blacks and whites. Over the two decades following the 1840 census, the intensive plantation society of northwest Louisiana gave rise to a slave population that outnumbered white landed men by over 50 percent. As it was throughout the slaveholding South, a small, relatively wealthy minority of whites—around 10 percent—held slaves; for example, of the 4,733 whites counted in 1860, only 490 were slaveholders.[20] Also characteristic of the region were plantations worked by fifty or more slaves; of the 7,338 slaves in the region, 2,493 were held on one of thirty-four large farms in Caddo parish. Across the unequal power structure institutionalized and forcibly maintained by slavery, ways of relating between blacks and whites were complex, as were the stratums within each racial group.

Unlike many frontier towns, Shreveport's earliest white pioneers were not only men but their wives and children, and they often lugged along all the family capital. As contemporary observer Albert Harris Leonard noted in his memoirs: "Many brought with them their slaves—horses, mules, cattle, hogs, wagons, farming utensils and tools with which to build houses and make other improvements. Among them were farmers, planters, merchants, mechanics, doctors, preachers, teachers, lawyers and gamblers."[21] Leonard's assessment of the occupational striae of white Shreveporters corresponds to the 1850 census.[22] Variety of profession, coupled with the relative ease of travel to and from the Creole Corinth of New Orleans, wafted a cosmopolitan air upriver to Shreveport. New Orleans was, in fact, the second largest U.S. port by the mid-nineteenth century, and the fourth busiest port in the world.[23] Primarily because of its connection with the Crescent City, Shreveport came into its own as a mercantile plexus capable of nourishing a unique social catholicity.

According to Leonard, the stable population of settlers contrasted with the character of Shreveport's "floating population," who often outnumbered its permanent residents. The transient congeries passing through on business or pleasure, kindled the rough and tumble atmosphere of "a typical 'wide open' frontier town." Leonard elaborated:

[The rowdy atmosphere in Shreveport was] . . . intensified by the presence of many steamboatmen generally lawless and reckless who came and went with the steamboats on which they were employed, and by the occasional appearance of quite a number of men generally toughs [*sic*] who were employed in cutting and rafting to Shreveport the timber used on building the town.[24]

"Rathole," as the earlier 1837 observer dubbed Shreveport, was probably an apt description of the nascent town. Shreveport was, in many ways, a typical river port, with the labor of its itinerant rabble, outside of trading cargo, mostly involved in swilling rye and rolling dice.

At the same time, Shreveport stood at the edge of the vast and lawless no-man's-land of Texas, lending it the quality of a rugged frontier settlement. A British-born settler arriving early in 1838 described the rustic accommodations of the bustling city in a letter to his sister:

They shewed [*sic*] the largest *Hotel* in the Place which was a Double log house and the logs were so wide apart that the Wind almost blew the teacup from your mouth as they had no tumblers at that time.

The table consisted of very fat salt pork, corn bread, and Molasses at times not often with a few turnips now and then. Their terms were $30 a month, had a bed on the floor and every morning there was an inch thick of Snow on the top Blankets![25]

Shreveport maintained its frontier ambience for the first few decades of its existence, even as its permanent population—with all attendant stability—continued to grow. Albert Harris Leonard was among them, arriving in Shreveport as a boy in 1849. Writing his memoirs nearly seventy years later, he described lawless gunfights in riverfront streets lined with brothels, taverns, and gambling houses.[26] Samuel Wear McCorkle, a traveling preacher who visited Shreveport in 1849 and 1850 at the age of 23, recorded a jeremiad about it in his journal:

It now becomes proper to describe the place called, Shreveport [*sic*]. . . . It is founded upon a body of red and very sticky clay, which is now from four to eighteen inches of depth through the streets. . . . At present, eastern Texas does a great portion of her dealing at this place, which fact keeps it alive and growing. . . .

I think that I may safely call Shreveport a "sink of pollution and wickedness" [*sic*]. On this morning . . . there was a difference between two men, which arose from card playing. After quarreling for a little time to no effect, they resorted to their "revolvers" [*sic*] to settle the difficulty. There were six shots fired, and three persons hit. Neither of the combatants were [*sic*] seriously wounded, but a man who was standing not far off was mortally wounded—died in a few hours. So much for Shreveport.

My ears have been almost continually ringing with vile blasphemy against God. Oh, the fuel that Satan will get in Eternity from Shreveport alone! The occupations of the majority of citizens are: stealing, gambling, swearing, lying, drinking, etc. The Sabbath here is no more regarded by the majority than a theatre is regarded as a place of seriousness.[27]

Needless to say, Shreveport's elected officials did not have much success upholding law and order. The town's first mayor, John O. Sewall, was killed in a duel; his successor, Alexander Sterrett, was also murdered in an argument with Charles Sewall, John's brother.[28]

Despite the various dramas played out in its streets, Shreveport became the economic center of a large region that included northwest Louisiana, southwest Arkansas, southeast Oklahoma, and northeast Texas, a position clinched when only months after Captain Shreve's project was complete, the log raft reformed above Shreveport.[29] Congress never allocated the funds that Shreve warned were necessary to maintain the channel. By 1841 the jam extended 20 miles.[30] Because these new Raft formations grew above the city, they were of great commercial advantage to Shreveport. In river navigational terms, Shreveport became a "division point," or the end of the line for large northbound steamboats.[31] By 1850 large vessels traveling to and from Shreveport regularly carried between 400 and 800 tons.

The foundation of Shreveport's commercial success was built with cotton bolls. The at-times priceless textile commodity was the most frequent and prolific cargo trucked down the Red River, though steamboats frequently trafficked animal hides, corn, sugar, mail, and people back and forth as well. The increased efficiency and reliability of steamboat service eventually leveraged human labor; thus, the cotton trade actually peaked in the area after forced labor became illegal and unconstitutional.[32] This resulted from the evolution of river transport through two types of large boats: transients and packets.

In the era following the 1820 Missouri Compromise, in which the Union held in tenuous balance until mid-century, the river most commonly carried transient boats. A transient lay in port until it acquired sufficient cargo or passengers to make the trip economically worthwhile. Transients were notoriously unreliable in their schedules for departure and return, not to mention destinations. A steamboat captain might advertise in a local newspaper that his boat would leave at a given date and time. He would ring his bell to announce an impending departure, only to remain anchored if not enough passengers showed up at the dock.

Packet steamboats became more common in the 1850s, the tinderbox decade culminating in the 1857 *Dred Scott* decision that foreshadowed Civil War. Packets made regular trips at set intervals, regardless of whether they were filled to capacity. A "line" was the expansion of packet service to two or more boats. Steamboat service further distinguished itself in offering either "way" or "through" traffic; way traffic stopped any time someone hailed from a small landing, whereas through traffic did not. This could make a huge difference for customers, given that in the 306 miles between Shreveport and the mouth of the Red River, there were 530 such small landings.[33]

The Civil War put a temporary damper on commercial steamboat traffic, as well as the progress of the railroads that were beginning to stitch the continent. Many riverboats were pressed into military service and girded with iron hulls made from rails. Despite this interruption, within six months of the war's end, steamboat commerce rebounded to antebellum levels. The cotton economy took longer to rebuild, with plantations and farms abandoned, and over half of all livestock devastated by the war.[34] Gradually former slaves were hired as field workers paid by the pound or, more commonly in the case of cotton, as sharecroppers; others became tradesmen—carpenters, bricklayers, blacksmiths, coopers, and other artisans. Although some whites were also sharecroppers, most were "yeomen farmers working their own land."[35] Despite the floods and cotton worms of 1866 and 1867 that destroyed crops and further delayed rebuilding, the cotton trade slowly gained ground after 1868.

By this time, Shreveport faced a new threat to its livelihood, which had emerged as quickly as the fickle shifts of the logjam.[36] Around 1860, as war reared its bloody head, the Raft's head lumbered southward to Red Bayou. In short, this new cluster ended Shreveport's division point status, as steamboats now traveled through backwaters to Jefferson, Texas, 50 miles west of the Red River. Stealthier vessels that during the 1850s used the backwater system to reach Arkansas now traveled to Jefferson, newly confounded in their efforts to skirt the jumble of fallen trees.[37] Contemporary newspapers document the competition between the towns. For example, the Shreveport *Times* on 23 December 1871 chastises the *Jefferson Democrat* for its criticism of the Shreveport Board of Trade; the *Times* editorialist recommends that local businesses give preference to boats that run exclusively from New Orleans to Shreveport, and not to Jefferson.

Shreveport eventually won out in this rivalry when Lieutenant E. A. Woodruff eradicated the Jefferson route on 27 November 1873. Sent to survey and make recommendations the previous year, Woodruff outlined the benefits of removing the Raft as opposed to carving a new channel around it. The reasons were much the same as they had been in the 1830s: reclamation of lands now subject to overflow, as well as the creation of a route for rapid, safe, and cheap transportation to the region above the Raft.[38] Woodruff used similar resources to those Shreve used more than three decades prior: several crews of ax men, a small battery of boats, and money from Congress. Unlike Shreve, Woodruff also employed nitroglycerine.[39] The downside of the project was the economic death knell it would sound for Jefferson.[40] Shreveport leaders understandably floated Machiavellian logic. They determined Jefferson's forced obsolescence a regrettable result of a necessary undertaking. Indeed, when the Red River again flowed freely, Jefferson's stature diminished almost overnight from the citadel of East Texas, under whose shadow a small Dallas labored, to a ghost town.[41]

Shreveport newspapers during the early 1870s reflect concern over two potential problems of the newly open river channel. For one, locals doubted the channel would remain open, given the Raft's history of intractability. Congress assuaged this anxiety when it appropriated in 1872 annual funds— $50,000 per year—to maintain the Red River. The other worry was the railway under construction nearby. This had not always been a concern. When railroads began development in the area in 1852, local residents welcomed them as a boon to the steamboats: they would actually expand the geographical scope of the river service, allowing goods to travel from greater distances to the Shreveport docks.[42] But now it was different. The new line would ultimately connect Shreveport to Vicksburg and, thus, to the Mississippi River — threatening steamboat business and, by extension, the city's livelihood. Unfortunately for Shreveport on this count, Congress was to give no aid, for the government was squarely on the side of railway expansion, as it was the prime tool for the nation's growth westward.

The papers remained Pollyannaish. A Shreveport *Times* editorialist on 25 June 1872 speculated that changes in steam navigation would allow the boats to remain competitive.[43] These predictions proved incorrect in a few short, disastrous years beginning a decade later, though the outcome would not be absolute for two-and-a-half more decades. For in 1880, income from cotton on commercial riverboats matched antebellum levels. Only a year later, some railroads began outpacing riverboats in the transport of Northwest Louisiana's most lucrative cargo.[44] Railroads connected Shreveport with New Orleans by 1882 and with Vicksburg, Mississippi (via a railroad ferry across the Mississippi River) two years later. One year more and passengers and cargo could travel through Houston to California by rail. Still, deficiencies in the railroad system—especially gaps in its service— were sufficient to keep steamboat business viable throughout the rest of the nineteenth century.[45] But the heyday for commercial riverboats was over.

The major problem for a town singularly dependent on the steamboat industry, in contrast to connections by rail or paved roadway, is the yoke of immutable geography:[46] that is to say, a port city is only as good as the reach and accessibility of its river. This explains why Shreveport was the economic and cultural locus in a region now commercially dominated by landlocked Dallas, Texas. The railroads changed the nature of business. Goods traveled faster between East and West by train than by the east– west Mississippi river trade route. And it is high irony that railroads progressed along lands protected from flooding by the same levees initially built to serve the nation's rivers.[47]

Around the turn of the century, Shreveport stood poised for change. In commercial terms, the river stopped flowing just as oil began to flow. At the same time Texas cowboys still brought their herds into the middle of town. One local resident recalled a downtown scene around the turn of the century, when the dynamics of the previous century still played out in its streets: "'They wasn't just cowboys. Farmers come into Shreveport in those wagons. Had at least four mules—sometimes six. And some of 'em, by George, even had oxen pulling those things.'"[48] A dozen or so saloons and gambling houses still lined the riverfront during this era. Steamboats, approaching extinction, still operated until 1898. But by 1900 they had all but disappeared, supplanted by the railroads. The discovery of oil in 1906 boosted the economy of the entire region and encouraged the movement of former rural dwellers to jobs in new boom towns like Oil City, 10 miles to the north of Shreveport. As the terms of its commercial vitality shifted, so shifted more slowly the rhythm of life in the region.

Shreveport in 1850 was caught between two identities: the burgeoning commercial center and the lawless hedonic port. The city existed at a strategic point for river and land traffic (a "division point" on the River, an "aiming point" on the Texas Trail), as well as a geographic and cultural border between the frontier West and the Deep South. At that time, Texas was still a largely unsettled, wild territory of the western frontier. Its ranchers and cattle drivers commingled with the more sedentary, conservative culture of the plantation. As the town took shape, the latter social order gradually dominated. In the words of Leonard:

> From the earliest settlement down to the close of our Civil War, two social systems struggled for supremacy in Caddo Parish. The Spirit of the frontier and the Civilization of the South. The first predominated during about two decades but all the time the second became more and more potent, and about the year 1860 was predominant, though largely modified by the manners and customs of the frontier.[49]

At the close of the nineteenth century, the frontier atmosphere on Shreveport's riverfront conceded to the civil stability of its churches, just as the steamboat bowed to the indefatigable chug of the steam engine. Churches became increasingly influential as the permanent population grew. With a shady boom past behind and steeples ahead, Shreveport faced the twentieth century as an economically tenuous, though ever more civil, nexus for culture.

2

Shreveport Music before Modern Media

I don't know where the hell it came from—but I know it's
claimed by people in the blues and people playing hillbilly.
—Mac "Dr. John" Rebennack, on the tune "Careless Love"

KWKH and the *Louisiana Hayride* nurtured a generation of studio side-men whose ease across country and rhythm-and-blues musical sensibilities prepared them to navigate the expanse of styles that mark late twentieth-century popular music. Earlier musicians attest that these players were not so much breaking new ground, but building upon a tradition. Long before the post–World War II generation was born, black and white musicians around Shreveport listened to one another and, at times, played together. Recordings by figures like Leadbelly and Jimmie Davis enter the story at a moment of transition between modern commercial recording and an earlier era. They raise critical questions. To what extent do recordings like theirs point to musical practices that predate mass media? In the case of Shreveport, to what extent do they complicate a picture of nineteenth-century musical life that may be oversimplified by the segregated categories of 1920s record sales (namely "race" and "hillbilly")? Through the piecemeal accounts of entertainment and musical life in nineteenth-century Shreveport, it is possible to develop a sense of context for Leadbelly, Davis, and other musicians at the cusp of the modern age of media. At the same time, this context becomes the background for the mass-mediated interactions across racial boundaries that happened after World War II. Perhaps their transformative power, which dramatically played out on the *Hayride* stage, resulted from a momentum that had been quietly building in places like Shreveport for at least a hundred years.

Music in Shreveport during the nineteenth century traveled the same river and land routes as the steamboats and overland pioneers. It also grew up in local practices that characterized the region's daily life. Along the Red River, occasional showboats joined the commercial traffic headed to the north end of a cotton line. Tent repertory and medicine shows rumbled into town via wagon and later trains, as did opera productions and theater companies. People gathered to celebrate and dance at high festivities like weddings and Mardi Gras balls, as well as everyday affairs like house parties or visits to a riverfront bordello.

From the river, one of the town's more frequent attractions was the *Banjo*, which before the Civil War operated as "the principal showboat of the Mississippi Waterways System."[1] A large portion of the entertainment aboard showboats like the *Banjo* consisted of blackface minstrelsy, a type of performance that began in the northeast before the mid-century, though its roots extend to at least the late 1700s.[2] The standardized tradition, developed in the 1840s, involved white performers in burnt cork or grease-based makeup performing musical vignettes and comedy sketches, allegedly based on slave life. At first, these routines generally featured burlesque stock characters such as "Tambo" and "Bones."[3] While they always portrayed African-Americans as socially and culturally inferior, the minstrel shows did not settle into the commonly cited stereotypes of the "happy slaves" and the unhappy, "incompetent Northern Negroes" until around the mid-1850s, when tensions over slavery heated up. According to blackface historian Robert Toll, the new set stereotypes "helped the Northern public to overlook the brutal aspects of slavery and to rationalize racial caste rather than face the prospect of fundamental social and political change."[4]

After the Civil War, African-American troupes began to perform, donning the face paint and adopting the musical style and comedy routines, but often imbuing the material with double meanings received differently, yet simultaneously, by white and black audiences. Although blackface minstrelsy experienced its greatest popularity between 1840 and 1890, forms of blackface entertainment lingered in rural southern life well into the age of radio. Its musical style and racist caricaturing found a home, for example, in the "Negro" or "coon" songs that populated phonograph record catalogues near the turn of the century. Limited by prejudices inherent in the entertainment industry, African-Americans as well as whites performed and composed "coon songs," and as with minstrelsy, these black artists often modified the form to include double messages, inside jokes, and transposed stereotypes. During the early twentieth century, George Walker and Bert Williams most famously navigated the era's difficult realities on vaudeville circuits and later wrote their own shows on Broadway.[5]

The presence of the *Banjo* on the Red River coincided with the age of minstrelsy. With seating for around 200 audience members, the *Banjo* made "an average run per day of less than twenty miles," stopping "at every landing that promised a crowd."[6] Performances on the *Banjo* followed the structure typical of most minstrel shows: The troupe formed a semi-circle with Tambo and Bones at either end, exchanging lively repartee that always got the better of the straight man in the middle. Performers interspersed the comedy with musical interludes on the banjo or fiddle, and with a song repertoire that balanced schmaltziness with light-hearted humor; they occasionally added skits, often poking fun at recent politics. Black and white performers, all in burnt-cork makeup, crowded the stage in the ensemble finale, called the "walk-around," which typically disintegrated into a showcase of "individual impromptu stunts."[7] On smaller showboats like the *Banjo*, nearly every member by necessity served a double role as both crew and cast.

The *Banjo* represents only a small portion of the river traffic in Shreveport, a periodic and exciting occurrence. More regularly, the crews of larger passenger and cargo steamboats also performed music to the delight of gathered locals. Nineteenth-century diary entries of steamboat travelers and Natchitoches area citizens record their impressions of the songs of "roustabouts," the longshoremen or riverboat deck hands. At first, these workers were mostly Irish and German—the two most numerous nationalities flocking to U.S. port cities in the antebellum years. At the mid-century height of Irish and German immigration, some 4,000 people reportedly entered New Orleans in the span of a week.[8] When African-American labor supplanted the Irish and German crews after the Civil War, some of their repertoire passed to the former slaves and survived as twentieth-century African-American songs. Thus, ethnic sounds of the Irish and Germans became part of the vast array of material performed by the "songster," an appellation many of the earliest blues musicians preferred. Two connotations exist for the word "songster." It can simply refer to a printed collection of song lyrics. But in African-American southern culture, the term "denoted a person who was a noted singer, played a stringed instrument, and possessed a wide repertoire of sacred and secular music."[9]

While the earliest white rousters sang for small crowds on docks up and down the river, it was the later African-American crews whose tradition of river work songs caught the attention of folk music collectors. Mary Wheeler, for example, published studies during the late 1930s and early 1940s that included descriptions of African-American roustabout performances of a bygone era: "As the steamboat was leaving port, all rousters were required to line up on the lower deck. When the vessel was loosened from the levee a song was 'raised.' This was always a hymn or spiritual."[10] For Wheeler, what began as spontaneous song to accompany work evolved into a departure ritual emphasizing sacred songs that, by the time of her writing, were part of vocal concert repertoire.

At the same time, however, these steamboat work songs bridge early commercial country music with an earlier context for black and white musical interaction. For example, Wheeler includes a transcription of the song "Beefsteak When I'm Hongry" (sung aboard the *Kentucky* and the *Joe Fowler*), the first verse of which appears nearly intact in the country song "Rye Whiskey," made famous by Tex Ritter but treated in print and recordings numerous times from the late 1920s onward. Another similarly ubiquitous tune is "Careless Love," which Wheeler describes as associated with the steamer *Dick Fowler* on the Ohio River. The tune was an early jazz standard and a staple of commercial recordings by both whites and blacks beginning in the late 1920s, recorded many times over in the first two decades of the industry. It lingered in repertoires of black and white musicians throughout the twentieth century. By the time Dr. John (Mac Rebennack) included it on his 1992 album *Goin' Back to New Orleans* he mused in the liner notes: "This tune is timeless and anonymous. I don't know who wrote it—I don't know where the hell it came from—but I know it's claimed by people in the blues and people playing hillbilly."[11] Tunes like "Careless Love" journeyed across racial borders long before song collectors and record producers captured them on paper or shellac. Before the age of recording, they wafted along the banks of the nation's waterways, carried by the voices of Irish, German, and African-American rousters as they hauled cotton on the Red River between New Orleans and Shreveport.

By the last two decades of the nineteenth century, most of the smaller passenger steamboats common on the Red River featured a pianist and fiddler duo or other small ensemble to entertain passengers or accompany nightly dancing. The musicians usually doubled as waiters, roustabouts, or firemen during the day. The larger "floating palaces" that characterize the pinnacle of the steamboat era generally included a six-to-eight-piece orchestra in the ballroom. Music was not restricted to nighttime. During the day, the rousters' chorus, often with accompaniment by the ship's bell or whistle, served the dual purpose of facilitating the heavy labor and luring patrons to the boat.[12] The greater formalization of the rouster singing coincides with the increased threat to river transport by the railroad industry, and the growing emphasis on musical entertainment aboard the steamboats indeed may have been a deliberate strategy to compete.

At a time when the Red River traced Shreveport's fastest link, economically and culturally, with the rest of the nation, some of its entertainments also lumbered into town by land. The extent to which these touring shows drew black and white audiences together is not specifically documented, but their arrival as entertainment in a town the size of Shreveport would have been circulated to a broad cross-section of the community. Many of the traveling circuses, medicine shows, and theatrical and variety troupes common in the nineteenth-century South came in horse-drawn wagons over land circuits. These established contexts and musical practices that lingered in country music of the early twentieth century. The medicine show, for example, appeared in the United States as early as the seventeenth century, but its precedents were the quack healers who attracted European audiences during the Middle Ages with music, magic, and trickery. These same healer types survived in the more modern rural South and made a living hawking tonics and laxatives to crowds drawn to the wagon by the sounds of fiddles and banjos. Bill Malone points out that many of these entertainers performed in blackface.[13] "Tent repertory" shows also commonly moved between rural communities and towns, staking their tents for more or less a week before moving on. Well into the early twentieth century, tent-rep shows continued to offer southern rural audiences a hodge-podge of human and animal entertainment—turning flips, making magic, dancing soft shoe and doing high kicks, yodeling mountain tunes and crooning sentimental ballads.[14]

Newspapers document formal theatrical performance in Shreveport as early as 1854, but it most likely occurred sporadically before then, with levee warehouses doubling as the staging grounds.[15] By 1859 the Gaiety opened as the first theater in the town; the second, Tally's Opera House, was finished in 1871. Many of the most famous actors of the era, including internationally known Adah Issacs Mencken, performed in Shreveport during the mid-to-late nineteenth century. Tally's Opera House featured local groups as well as traveling companies, and the entertainment ranged from *Macbeth* to P. T. Barnum's circus, from the opera *Prince Napoleon* to an appearance of the pianist Blind Tom.[16] Tally's eventually closed due to competition by the Grand Opera House, constructed in 1888. Music and drama, however, continued to thrive in the area during the last quarter of the nineteenth century, and Shreveport was a major stop for many of the traveling shows from Chicago and other major cities.[17]

Other common entertainments in nineteenth-century Shreveport were large-scale minstrel shows and the music of brass bands. Throughout the 1880s and 1890s numerous well-known minstrel troupes visited the city, including Callender's Georgia Minstrels and Al G. Field (with Dan Emmett). They performed at Tally's and the Grand Opera house, touted by advertisements like "Fanny Hill's Big Burlesque Company" or "Grand Parisian Ballet featuring sixty Beautiful and Lithesome Coryphees."[18] Inspired by these traveling shows, local citizens formed several minstrel troupes of their own. A white group was led by Sam Ford and Henry Pinckney Hyams, and two black troupes formed in 1881, the Brown and Williams' Colored Minstrels and the Gus Williams Company.

Brass bands were a common sight in communities throughout the United States during the era. A site for interaction between white and black musical aesthetics, brass bands were omnipresent during the nineteenth century in even the smallest villages. As historian William J. Schafer wrote, "Brass bands played for circuses, carnivals, minstrel and medicine shows, political rallies, churches, picnics, dances, athletic contests, holiday gatherings. The Salvation Army employed the small brass band as a potent weapon in its evangelistic crusade, and politicians and pitchmen of every stamp used brass bands for ballyhoo. Every military troop, quasi-military drill team, volunteer fire squad, lodge, or social club had its auxiliary band to swell holiday pageantry."[19] Shreveport was no exception and in the heyday of brass bands the city had several of its own, including the Gallery Slaves, the Continentals, Columbia Brass Band, and Professor Masino's Italian Band.

The organized music-making of minstrel troupes and brass bands created public spaces for the musical exchange between disparate groups of the region's residents. Likewise, high society affairs like the plantation balls and parties during the social season presented a circumscribed context for black and white musical contact. From the end of October through Mardi Gras, in early spring, the series of formal dances coincided with the season of high commercial activity along the river, as well as relief from summer heat. Sketchy contemporary records make it impossible to determine how often blacks and whites played together in the same social or "quadrille" orchestras—or simply string bands—that provided music for these events. Not surprisingly, most descriptions suggest that guests at these events would have been mostly white or Creole, while the musicians were most often African-American.[20] Clearly, however, these musicians navigated a broad range of styles. Depending on the occasion, their repertoire ranged from the raucous dance numbers of the "frolics" to more formal European-style dances such as the waltz, the polonaise, or the schottische.

Outside the realm of wealthy society, private parties and special occasions constituted an integral part of everyday life and featured music that people provided themselves or hired out. Again, many white community events like these included African-American musicians present as band members or soloists. In his recollections of nineteenth-century Shreveport life, Albert Harris Leonard described one typical setting, a wedding celebrated at the household of a man named John Walpole, whose son "married Miss Toinette Dupre, a pretty Creole brunette, with dark flashing eyes, and hair as black as night." Leonard describes the large wedding party arriving at the groom's house about 4 miles outside town, with the property illuminated outside by "torches of pit pine" and inside with "home run tallow dips." As Leonard recalls the scene:

> After the usual ceremony and congratulations, an old Negro with his fiddle woke the brisk harmony that country people love and to which they responded by "chasing the flying hours and flowing feet" until called to a substantial supper to which all did full justice. Then on with the dance till dewy morn, and all the while a barrel of whiskey, full when the first guests arrived stood on the front gallery, with its head knocked out. Near it in easy reach a gourd hung from a nail driven in the wall of the house. Those who wanted whiskey and all wanted it, that is all the men and some of the women, dipped this gourd in the barrel and from it drank their fill.[21]

In noting the Creole ethnicity of the bride, Leonard brings to mind Shreveport's proximity and connection to New Orleans culture and underscores the nuances of racial and ethnic identity that inform the region.

Celebrations were not unusual highlights of life in northwest Louisiana, and the African-American community hosted many of its own. Local black residents regularly held rural house parties, called "sukey jumps." A term of ambiguous origins, it was still used by Huddie "Leadbelly" Ledbetter, born near Shreveport in 1888, when he recalled his youth years later. In a 1940 Library of Congress recording, as he discussed square dances and sukey jumps, Leadbelly suggested an explanation for the last half of the phrase: "Because they dance so fast, the music was so fast and the people had to jump, so they called them sooky [sic] jumps."[22] Leadbelly biographers Charles K. Wolfe and Kip Lornell propose one explanation for the first half: "Sukey, or sookie, was apparently a Deep South slang term dating from the 1820s and referring to a servant or slave. A sukey jump, therefore, was once a dance or party in slave quarters."[23] Regardless of its origins, African-American sukey jumps shared certain characteristics with white house parties and "frolics." In both settings, drink flowed freely and people danced to sparse accompaniment, usually fiddle, guitar, or both. For the musicians involved, these parties were opportunities to sharpen their virtuosity.

The African-American guitarist Mance Lipscomb, born in 1895 in nearby east Texas, honed a broad repertoire by playing for the local dances of both blacks and whites during much of his life. "Discovered" in 1960, whereupon white festival audiences heralded him as a blues master, Lipscomb's mastery of varied styles might better be considered that of a songster. Less than a decade Leadbelly's junior, Lipscomb recalled how his eclecticism grew from meeting the needs of dancers in a variety of settings:

Yeah, them people would do all kinda dances behind my music. Waltz, slow drag, two-step. An then the one-step, swing-out, ballin the jack, buzzard lope, wringin the chicken's neck. Cakewalk come in somewhere in the midst a all that. Caint furgit that Charleston in there. Oh, buck dance was a little like that buzzard lope. An then, we had the blues.[24]

House parties made up an important feature of local life well into the twentieth century, affecting people across social classes and creating spaces where musicians like Lipscomb could absorb the diverse musical sensibilities all around him. These settings continued even as the era of the steamboat began to fade, when the river lost its central role in the region's economy.

As the twentieth century approached, new industry and means of transportation drew new urbanites to Shreveport. Radical social changes accompanied the dying out of Shreveport's river commerce and the swelling of its urban population. Whites and blacks moved from farms in the surrounding countryside to the city, both groups bringing their music with them to jobs in the oil fields or on the rail line. Amid these changes, local churches began exerting greater pressure in their efforts to darn the town's frayed moral fiber. The balance between what Leonard identified as a tension of "frontier" versus "civilization" slowly tipped toward the latter. These changing morays around the turn of the century can be measured by the growing public concern over Shreveport's many "houses of ill repute."

The city's infamous Fannin Street area was known for the potent blend of music and sex found in its brothels. These places existed in Shreveport from its earliest years, when the river lured the kind of rovers typical of a busy port. There had been occasional efforts to limit their operation. In the late 1860s the city passed two ordinances aimed at controlling prostitution houses: one set "a penalty for operating them 'in an indecent manner,'" and the other required their occupants to move to the outskirts of town.[25] However, prostitution as big business in Shreveport was not well documented until after 1900, when newspapers and city council records reflect a rising movement to regulate it.

The result was a city ordinance in February 1903 concerning the area known as St. Paul's Bottoms. The ordinance stated that "property within the prescribed limits shall constitute the red light district of the city of Shreveport to the exclusion of all others."[26] Before this time, brothels could be found throughout the city, many of them concentrated on the riverfront near steamboat and railroad business. By cordoning off a specific area for sin, Shreveport became one of only two cities in the nation, the other being New Orleans, to experiment with a legal red-light district. By 1917 Shreveport could boast "the largest red light district [legal or not] of any city its size in the entire United States."[27] This claim was made by the Council of National Defense in support of a movement to close the area, begun in July 1917 by the Anti-Vice Committee of the local Rotary club. The crux of the council's argument was that the legal district of bordellos, saloons, gambling houses, and even opium dens (though outlawed in 1907) threatened "the health, if not the morals, of the thousands of newly-drafted soldiers who were passing through the city."[28] On 15 November 1917, a city ordinance, narrowly passed in a referendum, officially reversed the 1903 designation and closed St. Paul's Bottoms.

Throughout its various phases of legality, Shreveport's red-light district played host to a regular congress of hedonists, rounders, and musicians of differing race and social stature, just as did other famous sin districts. As Malone points out, Shreveport's Fannin Street had parallels in Memphis (Beale Street), New Orleans (Basin St.), and Dallas (Deep Elm—"Ellum" in song). In these places, "one could find amusement in the white taverns or black juke joints, or listen to street singers—both white and black—who could be heard with frequency in any southern city in those days before ordinances drove them from the streets."[29] Guitar and piano players enlivened the atmosphere of Fannin Street, interacting in an environment that operated outside the confines of polite society.

Much of the music that existed in the Shreveport brothels and bars came from musicians like Pine Top Hill and Sycamore Slim, who played piano in the style that came to be known as "barrelhouse." In barrelhouse style, the left hand typically carried an emphatic bass beat while the right syncopated improvised melodic strains alongside dissonant chords. The overall effect was a rolling, rollicking sound that was of great formative influence on Leadbelly, the legendary folk musician from the Shreveport area. As a famous exponent of African-American folk musical styles during the 1930s and 1940s, Leadbelly remembered his musical experiences in Shreveport during the early 1900s:

Boogie woogie was called barrelhouse in those days. One of the best players was named Chee-Dee. He would go from one gin mill to the next on Fannin Street. He was coal black and one of the old-line players and he boogied the blues. At that time anyone could walk into a barrelhouse and just sit down and start playing the piano. I learned to play some piano myself by picking it out.[30]

Leadbelly adapted the characteristic bass pattern of the barrelhouse piano—what he called "walking the bass"—to his six-string guitar and, later, to a twelve-string guitar.[31] It became a hallmark of the singer's sound, a full sound born of the necessity to oftentimes single-handedly keep the dancing going all night long. Like Mance Lipscomb across the Texas border, Leadbelly developed his guitar playing in the era's singularly demanding contexts. As Lipscomb put it, a situation like a house party needed a single musician who was "four men deep," that is, who could sing, keep the beat going, and play both bass and lead parts. Thus, Lipscomb learned "a whole lot a ways" to play his instrument.[32] Leadbelly began a similar tutelage in rural settings around northwest Louisiana, but carried his talent even further. Indeed, few guitarists parallel Leadbelly's mastery of ways to play his twelve-string guitar, a skill he began to hone on Fannin Street.

The known facts of Leadbelly's early life are few, but some things are certain: as a youngster growing up around Mooringsport, Louisiana, Leadbelly began playing music for rural Saturday-night sukey jumps and occasionally for Sunday morning church. In 1904, when he was 16, Leadbelly left home, probably because he fathered an illegitimate child.[33] The singer did not roam far, settling in Shreveport where he lived on and around Fannin Street, soaking up the music of the Bottoms nightlife. Ledbetter left Shreveport in 1906, after only two years. Even so, the music and experiences he absorbed there remained with him throughout his life.[34]

Leadbelly recorded several tunes that pay tribute to his formative experiences in Shreveport, including one named "Fannin Street" (also recorded as variants, "Tom Hughes Town" and "Follow Me Down"). Leadbelly begins the recording with a spoken aside that reveals the family tensions arising from his attraction to Shreveport's nightlife and the deceptions he employed to get there. It also calls attention to a particular "crying" guitar figure that punctuates many of the verses: "That's my mama crying about me, didn't want me going on Fannin Street. Just the place I wanted to go. Sent me to the fair five times, I ain't got to the fair the first time."[35] Once the song begins, it slowly builds in intensity. The barrelhouse bass signature fills in spaces between the rhythmically edgy verses, whose short, angular melodic ascents cram in more and more lyrics as the music proceeds. During instrumental breaks, the vocals punctuate with hums and moans as the guitar increases in complexity and speed. Leadbelly is at least "four men deep" by the end of this song tribute to the place where he first encountered barrelhouse and blues and added them to his repertoire of country songs, work songs, and ballads.[36]

Later chapters in Leadbelly's life are the stuff of legends, including an incarceration on a Louisiana chain-gang (from which he escaped), another in Texas under the pseudonym Walter Boyd, and a third at Louisiana's notorious Angola State Penitentiary. While in prison, Leadbelly further honed his skills as a musician; it even appears that he sang his way into a pardon from Governor Pat Neff in Texas and tried to do the same in Louisiana.[37] During his prison term at Angola, Leadbelly met John and

Alan Lomax, the father-and-son team then traveling to prisons throughout the South collecting folk music for the Library of Congress. Shortly after his release, Leadbelly contacted John Lomax and asked him for a job. Thus began a long and complicated relationship with the Lomaxes that eventually led Leadbelly to fame. Moving to the East Coast, he performed for upper-class white audiences at places like Harvard and the Modern Language Association, at first in prison stripes, accompanied by the scholastic lectures and explanations of John Lomax. Leadbelly and John, after a time, ran aground and afoul; but Leadbelly remained on good terms with Alan, who later took over his father's post as head of the Archive for American Folk Song at the Library of Congress.

Leadbelly's later episodes include international recognition as a folk music performer and participation in the 1940s New York folk music scene along with Woody Guthrie, Pete Seeger, Burl Ives, Josh White, Sonny Terry, Brownie McGhee, and others. He constantly struggled to control his temper and, while in New York, served another year prison term on Riker's Island for stabbing a man. Meanwhile, Leadbelly played his extensive repertoire for audiences in Carnegie Hall as well as for his own regular radio program on WNYC in New York (beginning in 1941) and for a short time on KRE in Los Angeles.[38] Despite his prolific recordings and his recognition as the avatar of American folk music in all its depth and breadth, he died penniless on 6 December 1949 of Lou Gehrig's disease[39] (fig. 2.1).

Upon his death, Leadbelly's wife traveled with his body down to Mooringsport, Louisiana, and he remains buried in the graveyard of the Shiloh Baptist Church; at the time he died, his family could afford no marker for his grave. Back home in Louisiana, Leadbelly's death and burial received little notice. While his death was reported in the *New York Times*, none of the four area weekly newspapers covered the story and the daily Shreveport *Times* printed only a brief article taken from a wire service.[40]

In 1982, sixty-five years after Shreveport's legal red-light district closed, the city council changed the name of the neighborhood still known as "St. Paul's Bottoms" to "Ledbetter Heights" in an effort to honor the singer and inspire community revitalization. The area also was declared a National Historic District. That same year, the Louisiana Tourist Commission placed a historical marker near Caddo Lake in Oil City, near the site of Leadbelly's childhood.[41] In 1993 the Caddo Parish Police Jury used its memorial fund to erect a granite monument over Ledbetter's grave, replacing the state marker put in during the early 1980s.[42] On 22 October 1994, the Shreveport Regional Arts Council sponsored the downtown construction of a $25,000 bronze statue of Leadbelly pointing away from the riverfront toward Ledbetter Heights. People visit the musician's grave, often leaving behind a guitar pick or a penny. To get there, they venture a long country road to the graveyard behind the Shiloh Baptist Church, about a mile from the Texas border. There they can still see many of the surrounding graves of poor rural African-Americans marked as Leadbelly's was for more than twenty years—with a plain steel pipe sticking out of the ground.

Such an impoverished burial belies the musical affluence of Leadbelly's

Fig. 2.1 Leadbelly in a publicity shot. Noel Memorial
Library Archives, LSU in Shreveport.

life. His recordings attest to a broad range of musical experiences, most of
which predate the era of commercial records. His songs fall under a variety of genre headings: ragtime, barrelhouse, blues, country ballads, cattle
calls, work songs, field hollers, gospel, spirituals, string band music, folk
songs, children's songs, play/party songs, topical songs; even Tin Pan Alley,
Broadway, and popular songs of the early twentieth century were part of
his repertory. Nearly any compilation of Leadbelly's music reflects the
breadth of his guitar playing, equal in its dynamism and athleticism to his
singing.[43] His style can be understated, a fairly simple alternation of bass
notes and turns with strummed chords in a tune like "You Cain' Loose-A-
Me Cholly" or a melodic blues accompaniment in "Sweet Mary Blues." At
other times, he maintains a simple but steady undercurrent on one or two

chords as in the song "Alberta," or weaves a delicate instrumental tapestry in tunes like the self-described "twelve-string rag," "Easy Mr. Tom." His vocals are equally impressive. Alternately moaning, shouting, or declarative, even yodeling in tunes like "When I Was a Cowboy," Leadbelly's songs extend far beyond later commercial stereotypes about how and what a black man sings.

Leadbelly's corpus, prodigious and diffuse, evinces a cultural dynamism between blacks and whites that occurred during the nineteenth and early twentieth centuries, particularly in the northwest Louisiana region. The unique circumstances of his life allowed his vast repertoire to be recorded largely outside the terms of the commercial music industry. In his musical breadth, he stands out both because of his extraordinary musicianship and because his corpus troubles the neatly segregated distinction between black and white music institutionalized by the phonograph industry nomenclature "race" and "hillbilly." By the time record producers in search of material to feed the growing demand for rural sounds reached Deep South regions like Shreveport, these categories defined their task. In Shreveport they found African-American artists who ably fit their needs. Wolfe and Lornell list a number of Shreveport area artists who made commercial recordings during the 1920s and 1930s, including Elzadie Robinson, a "rough-voiced vaudeville singer" who recorded for Paramount from 1926 to 1928; Lillian Glinn, who recorded "Shreveport Blues" for Columbia in 1929 (the more well-known performer Memphis Minnie also recorded the tune); Oscar "Buddy" Woods and Ed Schaffer, who sometimes played guitar Mississippi Delta style, on their laps with a broken bottleneck used to "fret"; Williard "Ramblin'" Thomas, who sang and played slide guitar in twenty songs recorded between 1928 and 1932 for Paramount and Victor.[44]

It is not possible to ascertain the degree to which recordings by these artists accurately represent the breadth of their musical life. But the question may be worth bringing up nevertheless. How much did the formulaic thinking and myopia of commercial profit shape the recorded output of black and white rural musicians alike? How often by the late 1920s and early 1930s were artists encouraged to fit their repertoire and performance styles to whichever audience the record company wished to target? Leadbelly experienced this pressure. During Leadbelly's encounter with commercial recording for the American Record Company, Art Satherley encouraged him to emphasize blues because blues was the style Satherley expected black audiences to purchase. But to what extent does Leadbelly's encounter parallel that of other roots performers from places like Shreveport where a history of cross-racial proximity brought divergent influences to developing musicians?

Northwest Louisiana adds a critical dimension to this question, which regularly rises in roots music scholarship both in cases of specific musicians and as an issue of larger cultural dynamics. One of the most notable contributions to this dialogue is the landmark collection of recordings, *From Where I Stand*, which purposefully explores the relationship of black performers to country music. In the liner notes to the collection, former director of both the Country Music Foundation and the National Endowment for the Arts Bill Ivey considers the connection between early phonograph records and the musical practices that preceded them: "It is doubtful that record label executives [during the 1920s and 1930s] would have dredged up much enthusiasm for musicians who did not fit easily into the 'race' or 'hillbilly' designations, and it is probable that recorded examples document only a handful of the multi-racial ensembles or the black old-time musicians who actually performed in a country style."[45] Ivey suggests that music that did not fit racial preconceptions simply may not have found a place on early discs.

Other brief glimpses into the makeshift studios of early recording companies bear this out. Charles Wolfe, for example, recounts the story of a black string band dismissed from a Vocalion session in Knoxville because the producer felt that it "'doesn't sound like anything I've ever heard.'" Wolfe reflects, "Black bands playing something other than blues didn't fit into either stereotype, and so few of them were recorded."[46] If commercial producers pressured Leadbelly to play parts of his repertoire that conformed to stereotyped notions, these same stereotypes continued to demonstrate power in the many posthumous releases of Leadbelly material. Although most often anthologized in blues collections, as Ivey says, "both his songs and his performance style fit 'country' criteria more completely. Leadbelly is, in many ways, the quintessential folk master of his era."[47] But Leadbelly's importance goes deeper than his talent as an individual. Leadbelly points to a richer dynamic within the history of southern roots music than the artifacts of phonograph records portray. Leadbelly's repertoire reflects the kind of musical fluidity across racial and cultural borders, necessarily tacit yet profound, that emerged from day-to-day realities of life in Shreveport.

Other contemporary musicians broaden the context for Leadbelly and further the idea that exchanges of musical ideas and sounds were sought out among black and white musicians alike. They also suggest other deep southern regions where similar exchanges occurred. In 1930 Polk Brockman held sessions for Okeh Records in Shreveport, where he recorded an African-American string band from Jackson called the Mississippi Sheiks.[48] The Sheiks are famous as Mississippi's most commercially successful blues group during the pre–World War II era. Several songs from their repertoire, "Keep My Skillet Good and Greasy," "Sitting on Top of the World," and "Yodeling Fiddling Blues," reflect an active relationship between country and blues musicians from the late 1920s through the 1930s. "Sitting on Top of the World," the Sheiks' top-selling song, was performed by white groups during the 1930s and today remains a staple in bluegrass and blues repertoires.[49] But the musical ideas flowed both ways. As music historian John Rumble points out, the song "'Yodeling Fiddling Blues' shows the influence of country great and Sheiks contemporary Jimmie Rodgers," also a native Mississippian.[50] Rodgers himself is another example of interaction across musical borders, as a white musician with overt and widely acknowledged blues influence.

Recordings by Oscar Woods and Jimmie Davis present yet further context. Woods, an African-American player with a broad mastery of regional traditions, recorded for John Lomax in Shreveport in 1940. Davis is most famous for his sentimental country and gospel recordings, as well as for his two terms as governor of Louisiana, 1944–48 and 1960–64. However, during the 1930s, Woods had performed and recorded with Davis, joining him in sessions not only as an instrumentalist but as a singer in vocal duets. For Davis, these 1930s recordings stand in sharp contrast to his more genteel later material. The early songs are rife with sexual innuendo absent from the records he made after he won the political limelight.[51] A list of titles is ribald enough: "She Left A'Runnin' Like a Sewing Machine," "Red Nightgown Blues," "Tom Cat and Pussy Blues," "She's a Hum Dum Dinger from Dingersville." But lines like "you ought to see that cock and pussy roosting in the Chiney [sic] tree" leave no room for doubt that Davis was as well versed in a red-light north Louisiana blues tradition as he was in the popular recordings of Jimmie Rodgers.[52] His vocal style in delivering these lines communicates a comfort and fluidity across a broad range of roots musical traditions. More specifically, the early Davis recordings reflect the deep influence on his musical style by African-American musicians from northwest Louisiana.

As examples of interaction between white and black music in the South, the Sheiks, Rodgers, Woods, and Davis suggest that cultural "cross-pollination," as heard in the music of Leadbelly, was not an isolated phenomenon.[53] Leadbelly's musical talents were neither typical nor anomalous, but represent a deep and widespread process that occurred throughout the South. Emphasizing these interactions between black and white musicians during the late nineteenth and early twentieth century dilutes neither the potency nor distinctiveness of either African-American or Euro-American musical styles; but, rather, acknowledges their cross-fertilization and mutual enrichment.

Two Leadbelly recordings included on the *From Where I Stand* collection present examples of songs that bridge a musical border between southern whites and blacks, even after the beginning of the recorded era. These include "Midnight Special," which Leadbelly first recorded in 1934 for the Lomaxes and which later became a hit for the white duo Wilma Lee and Stoney Cooper in 1959. Both black and white artists cut versions of the tune during the late 1920s, including Sam Collins's 1927 "Midnight Special Blues" and Dave Cutrell's 1926 recording in St. Louis, "Pistol Pete's Midnight Special."[54] Another train song, "Rock Island Line" was cut by Leadbelly in 1934 but, as Rumble suggests, the tune "probably dates to the early 1900s, when the Chicago, Rock Island & Pacific Railway first entered Arkansas."[55] Among white country performers who have treated the song, both Johnny Horton and Johnny Cash sang it at the *Louisiana Hayride* during the mid-1950s.[56]

Leadbelly's extensive repertoire, including songs that he wrote, songs that he absorbed from the culture around him, and folk material to which he added his own unique voice, offers material that predates blues and country as national phenomena with rigid racial associations. His eclecticism demonstrates the ease with which musical border crossings occur, particularly during a transitional period that predates the racially circumscribed commercial categories of the 1920s. Drawing equally from his own compositions and from the anonymous wellspring of folk material that he popularized and preserved on phonograph records, Leadbelly's legacy is the ability to communicate broadly. Thus, Leadbelly tunes have been treated by a long list of widely different artists, from the Rolling Stones to Nat King Cole, from Aerosmith to Lawrence Welk.

The list of Leadbelly covers could be viewed in two ways: (1) as the result of a hegemonic and monolithic recording industry machine that encourages the appropriation of musical material from the folk artist to be exploited solely for profit; or (2) as the extension of a tradition of musical exchanges across the black–white border that likely began in places like Shreveport's Fannin Street, or even before, on the loading docks and in railroad work gangs, at the camp meetings and traveling entertainments of nineteenth-century Shreveport. In this latter sense, Leadbelly epitomizes the potential for musical exchange in Shreveport and its environs. He also troubles any notion of black and white music developing along simultaneous but parallel lines. In light of Leadbelly, the sharp segregation of southern roots musics seems more the work of commercial forces to define their markets.[57] If this is not to some degree a construction or simplification of a musical reality that was far more complex, then the cultural significance of Leadbelly is little more than that of a peculiarity; but then such is the case for the Mississippi Sheiks, Oscar Woods, Jimmie Davis, Jimmie Rodgers, and many other early recorded artists, black and white.

The far-reaching process of musical exchange affected southern musicians far outside of Shreveport, and happened outside of face-to-face music-making and electronic media. Uncle Dave Macon, the white banjo player, recorded material that reflects the wealth of potential musical sources available to southern musicians in the decades before and after the turn of the century. Among Macon's standard repertoire were African-American songs and dance tunes like "Rock about My Saro Jane," which he described learning by "hearing a[n African-American] steamboat's crew on Front Street in Nashville, Tennessee, in 1887."[58] Another report comes from Big Bill Broonzy, who once described his childhood musical experiences in Mississippi and Arkansas as a fiddler at "two-way picnics and barbecues," where musicians moved across a single stage playing "old country songs and popular tunes of the day" for the white and black audiences that flanked either side.[59] Broonzy experienced the racism that often governed performance opportunities for black rural musicians. In another interview, he explained why he played mostly for white audiences as a young working musician: "Because, you see, if you play for colored people, why they just pronounce—just consider you as a bum musician down there. The white folks want all the good things for themselves." The bitter constraints of racism eventually drove Broonzy to relocate to Chicago.

Musical interchange also occurred via hymn books found in homes of both blacks and whites. Especially during the 1930s and after, these often included similar, if not identical, selections. Thus, the white-composed "I'll Fly Away" was commonly in black repertoires, while the African-American-penned "Precious Lord, Take My Hand" was a white sacred standard.[60] Like all books, hymnals were no respecter of race and, as through radio and phonograph records, the sharing of white-created and black-created musics occurred independent of the society that bred racial categories in the first place. Moreover, the hymnbooks show that songs did not have to be a part of the oral tradition to be embraced across racial lines. These songs were all written compositions.[61] But the tradition of exchange extends at least a hundred years before, when traveling preachers printed text-only songbooks to aid the scores of worshippers who gathered under the "brush arbor" to express their religious sentiment and sing songs unsanctioned by the established denominations and their hymnals.[62]

These broader examples suggest that Shreveport is at once historically unique and archetypically mid-sized, mid-southern. Racial prejudice and social convention governed the interactions between whites and African-Americans, even in this border region between South and West. Any clues that cultural borders were fluid dispel neither the specter of slavery nor its twin legacies of injustice and inequality. Yet, amid entrenched racism, interaction between black and white musicians happened in the South in settings that were worldly, sacred, and somewhere in between: African-Americans and Euro-Americans shared musical experiences at vaudeville and medicine show performances, in church music, and informal settings such as house parties and picnics. The mingling of black and white cultures is one reason northwest Louisiana created a musical dynamic so distinct from that romanticized matrix of early country music, the Appalachian mountains. African-Americans and Euro-Americans lived in proximity to one another in flatland areas like Shreveport and their musical voices reached one another across the borders—South and West, black and white, sin and religion—that lend the region its unique character.

The commercial destiny of Shreveport took shape over the course of the nineteenth century. By the time Leadbelly began touring with John Lomax, the city's original purpose for coming into being—the river and the commerce drawn to its levee—had long since died. River commerce was replaced by the railroads and by the regional oil business. But the cultural forces spreading from the river remained like so many bayous and lakes. The musical entertainment found in nineteenth- and early twentieth-century Shreveport, especially along its riverfront and in its red-light district, laid the foundation for Leadbelly's corpus just as it formed the eclectic backdrop for the radio industry that began flourishing in the 1920s. Echoes of the past could still be heard in the musical sounds of mid-twentieth-century Shreveport, when the city emerged as a cultural locus for country music.

3

Hillbilly Music and the Phonograph

Uncle Dave, you're not before an audience now; we're putting
this on wax.
—Jack Kapp, recording engineer (as told to
Charles Wolfe by musician Sam McGee)

The first few decades of the twentieth century epitomized the American
ideal of progress, as cities burgeoned into metropolises and technologies like washing machines and Model Ts revolutionized modern life. Yet
it was a complex and dynamically ambivalent time as well, when nearly
every push forward was met, point for point, with a push backward: the le-
galization of women's vote and the outlawing of booze; the optimistic crusade of trust-busting and the anxious enterprise of global war; egalitarian
hope with the formation of the NAACP and reactionary hate with swelling
membership in the KKK.[1] Among the vicissitudes that marked the time
from the turn of the century to the stock market crash, the birth of mass
media forever changed the way people experience the world around them.
Recorded music brought to bear myriad changes upon U.S. culture as it
became, in a word, popular.

Shreveport entered the story of the phonograph industry only indirectly,
as it existed far from the centers of development or commercial exploita-
tion. Yet, positioned on the periphery of the phonograph industry's power,
Shreveport contributed the unique perspective of an outsider, adding
depth to the picture of the phonograph's role in popular music, just as in
the last chapter, Shreveport suggested a dynamic picture of nineteenth-
century roots music. During the 1920s and 1930s, Shreveport eventually
became a cultural way station, its platforms packed with the roots music
that recording executives so earnestly sought. Recording companies were
quick to market this roots music by classifying it in terms of a racial society, "race" for black and "hillbilly" for white. While blacks and whites certainly developed distinct traditions, the industry paradigm emphasized
and ensconced their separation. The terms oversimplified the social and
cultural complexity of music in places like Shreveport and, in so doing, ob-
fuscated not only the richness of the music in its own day but dictated the
terms of musical identity far into the future. In the case of hillbilly music,

Shreveport complicates the preconceived notions of white racial identity, class, and cultural stasis that the hillbilly music label brought to early commercial popular music. To understand Shreveport's position in relation to the broader world of commercial hillbilly music, we must first follow the development of the phonograph industry from its beginnings to the change of identity that occurred during the 1920s.

In the early 1900s, the United States was just beginning its love affair with the phonograph. Although the industry technically began with Thomas Edison's 1878 patent of the phonograph, it was Alexander Graham Bell and his research team who pushed forward the invention's slow evolution into a consumer product. In May 1886, Bell patented the "graphophone," which featured relatively durable cylinders of wax-coated cardboard to replace Edison's delicate tinfoil-covered originals. This improved model made a false start into the world of consumer goods when, in 1888, entrepreneur Jesse H. Lippincott bought both the Edison and Bell patents, formed the North American Phonograph Company, and created thirty subsidiaries through the sale of franchises around the country. Lippincott envisioned the machine as useful in business, a dictaphone to replace much of the work done by stenographers. Unreliable, prone to battery surges, laborious in its operation, and smelly, the Lippincott product failed to find its place alongside the office typewriter.[2] In the meantime Edison saw his own vision of the phonograph's potential use, and in 1891 he purchased the floundering company from Lippincott.

Soon after, phonographs began to appear in drugstores and bars as "coin-in-the-slot" machines throughout the 1890s. For a nickel, patrons heard a cylinder reproduction of music, two minutes long and randomly selected by the machine. The success of these jukebox prototypes, which averaged a return of $50 per week for proprietors, made manifest the phonograph's future as entertainment.[3] Constrained to a narrow spectrum of frequencies, the most successful early cylinders captured brass bands, solo banjo and xylophone players, solo whistlers and singers. Since mechanical mass reproduction of the still-delicate wax cylinders had yet to be realized, recording sessions were tedious both for artists and engineers.[4] Edison's sole contender was the Columbia Phonograph Company, the only Lippincott franchise to survive. Columbia competed with Edison largely on the strength of its exclusive contract with John Philip Sousa and the popularity of its singer/whistler John Y. AtLee.[5] Both companies vied for the consumer dollar by introducing models inexpensive enough for home use during the mid-1890s.

In the meantime, the German-American inventor Emile Berliner had acquired enough capital to produce and market his "gramophone," which replaced the cylinder shape with discs of vulcanized rubber (later shellac), and vertical cuts with lateral grooves.[6] When first introduced, this invention seemed destined to be a stepchild of the more well-established cylinder machines. The perception quickly reversed when litigation over patent rights mired the industry and opened an opportunity for Eldridge R. Johnson, the machinist who had improved upon Berliner's machine. In 1900

Johnson began his own business selling the gramophones he had until then built for Berliner. Johnson's venture started the rapid expansion of the phonograph industry in the United States, with his profits reaching $180,000 after only one year.[7] The following year, Johnson and Berliner (once Berliner's patent rights were upheld in court) agreed to incorporate, with Berliner contributing the patents and Johnson contributing the plant facility and his own expertise. Thus the Victor Talking Machine Company formed in October 1901.[8]

Victor soon dominated the market with a technically superior machine and aggressive advertising that emphasized the prestige of its recording artists. Enrico Caruso, the internationally acclaimed tenor, symbolized this stature. The company promoted him as the hallmark of its Red Seal series of grand opera and instrumental classical music.[9] Besides Caruso, nearly every notable New York Metropolitan Opera singer eventually signed an exclusive Victor Red Seal contract, thus clinching the company's image as a purveyor of quality. Victor also introduced a new design, the Victrola, which encased all the workings of the talking machine within a handsome wooden cabinet. This design further elevated the Victrola's image to that of a musical instrument fit to grace the wealthy parlor alongside the piano. Selling for $200, the Victrola's upper-class appeal lay in the fact that it looked like a piece of fine furniture for the home.[10]

The affluent image, along with the content, of phonograph records began to broaden in 1920 through a complex series of events. This shift centers around the figure of Okeh Record executive Ralph Peer, who christened two new categories of phonograph records, "race" and "hillbilly." Race records emerged after the 1920 Okeh release of Mamie Smith singing "Crazy Blues" and "It's Right Here for You"—the first songs by an African-American blues singer put to shellac.[11] The recording sold so well, an unanticipated 75,000 copies for $1.00 each in the first month, it inspired Okeh Records to seek other ethnic and grassroots performers. Although Peer is credited with denoting this new category of recordings by African-American artists, music business insider and historian Russell Sanjek suggests the possibility that "race" was chosen because it was the word black leaders used to refer to themselves ("race leaders" and "race spokesmen") during the post–World War I era.[12]

A few years later, this same Peer became preeminent in recording white "hillbilly" music. He established what would become the genre nomenclature in 1925 when he dubbed the previously nameless Galax, Virginia, band led by Al Hopkins as The Hill Billies. The story of hillbilly recordings, however, predates Hopkins's band. In March 1923 the Virginia harmonica player Henry Whitter entered Peer's New York office and cajoled him into recording six sides. Peer promptly shelved them. Several months later, Peer traveled south to Atlanta where he set up a temporary studio in an empty loft. There, on portable equipment, he recorded Fiddlin' John Carson's versions of "The Little Old Log Cabin in the Lane" and "Old Hen Cackled and the Rooster's Going to Crow," which became the first hillbilly record released. Carson's recording sold out its first 1924 pressing.

Many of Peer's decisions, attitudes, and business practices resonated in the commercial music industry for years to come, some longer than others. For example, he set a precedent for field recording, which was a common source of 1920s commercial roots releases thereafter.[13] Before Peer quit Okeh Records in 1925 to begin his own business, he recorded many artists this way, both black and white, mostly in Atlanta but also in Dallas. Other record companies followed suit, and their announcements of makeshift sessions in local newspapers drew professionals and amateurs alike. Geographically concentrated in the southeast, the earliest discs preserved the repositories of folk songs, instrumental tunes, ballads, and Tin Pan Alley numbers long forgotten by mainstream popular culture.

A shift toward newly composed material followed, partly motivated by exhaustion of the older repertoire and partly by the business acumen of Peer. He quickly realized the value of owning copyrights for original musical works and subsequently demanded that musicians compose new songs. Record manufacturers normally set aside two cents per record as a "mechanical" royalty paid to the copyright holder. While still working for Okeh, Peer established the practice of securing copyrights for the record company from composers, in exchange for a half-cent royalty per record sold. At first, Peer gained no personal profit from this arrangement, as he was still employed by Okeh Records. Rather, he saw this as an equitable symbiosis between the record company and the composers who supplied it with new material.[14] From the artists' perspective, Peer's royalty contracts were an improvement on the practices of other companies, who most often paid a flat fee for their songs. Ultimately, Peer's practice improved long-term relations between musicians and record companies. It also served him well. Eventually, after years of amassing copyrights and collecting royalties for the use of tunes, Peer became a wealthy man during a time when few enjoyed affluence.

Peer's deliberation and foresight in issues of ownership still resonate throughout the popular music industry. Yet his attitude about the music he recorded reflected broader social tensions and class anxieties of the era and the terms he coined somewhat off-the-cuff to define commercial roots music resonate even more deeply. Race and hillbilly music together form the bedrock of the popular music market today and the later name changes to rhythm-and-blues and country-and-western did not entirely free the music from the burdens of the 1920s. The labels are products of their time, bearing all tensions within society along lines of generation, region, race, and class that uniquely characterized the early twentieth century. In the specific case of hillbilly music, both the genre and its early musicians embody the era's ambivalence over the nature, meaning, and price of progress.

The phonograph's evolution from quaint curiosity to influential mass medium coincided with an era in U.S. society particularly pregnant with anxiety over its experience of rapid social changes and self-conscious over its identity and role in the world. Steady emigration from hinterland to city transformed the complexion of the entire country while a new moral interventionism changed both the posture and stature of the States abroad. Understandably, the 1920s realized a domestic correlative to such cosmopolitan progress—the equal and opposite force of popular nostalgia, which came to be characteristic of hillbilly music. Cultural historian Lawrence Levine notes that the tension between progress and nostalgia in the 1920s "was not merely present in the antithetical reactions of different groups but *within* the responses of the same groups and individuals. Americans were still torn between the past and the future, the individual and society."[15]

Many early hillbilly musicians themselves portrayed the stresses and ambivalences of the era when mass media began to change the music and practices that up to that point had been grounded in face-to-face communication. The early recording pioneer Uncle Dave Macon is the archetype of the hillbilly musician who made the transition from live stage entertainment to phonographs, radio, and "talkies," all of which gradually supplanted their predecessors by the mid-1930s. Born in 1870, Uncle Dave had been exposed to vaudeville, tent repertory, medicine show, and circus entertainers from his boyhood on, growing up in the downtown Nashville hotel his parents owned, a hotel that catered to transient show business folk. At the age of 15, he learned to play the banjo and for the next thirty-five years absorbed music wherever he traveled, adding to the vaudeville repertoire he already knew with an unusual capacity for retaining songs. In 1900 he founded his Macon Midway Mule and Wagon Transportation Company, which he operated for the next twenty years. Until he reached his fifties, Macon kept his day job and performed as an exuberant amateur with a comic, gregarious stage presence.[16]

In 1921, at the age of 51, Uncle Dave played in a schoolhouse in Morrison, Tennessee, to raise money for a local Methodist church. Two years later, he was hired to play Loew's Theater in Birmingham, Alabama, which led to an offer to tour the circuit of Loew's Theaters throughout the country. Macon became one of the most sought-after vaudeville entertainers of the era and one of the first hillbilly recording stars. He was also a headliner on the *Grand Ole Opry* for its first fifteen years. Macon's heart remained in vaudeville tours, even though he was a working-class celebrity in the newer forms of entertainment—namely records and radio—that heralded the inexorable demise of those tours. (The next entertainment wave, the "talkies" or sound motion pictures, dealt an injuring blow; the Great Depression, a mortal one.)

Macon's music expressed the ambivalence experienced by many southerners, especially those outside larger cities, toward technological change in the twentieth century. For country music scholar Charles Wolfe, Macon's attitude about the car epitomizes his generation's hesitance toward technology: "Like many of his peers, he had mixed feelings about the automobile; he never forgot that trucks once put him out of business, and sang: 'I'd rather ride a wagon and go to heaven / Than to hell in an automobile.' At the same time, he was singing the praises of the 'Henry Ford car' in 'On the Dixie Bee Line.'"[17] Furthermore, Macon's career parallels that of other traditional southern musicians, both frustrated and accelerated by the changing technology. Much more so than early radio, phonograph records perturbed musicians because they placed a new set of constraints upon entertainment, the most obvious being the time constraints dictated by the 78-rpm disc. Other constrictions were less obvious. Wolfe quotes an interview with musician Kirk McGee, reflecting on his mid-1920s sessions with Uncle Dave:

> Uncle Dave . . . wouldn't stay put. He kept getting closer and closer to the mike. He was an old stage man, and he wanted to do it just like he was doing for an audience. And Jack Kapp, the recording man, said "Uncle Dave, you're not before an audience now; we're putting this on wax." And then Uncle Dave would get to reeling and rocking and stomping his foot on the floor and this would shake the floor, cause the recording stylus to vibrate. So they went and got this pillow for him to put his foot on, to stomp on. Uncle Dave said, "I don't like that, because I can't hear my foot; that'll ruin my rhythm."[18]

Despite all the hurdles of the medium, records made by Uncle Dave and other southern rural musicians sold well throughout the country and they became known far beyond the scope of any theater or tent circuit they had worked before. Uncle Dave, like many musicians, reflected in his music the same tensions experienced by many listeners in an era of rapid change. His type of music made the transition from live performance to modern recording, acquiring the label "hillbilly music" in the process. The recording executives in the East and Midwest who identified this market felt they had discovered a hidden cache. But the passage into modern commercialism involved more than the simple capturing of white rural sounds in a more permanent and portable form. It involved a degree of transformation of those sounds, from a more organic state to a more concrete, defined body of music. By the mid-1930s, the corpus of rural white southern recordings formally assumed Peer's tag, "hillbilly," but before then, it had no set label. Initially dubbed "old-time," "folk" tunes, "songs from Dixie," "old southern tunes," and so on, commercial hillbilly music as such was a new entity, connected to the past, but occupying one among several emerging public spaces for working out the era's tensions of identity in relation to region, race, and class.

In terms of region, hillbilly music represented the South, which suffered from a conflicted self-image from within and contending impressions about the South from without. The music alternately stood for all that ailed contemporary society and all that woefully had been lost in the face of modernity. On the one hand, outsiders during the 1920s increasingly saw the South as a "benighted" region of bumpkin racists and ignorant hayseeds.[19] Intense scrutiny and criticism of southern culture were common themes in newspapers of the day, ranging from measured commentary on the region's social problems to the vituperations of H. L. Mencken published in the *Baltimore Sun*. After witnessing the horrors of the Scopes trial in Dayton, Tennessee, Mencken deemed the South the "bunghole of the United

States, a cesspool of Baptists, a miasma of Methodism, snake-charmers, phoney real-estate operators, and syphilitic evangelists."[20] The ambiguous figure at the center of Mencken's popular tirades was the white rural southern straw man, the "poor white," whose hillbilly music also embodied all the conflicting images associated with the South since the nineteenth century.[21]

Alongside portraits of the South as a stagnant backwater were its portrayals as a region of pastoral mollifications and idyllic probity, as ennobled in folk music and popular nostalgic music since before 1900. Nostalgia, especially for the Old South, took root as a theme in popular songs long before the phonograph when current tunes from Tin Pan Alley composers sold millions of copies of sheet music for the parlor piano.[22] The idealized South thematically dominated minstrel songs, and many compositions by Stephen Foster and other nineteenth-century tunesmiths. Romanticizations like James Bland's "Carry Me Back to Old Virginny" were extremely popular throughout the entire nation as both sheet music and cylinder recordings.[23] They expressed nostalgia for a southern rural farm life free of deprivation, hardship, and the encroachments of modernity—in other words, a life that existed only in the imagination.

Popular song was not the only source of fuel for the developing nostalgia for an idealized South. The work of academic folk song collectors added yet another layer. Most notably, Cecil Sharp's 1917 publication of *English Folk Songs from the Southern Appalachians* represented a tremendous contribution to scholarly knowledge about the survival and evolution of British folk songs in the New World. At the same time, it supported a reified notion of southern white music and unintentionally established a set of values by which later commercial hillbilly music would be measured. Based on his field work in the mountains of North Carolina, Tennessee, and Virginia, Sharp presented the people he encountered as the descendants from the halcyon days of Great Britain, reclusive folk from the Tin Pan Alley pop culture of the United States. In his introduction, Sharp portrays a people in total isolation:

> [T]he cultural value of singing must depend upon the kind of songs that are sung. Happily, in this matter the hillsman is not called upon to exercise any choice, for the only music, or, at any rate, the only secular music, that he hears and has, therefore, any opportunity of learning is that which his British forefathers brought with them from their native country and has since survived by oral tradition.[24]

While remnants from British tradition certainly were abundant in these relatively remote regions of the United States, Sharp's description of Appalachian people conformed to a then-current popular conception of southern mountain folk as "our contemporary ancestors."[25] Sharp's ears listened for the sounds of British roots to the exclusion of other facets of vital tradition among the same people. For instance, he neglected church and instrumental music outright; nor is there indication that Sharp ever questioned his informants as to their knowledge of contemporary popular music on phonograph records or sheet music.[26] These limitations do not negate the value of Sharp's contributions, but they raise questions not only about the music he neglected to note but about the extent to which his conclusions weighed on the future understanding of commercial hillbilly music. Sharp's presentation confirmed a widely accepted ideal of the rural mountainous South as a living diorama of an older, more congenial way of life, rapidly disappearing in the wake of industrialization and urbanization. Both the sense of cultural inertia and the tone of nostalgia in Sharp's work contributed to the backdrop for hillbilly music to come. Nostalgia for the romanticized South, mountainous or not, would remain a prominent theme in hillbilly music and, in its later appellation, country and western.

The notion of Appalachia as an Anglo culture preserve moved from the realm of folk song scholarship into the echelons of classical concert music, acquiring associations with class identity along the way. As Bill Malone summarizes, "proponents of high-art music had discovered two general types of southern folk music and had mined them for artistic purposes: the Negro spirituals, and the mountain ballads. But in each case, the form had been heavily romanticized, and consequently the lives of their creators were greatly distorted."[27] If nostalgia attended to some degree many forms of white rural southern music, a certain mantle of respectability and purity elevated mountain ballads in relation to commercial rural music. Concert audiences embraced Appalachian ballads that demonstrated a distinct Anglo lineage just as they did African-American spirituals. In the case of African-American spirituals, the music would be starched and powdered, fit into corsets and cutaways for the concert hall. In the case of Appalachian ballads, songs became pieces in an Anglo-Saxon museum of the mind. Commercial hillbilly music shared with the ballads a tradition in rural white southern culture and, today, all of this music would be called "roots music" of one sort or another. But the period's preference for styles that floated a purer, more authentic sense of cultural refinement reflected not only the binary tension pandemic in the United States but the status anxiety of the era as well.

Even among early industry pioneers, hillbilly music seems to have rubbed against their notions of respectability. Some of them nursed antipathy for the music they recorded, but pursued it nevertheless for the lucrative sales it promised. Peer, for example, has been called an "unsung folksong collector" and "a cultural documentarian of the first rank" for his role in founding both the "hillbilly" and "race" record industries.[28] At the same time, he was known to detest hillbilly music, which, it seems, fit neither his notion of legitimate music nor his personal aspirations toward social distinction. When once asked by an interviewer to name some hillbilly musicians he discovered besides Jimmie Rodgers and the Carter Family, Peer replied, "Oh, I've tried so hard to forget them."[29] This attitude of condescension echoed the class discomfort of some whites who winced in the face of hillbilly music's questionable respectability and its implications for white identity. For example, one *Chattanooga Times* reviewer recounted the packed house performance of Jimmie Rodgers in 1929 with a tone of distanced scorn, noting that "more people were entertained by the yodeler and his assistants than witnessed any performance of grand opera presented in the auditorium last week."[30]

In practice, the potential negative connotations evoked by the music troubled early recording executives very little: They just wanted the product to sell well. And hillbilly music fulfilled their hopes as a commercially potent formalization of white southern culture. Between 1925 and 1929, the peak of phonograph sales before World War II, hillbilly releases grew from 225 to 1,250.[31] Even during the Great Depression, when record sales dropped by 1933 to 7 percent of their 1929 levels, hillbilly records remained surprisingly resilient. At that time, when hillbilly music received little exposure on the radio networks, it remained a relatively viable entity on phonograph records. Perhaps this success related somewhat to the music's nostalgic connections to the idealized hillbilly as an icon of a gentler, simpler time; or the appeal of "old-time" tunes, sentimental ballads, and newly composed material in those styles as an antidote to the hardships of the day.

Hillbilly records also remained relatively affordable. The record industry subsisted during the 1930s on the small sales of low-cost budget records, allowing them to sell fewer copies but still maintain profits. Companies reduced costs by recording hillbilly music on discs that sold for 25¢ to 50¢ each.[32] Many labels also avoided paying copyrights when they could, a task easier to do with rural poor performers who often enjoyed exposure and expected little financial return.[33] The record companies that survived the Depression also benefited from the increasing demand for records by that heir of the coin-in-the-slot phonograph, the jukebox. After the repeal of Prohibition in 1933, the jukebox became a fixture in every beer joint and dance hall. Jukeboxes accounted for over half of all records sold in 1936, marking a shift in the function of the record industry from home entertainment back to its role as public diversion.[34]

Many of the beer drinkers and dancehall shufflers who dropped their coins into jukeboxes during the 1930s heard an increasingly wide array of hillbilly sounds. Post-Depression country music reflects more diverse regional traditions as recording emphasis moved away from the mountainous regions of the Southeast and into other parts of the South and Southwest. "Hillbilly" seemed ever less adequate to describe the range of blues, cowboy ballads, string band music, brother duets, and Western swing that marked the westward shift in recordings by white rural southerners. By the late 1940s, it would be replaced by "country-and-western" in a conscious effort to distance the music from the pejorative connotations of the term "hillbilly."[35]

But the implications of hillbilly music as a category for southern sounds extended beyond its negative undertone. As a fundamental way that people make sense of the world, categories contain the power to structure knowledge. In the case of race and hillbilly, the potential problem lies not with the categories of black and white musics themselves, but with how those categories are perceived. As linguistics professor George Lakoff discusses, the "classical" notion of categories assumes that any given category is characterized by distinctive features, contained within distinct boundaries, isolated from other categories.[36] Race and hillbilly made sense as the typography for southern music during the 1920s. Their names arose during the period that has been called the "Age of Segregation" and they iterate the ethos of Jim Crow.[37] In other words, the acceptance and circulation of the industry terms coincided with and inadvertently confirmed the paradigm of racist segregation that during the 1920s was violently enforced by the white political establishment in defensive reaction to heightened activism among African-Americans.

The race-based division for southern music led to real consequences during the 1920s. Charles Wolfe tells the story of the Allen brothers, Lee and Austin, who recorded a large number of "white blues" during the late 1920s and early 1930s.[38] In 1927 the brothers recorded for Columbia's field unit in Atlanta, Georgia. They were the final group appearing before chief engineer Frank Walker, who had spent a long day recording songs of both black and white southern folk artists. As Wolfe writes, "though the music was segregated when it came out on disc, in the field it was a different story."[39] Walker himself, who had extensive experience making recordings in the South, later recalled the demographics of musicians he encountered during these field trips:

> If you were recording in Texas, well, you might have a week in which you recorded your country music; cowboy music thrown in and a little Spanish music from across the border. . . . And the next week might be devoted to so-called 'race music,' because they both came from the same area and with the same general ideas.[40]

Following the Atlanta session, confusion ensued in Columbia's New York office, due to the large number of masters they received and an unfamiliarity with southern accents or music. Subsequently, the Allen brothers' recording of "Chattanooga Blues" and "Laughin' and Cryin' Blues" was released on the "race" series (14000), rather than the "hillbilly" series (15000, at that time labeled "familiar tunes").[41] Wolfe describes the Allens' reaction: "They frantically wired Walker to ask him to correct the mistake before it went any further, but over six thousand records had already been pressed, and there was not much he could do."[42] The brothers threatened to sue Columbia for $250,000 for damage to their reputations. They eventually dropped the lawsuit and signed on to record for Victor. But the story shows how the "race" and "hillbilly" categories, assigned arbitrarily by a recording executive, obtained currency in everyday life. Regardless of the Allens' obvious familiarity with and constant musical reference to black southern styles, the salient feature of their music in the commercial marketplace was its whiteness.

During the 1920s, the label hillbilly music and its equivalents applied willy-nilly to a variety of southern sounds, so long as they were white: the fiddle-scratching of John Carson, the energetic nasal crooning of Uncle Dave, the constrained tenor balladeering of Vernon Dalhart, or the blues yodeling of Jimmie Rodgers. Today, whiteness no longer solely demarcates the hillbilly genre from the perspective of historians. But race-based categories are deeply ensconced in U.S. society. Despite their limitations, they retain power to structure thinking about southern music, propagating long-standing, hackneyed metaphors for its development (like two streams running in parallel). Viewing the early commercial roots music industry from the distance of Shreveport invites a self-conscious inquiry into how early commercial categories shape the country music story. Shreveport's history suggests different metaphors (like a single tree sprouting numerous branches) as alternative models for setting up discussions of past music, or even a deliberate reconfiguration of the categories themselves. To use Lakoff's terms, race and hillbilly might be conceived not in a relationship of "classical categories" but as "radial categories," where the center is most predictable and other elements spiral out, bearing "family resemblances" to the prototype.[43]

From Shreveport, it becomes easier to see how the polychrome musical cultures shared between black and white were effectively lost to the monochrome of commerce. After such loss, faithful music history can recover only by re-listening to familiar music for sounds left unheard and rethinking ideas assumed proven as good as law. In the case of country, such reevaluation leads to an understanding of how much music sprang from the unique, intense juxtaposition of black and white repertoires, styles, and sounds in the South, in general, and in places like Shreveport, in particular. This would alter parts of the standard story of country, particularly affecting its canon. Leadbelly, for instance, could easily be considered a seminal country artist.

By peeling away layers of associations with race, region, and class, and more elusive issues that frame discussions of race and hillbilly music like authenticity, new ways of conceiving the whole of southern music might arise. Different categories altogether could be newly applied to familiar material. An alternative distinction like urban versus rural, for example, creates more space for a figure like Vernon Dalhart than the perfunctory treatment he usually gets in country music history. Growing up in the bucolic backwater of Jefferson, Texas, and branding hide as a cowpuncher in the deserts of West Texas, Dalhart turned to a career as a singer and eventually recorded the first million-selling hillbilly record in 1924 ("The Prisoner's Song" and "The Wreck of the Old '97"). He followed this success with "The Death of Floyd Collins" and a list of country material embraced by a national audience.[44] It seems that, in the pantheon of country music, Dalhart's earlier aspirations and success as a light opera tenor and popular singer (treating a range of current genres that included patriotic songs, comedy numbers, Hawaiian novelty tunes, and so-called "Mammy" songs) annul any claim to hillbilly authenticity that his east Texas upbringing might have earned him.

Dalhart has been neglected by music scholars and by record companies alike. Reissues of his music understandably are rare because his style reflects, like the earliest records of Jimmie Davis, an outmoded parlor fashion. But he is dismissed most often on the grounds of his authenticity. Ralph Peer himself voiced this summary dismissal in a letter to the editor of *Variety* magazine in November 1955:

> Vernon Dalhart was never a hillbilly and never a hillbilly artist. Dalhart had the peculiar ability to adapt hillbilly music to suit the taste of the non-hillbilly population. Perhaps we could characterize him as pseudo-hillbilly. Dalhart was extremely successful as a recording artist because he was a profitable substitute for a real hillbilly. . . . He was a popular artist who sang hillbilly songs for the northern and central western population.[45]

Scholarship tends to echo Peer's sentiment. Dalhart was once called "the John Denver of old-time music," a statement that would have been loaded in 1979 when it appeared in print; he was dubbed "coolly commercial" or, in one case, erroneously characterized as a Northerner profiting from the popularity of hillbilly music.[46] More recently, Bill Ivey grouped him with cowboy song interpreter Carl T. Sprague, writing that "neither singer was the real McCoy—that is, a genuine amateur folk talent from the rural South."[47] Perhaps without the burden of authenticity, Dalhart gains new relevance. His background in a border region between South and West, the class identity issues arising from his conflicting professional aspirations, and the complexity and broad success of his recording career position Dalhart to complicate the picture of southern roots musicians.

A celebrated figure like Jimmie Rodgers, on the other hand, already complicates the racially overdetermined borders of Peer's paradigm. Yet discussions about Rodgers remain guided by it. Acclaimed as the "Father of Country Music," the bulk of Rodgers's repertoire is blues material that clearly crosses racial boundaries. Rodgers even recorded with jazz groups, most notably on a 1930 recording, "Blue Yodel No. 9 (Standin' on the Corner)," with Louis Armstrong on cornet. In this recording, black and white southern styles mingle comfortably. The tune opens with an introduction on trumpet and piano, whose barrelhouse undercurrent remains prominent throughout the record. From this follows an ongoing dialogue between Rodgers's lyrics and Armstrong's lyrical playing. Periodic yodels and a long trumpet solo mark the signatures of both musicians.[48]

In a biography of Armstrong published the year of his death (1971), authors Max Jones and John Chilton describe the date as a "semi-informal moment in Louis' crowded career," one whose circumstances the jazz legend did not clearly recall in 1970 when they were writing their book. They muse: "How this improbable partnership came into being remains one of jazz's unsolvable riddles." Rodgers's biographer, Nolan Porterfield, responds, "I suppose we are entitled to say that it is also one of country music's unfathomable mysteries, . . . Jimmie was, after all, a bluesman, despite the pallid pigmentation of his skin, and had been making jazz-oriented recordings since early in his career." When Armstrong released a 1970 album titled *Louis "Country Western" Armstrong*, which he promoted via an appearance on the *Johnny Cash* television show the year before his death, Jones and Chilton report an unnamed observer's bewilderment and Armstrong's clear response: "No change for me, daddy, I was doing that same kind of work 40 years ago."[49] The tone of bafflement rings through these reports on moments of musical exchange, but it springs more from a sense of dissonance with Peer's paradigm than anything else. Certainly from the perspective of Shreveport history, not to mention broader southern history, Rodgers and Armstrong's collaboration seems more a matter of course than an improbable happenstance.

In the paradigm that assigned whiteness, not to mention the burdens of nostalgia and class identity, to hillbilly music, Shreveport musicians like Leadbelly and Jimmie Davis, or Rodgers and Armstrong, for that matter, seem more like exceptions to a Jim Crow rule than what they really are: representatives of a complex and dynamic musical process. For, while the musical distinction along racial lines was indisputably a pragmatic, profitable tactic to label and sell records, it did not portray the complexities of music in southern culture in general, Shreveport in particular. As a result, the segregated concepts of white and black identity that once had been the cornerstone of slave society defined the parameters of new musical markets and shaped popular music for decades to come.

Yet at the same time the phonograph industry froze block-solid a race-based paradigm for understanding southern roots music, it also birthed a new way to experience music. The phonograph record was a novel medium for musical exchange between blacks and whites and, thus, a new context for musical border crossing that depended neither on face-to-face contact or even geographic proximity. Throughout the stonewall culture of the South, where music once seeped through mortar gaps in the breakwaters between race and class, it now gushed forth as never before. Musical sharing across racial borders within nineteenth-century southern culture was a mundane exchange of proximity. Euro and Afro, in close and constant contact, continually listened, remembered, and adapted bits and snatches of what the other was doing in contexts that were continuously constrained by power relationships based on race. After the 1920s, blacks and whites could buy phonograph records of musicians they might not otherwise hear because of social convention or a lack of opportunity. Listeners could purchase music in a form disembodied from its performers and absorb it privately via the family record player.[50] Later hillbilly musicians reflected the rich new possibilities for exchange via records. Post-Depression hillbilly musicians like Milton Brown, and Bob Wills—members of the first generation to be influenced more by phonograph records and radio than by the stage and tent entertainments—often simply mimicked the recordings of earlier artists, down to the last verbal gesture.[51]

Early commercial recordings of Davis, Dalhart, Woods, the Sheiks, Rodgers, the Allens, and others make clear that record label categories and their attendant genres were primarily prescriptive, with descriptive accuracy evidence only of later successes in circumscribing music into discrete race-based categories. But it was more than a matter of "hillbilly music" simply being inadequate to encompass the breadth of early white southern commercial sounds, although that could certainly be said. Hillbilly music acted as a paradigm for historical thinking that, in light of the dynamics of a place like Shreveport, creates more dissonance than clarity. Grouping all white southern sounds under the rubric "hillbilly music" brought to bear associations of region, race, and class that lingered long after the 1920s and, to a degree, continue to inform discussions of places, people, and sounds that are critical to the music's history. In effect, the 1920s established the commercial currency of a racial paradigm for southern music, but also intellectually segregated the music in much the same way southern society had polarized itself. The record industry simultaneously bolstered racial walls of southern music and created an avenue of profound possibility for interaction. Despite the inherent design of industry categories, the process of musical sharing survived, and eventually flourished, in the era of recorded music.

During the same era, mass media opened yet another door for musical exchange, one much less dependent on capital outlay and, therefore, much less concentrated geographically and constrained by industry norms. In the context of popular music history, radio brought opportunity to places it never existed. The spread of broadcasting during the 1920s opened new prospects for musical communication and also proved to be one of the biggest challenges to face the phonograph industry. Initially dismissed by record executives as a passing fancy, the threat from radio grew painfully real by 1924 when Victor's sales dropped 60 percent and Edison's dropped 50 percent.[52]

The late 1920s saw a trend toward record company consolidation, as small record producers were bought out by large corporations with interests in radio, records, and sound motion pictures. This pattern accelerated after the crash of 1929. Smaller companies could not survive the austerity of the Great Depression and many larger companies barely endured. Beginning in 1930, recording activity dwindled almost to a standstill, and companies unearthed older recordings from their vaults to release on phonograph discs. Hillbilly music remained an inexpensive means to stay afloat. As Nolan Porterfield described the situation during the early 1930s: "Record sales were practically at a standstill, although hillbilly discs continued to withstand the Depression better than some others: 'Billy Tunes Still Bullish,' reported *Variety* in undisguised amazement, noting in particular that Sears, Roebuck's 'hick disc' market had tripled since 1930."[53]

As phonograph companies struggled, radio moved to center stage as the medium that would determine fame and fortune in popular music for decades to come. But it was local rather than network radio that first realized the mutually beneficial relationship between records and the broadcast spectrum. The large networks, which had grown rapidly during the Depression, avoided records whenever possible, favoring live performance and electrical transcriptions of live programs. Local radio, on the other hand, played records, featured local musicians, sponsored political debates, and otherwise filled the airwaves in any way they could to reach their regional audiences. From these local practices on stations like KWKH, the music and culture of Shreveport and its environs played a key role in the changing course of country music.

4

Hillbilly Music and KWKH Radio

Hello, World. It's W. K. Henderson talkin' to you and I'm not
afraid of anything but pneumonia.
—W. K. Henderson, KWKH founder

The story of hillbilly music on radio weaves together several of the
more rough-hewn, colorful twines of the medium's history—including
the often stormy relationship between radio and records, the tribulations
of local ownership and national networks, the tug of war between individual freedom and government regulation played out over the ether, and the
effects of World War II on the industry. Shreveport plays an active role in
this story, since its station KWKH began during the freewheeling early days
of local radio and exerted a degree of influence possible only through the
singular power of broadcasting. The history of KWKH demonstrates the
potency of radio signals in communicating a regional culture to a national
audience. Early radio created new opportunity for otherwise isolated theaters of music and culture like the one that existed in Shreveport. In so
doing, it opened new contexts for the exchange of business, ideas, and, most
central to this story, music.

The public broadcast and private reception of everything from fifes and
sermons to sales pitches and sousaphones made it possible for anyone with
a radio to hear what anyone with access to a broadcast station was playing or saying. The result was a process of accelerated cultural exchange,
but one that was slow and gradual. Face-to-face interaction remained the
most potent means of musical communication for a while yet, especially
in rural areas. According to the Federal Census, which included a question
about receiver ownership, urban, white families in 1930 were statistically
more likely to be radio owners than southern, rural, black families.[1] Ownership of radio receivers burgeoned during the subsequent decade, as they
became cheaper and battery-operated sets became available to serve rural
citizens who lacked electricity.

Over time, radio's potency resulted in the creation on a national level
of a racially hybridized music culture—the likes of which was the essence
of the southern roots sound in general, the heritage of northwest Louisiana in particular. Over the next several decades, radio was the aural uni-

verse where blacks tapped their feet to "Turkey in the Straw" and "Soldier's Joy" and whites snapped their fingers to "Caravan" and "Jiveola Brown." Eminent among these latter listeners were Elvis Presley and his musical contemporaries—ambitious and adventurous white musicians who fused country music with rhythm-and-blues to create "rockabilly" during the mid-1950s.[2] The music they heard flowed from independent local stations in places like Shreveport, where in the mid-1920s music first found new freedom in the airwaves. KWKH eventually rose to prominence in popular music history, most notably after World War II when it broadcast the *Louisiana Hayride*. But its significance begins decades before, when people were only beginning to fathom the opportunity radio represented to regional hotbeds like Shreveport.

Station KWKH began as the hobby of a wealthy businessman with a penchant for technology and a hankering for a soapbox. W. K. Henderson belonged to the pre-network era when independent radio stations proliferated in the United States. He accumulated capital via the family business, the Henderson Iron Works and Supply Company, and with it bought an extensive private telephone system.[3] Like many early twentieth-century individualist entrepreneurs, Henderson harbored antipathy for large corporations and federal bureaucracy. He quickly realized radio's potential for his quixotic fight against what for him constituted an evil trinity threatening the flow of free ideas and free enterprise: the United States Department of Commerce (after 1927, the Federal Radio Commission), chain radio stations, and chain retail stores. An apropos transcription of one of Henderson's 1930 monologues blasts all three villains:

Hello, world. It's 8:00 o'clock. This is old man Henderson talkin' to you. . . . My friend, this station KWKH is supposed to be on 850 kilocycles, and we are bein' interfered with by several other stations, powerful stations—WABC in New York. That's a chain outfit. They drowned us out up in that part of the country, doggone 'em. Then there's that Sears Rareback [*sic*] outfit, WLS in Chicago and WENR. They have plenty of power, and while they may be on their wavelength, they sideswipe us all over the country, doggone 'em. I wanna say this to you, my good friends and listeners. I don't believe that those stations are doing this purposely. The fault is with the Federal Radio engineers. They have put these stations too close together. There should be a separation of more kilocycles. But I'll say this, if I was one of these chain stations, I'll guarantee you they would clear it up mighty quick.

My friends, I want you, everyone [*sic*] of you, to demand of that branch of government, the Federal Radio Commission, that they have their engineers figure out a channel, 850 kilocycles, that we may use that you may hear us that we will not be interfered with. There's no excuse for this. All the chain stations are using cleared channels, the best wavelengths, and they should be put on one wavelength, giving a place for independent stations. But that's not the idea this day and time. The idea is to chain everything, confound it and plague take it. You wanna write to yore [sic] senators that the independent stations have equal rights as to kilocycles and as to power and so forth.[4]

In addition to airing his antagonisms, Henderson made his station both a powerful musical vehicle and a political tool in its infancy, with live country music—then "hillbilly"—appearing occasionally as one of several types of performances heard between records and political diatribe.

Henderson's KWKH broadcast the earliest Shreveport hillbilly music of national significance, the *Jimmie Davis Show*, first heard in late 1927. Thereafter, hillbilly music became a more prominent feature on the station, presumably as demand for it increased and hillbilly performers began to realize the value of radio broadcasting.[5] In a national context, Henderson's radio station adds a level of depth and concrete detail to the history of the broadcast medium. Furthermore, it epitomizes much of the dynamic between local and network radio. The national realization of radio's promise arose from the contexts of local stations like KWKH. And many of the tighter government regulations of the 1930s and the overall standardization of the medium emerged in response to the idiosyncratic practices of station owners like Henderson. In order to understand how KWKH typified the struggles of early radio and gradually carved a regional niche of national significance, we must examine the broader context of radio's development into the most influential medium of the next several decades.

In the current era of increasing media conglomeration, it is important to recall that the innovations, ownership, and ethos of mass mediums developed independently from one another. Giant mergers like the one between Time-Warner and America Online in recent history mean that Internet, magazine, movie, and recorded music dwell together under a single corporate umbrella. Early radio, however, evolved distinct from its competing medium of phonograph records. In fact, the two spent a good part of their early history in conflict over the use of records as radio programming. They eventually realized their two-way relationship, namely that of radio broadcast as an excellent promotion for recorded music and recordings as cut-rate broadcast material. But recognition of the commercial promise in this symbiosis came very slowly. In fact, the commercial viability of radio broadcasting remained shrouded for years. Nor could radio's inventors around the turn of the century have anticipated the eventual pervasiveness of the medium.

The pioneers who developed radio technology in the late 1800s envisioned it not as a source of entertainment at all. They saw it as merely an improvement of wireless communication used by the military and a small number of amateur enthusiasts with handmade receivers and a handbook of Morse code. Radio was a fascinating but problematic extension of technology patented in 1897 and originally conceived as a "wireless telephone."[6] Its initial conception as a voice transmission device misguided the earliest predictions of its potential usefulness. The "radio telephone," as it was sometimes known, seemed a poor substitute for the real thing, as it was subject to "weird and little-understood conditions of the ether, static electricity," and, most egregiously, it lacked "the privacy of the wire."[7] Of course it was this inherent lack of privacy—indeed, the possibility of broad access to audible sounds transmitted via radio waves—that would spark one of the biggest technological transformations of the century.

The initial glimmer of radio's potential occurred in Pittsburgh on 2 November 1920 when Dr. Frank Conrad, the Westinghouse company's Assistant Chief Engineer, conducted the first scheduled radio broadcast: the election returns of the Harding–Cox presidential race. The event incited hobbyist enthusiasm among radio amateurs. Receiving sets and the supplies to construct homemade receivers were sold out in Pittsburgh and the surrounding areas and Westinghouse Vice-President H. P. Davis distributed simple receivers to friends and company officers to further enlarge the audience.[8] Throughout the night, station KDKA, newly licensed by the Department of Commerce, broadcast election returns as they were telephoned in by the *Pittsburgh Post*. Unsure of the size and range of the audience, announcers requested that anyone hearing the broadcast contact the station to let them know they had received the signal. Response to this request indicated that anywhere "from five hundred to a thousand listeners, equipped with earphones or gathered in stores," heard the returns.[9] After this success, the company went on-air nightly between 8:30 and 9:30 p.m., initially playing phonograph records that Conrad borrowed from a nearby music store in exchange for on-air promotion. Sales shot up for the tunes Conrad broadcast, thus hinting at the future cooperative relationship between radio and phonograph.

For the moment, however, Westinghouse officials remained blind to any lucrative potential in shared interests with phonograph record companies. Westinghouse Vice-President Davis assumed that, once the novelty of broadcast wore off, audiences would ultimately prefer listening to their own records to those played on-air. Instead, Davis sought out live entertainment in order to exploit what he called the "instantaneous collective communication" of the medium. KDKA added live music to its schedule, often featuring the Westinghouse Orchestra. During the landmark year of 1921, the station also pioneered broadcasts of church services and sports events, destined to become staple crops for radio.[10] Davis sensed that his company stood at the cusp of a technological breakthrough in a league with the telegraph, the telephone, or electricity, a means of communication and even "mass education" such as the world had never seen.

Within seven years of KDKA's formation, some 700 stations sprang up from coast to coast, creating a chaos of the airwaves. The Department of Commerce weakly tried to regulate the bedlam, but ultimately lacked well-formed guidelines, not to mention legal authority, to enforce order in the midst of this newly opened audio frontier. Frequencies often became the object of territorial disputes. If and when these resolved, their reception was muddied by errant, crossover interference from unfixed signals and a lack of precision in both broadcast and receiver technology. Arrangements to divide up hours of the day between competing stations often failed and many rival stations engaged in purposeful attempts to drown out another station's signal, with the net result that neither signal could be heard by listeners. In the mad scramble for frequencies, new stations folded nearly as fast as they formed. The failures were due, in large part, to lack of revenue, as there was little profit to be shared in an industry where almost all early income came from the sale of receivers. To exacerbate the financial instability of radio, the American Society of Composers, Authors, and Publishers (ASCAP) began to demand royalties for broadcast phonograph records and live performances, thus establishing a long-standing adversarial relationship between ASCAP and broadcasters.[11]

The earliest hint of radio's profits outside receiver sales came in 1922, when WEAF in New York aired the first sponsored radio program on August 28. A Long Island real estate firm bought ten minutes of air time for $100 to advertise two apartments, which sold quickly. Within seven months, Macy's department store and Colgate had joined a roster of twenty-five program sponsors at WEAF.[12] Few other stations followed the example of paid sponsorship, however, and a number of alternative models characterized the medium's first few years. Radio in its infancy attracted a mishmash of station owners, nearly everyone from hucksters to pedants, from carnival barkers hawking snake oil to pedagogues explaining economics. Commercial interests like electric companies and radio equipment manufacturers created stations in order to stimulate sales and increase the use of electricity. Newspaper owners used radio for promotions, and by 1924 more than 100 daily papers also operated radio broadcasting stations.[13] Early radio's noncommercial operators included preachers, cities, and universities—all who saw radio as a chance to evangelize, inform, or educate the hoi polloi.

Most of these owners were slow to realize the commercial potential of sponsoring a medium whose immediacy and aural intimacy captivated audiences. Of the 526 radio stations in 1924, over 400 refused to accept paying sponsors. In this regard, many of the most influential figures in early radio, including onetime Secretary of Commerce Herbert Hoover, lacked vision. Before he became a presidential harbinger of business-minded twentieth-century Republicanism, Hoover seemed attuned to the public utility of the airwaves at the expense of radio's private profitability. At the first National Radio Conference in 1922, he announced: "It is inconceivable that we should allow so great a responsibility for service to be drowned in advertising chatter."[14] Within a few years of Hoover's comment, commercial sponsorship became not only commonplace, but the modus operandi that would guide the substance of radio broadcasting. Eventually, educational and other noncommercial stations died away and national commercial networks dominated the airwaves from the 1930s until the early 1950s.

Within a few years, radio overtook the phonograph in its primacy in American media, a position it occupied until television pushed it aside. The initial momentum of radio was fueled by the formation of large broadcasting chains, known as networks, which began in 1927, when RCA formed its National Broadcasting Company (NBC) with the separate Red network and Blue network; that same year, the Columbia Broadcasting System (CBS) also formed.[15] The young networks experienced great financial success, in spite of the economic strains of the Depression. Advertising agencies played a critical role in building this rapid success and did much more than buy time; they actually produced much of the network programming, dictating the content during prime listening hours.

This relationship between advertisers and the networks profoundly affected the tone and content of network radio. As broadcast historian Erik Barnouw sums it up: "With rare exceptions—such as *The March of Time*, the work of *Time* magazine—there was a blackout on current problems."[16] Comedy and variety shows dominated the 1930s starring former vaudevillians such as Eddie Cantor, George Burns and Gracie Allen, Jack Benny, and Amos 'n' Andy (Freeman Gosden and Charles Correll, who developed the show from their earlier effort, Sam and Henry).[17] Most dramatic programs were devoid of social context. Sponsors wanted no association with the plight of Oklahomans in the dust bowl or the Nazi march into Austria. The leading network, NBC-red, did no news, while NBC-blue had one news show. CBS had one national and world news program, one human interest news program, and a few scattered commentaries.[18]

This situation gradually began to change by the late 1930s, when the major independent news gathering organizations—the AP (Associated Press), UP (United Press), and INS (International News Service)—began "wire services," selling news copy to radio stations via teletype technology. Rising international tensions further stimulated radio's increasing presence as a news source, as interest grew in what was happening around the world and powerful sponsors, such as the oil giant Esso, began sponsoring news broadcasts. News coverage further expanded as more newspapers began operating radio stations or purchasing existing ones, as happened in Shreveport during the mid-1930s.

The national ascent of network radio coincided with the Depression. During the 1930s, radio moved to the center of the living room where three generations often gathered around a cabinet receiver and listened to lullabies, laments, barroom stomps, and rail-fence jokes. It was magical entertainment, invisibly transmitted albeit static-plagued, and unlike any amusement before. Barnouw puts radio's power into perspective when he notes that "according to social workers, destitute families that had to give up an icebox or furniture or bedding still clung to the radio as to a last link with humanity."[19] Radio's singular power inspired theorist Marshall McLuhan to ponder its power to "retribalize mankind, its almost instant reversal of individualism into collectivism" and psychologist Morton Bard to theorize about radio's ability to cut "through the sense of aloneness. It's like touching someone without actually having that other person there. . . . The person on the radio is a person with whom one can be close without having to tolerate all of the disadvantages of closeness."[20]

The unique immediacy of radio was a quality shared by local and network programming alike. In its powerful way, radio communicated not only music but passionate political as messages well. Sometimes the two were linked. In fact, independent radio enabled the success of several well-known politicians, notably Texas governor W. Lee O'Daniel and Louisiana governors Jimmie Davis and Huey P. Long. Country music icon Roy Acuff won the Republican nomination for governor of Tennessee in 1948, but lost the election. Although he never ran for office, Father Coughlin in Detroit wielded tremendous political influence through his radio broadcasts. The distinct potency of radio is difficult to apprehend now, when broadcasting is so pervasive. But it may explain the impact of figures like W. K. Henderson during the 1920s and of popular radio programs, the *Louisiana Hayride* among them.

Generally, hillbilly music assumed a place on the audio stage set apart from the network programming produced by ad agencies. Although hillbilly musicians were often relegated to wee hours, radio barn dance programs aired weekly during prime time by the mid-1920s on at least three major radio stations, including Fort Worth's WBAP, Nashville's WSM, and Atlanta's WSB.[21] In coming years, small and independent rural radio proved ever more decisive in the widespread popularity of the hillbilly sound, eventually drawing the network attention that would take country to a national audience and change the course of popular music forever. By that time, hillbilly music occupied predictable slots in the schedules of local radio stations: early in the morning, late at night, or during mid-day interstices between network programming. Bob Sullivan, radio engineer at KWKH from 1949 to 1959, recalled his regular morning schedule between 5:00 a.m. and 1:00 p.m.:

Back then we didn't play records in the morning. We had live bands on. We opened at 5:00 with Mac Wiseman. 5:15 we had the Bailes Brothers. 5:30 we had Johnnie and Jack. 5:45 was Harmie Smith. And then we had a 15 minutes news break and we went back to Webb Pierce and Hank Williams and all these guys. And we had live bands until 9:00 in the morning when we, what we called "hit network," or starting taking our feed from CBS with Arthur Godfrey and those guys. So we were on network until noon and from noon to 1:00 was local programming with news and whatever.[22]

For many listeners, the core spell of radio's magic was the live hillbilly music blasting from stations like KWKH.

Naturally, smaller rural stations in the South, Midwest, and on the West Coast featured more hillbilly music than did their large urban counterparts. Initially operated by a motley cohort of radio entrepreneurs with idiosyncratic programs of regional interest, these stations pushed country music to broader prominence and formed the undercurrent of radio's success. The longtime sales manager of RCA, Elmer Bucher, once observed that the glut of local and independent radio mavericks were as responsible for the landslide sales of radio receivers as were the citadel stations owned by corporate giants.[23] It was largely their diffusion of grassroots music, entertainment, and information over their airwaves that sparked the radio consumer revolution. Moreover, not only did the early local stations spread hillbilly sounds, they partly motivated the competing record companies to cast their nets more openly in search of a wider variety of "race" and "hillbilly" musicians. The result was a broadened catch of string bands, songsters, and folk of all stripe and color playing at and on everything from washboards and whiskey jugs to Jew's harps and kazoos. Without the urgency of radio competition, it is doubtful whether record companies would have been as quick or vigorous to net the plethora of white and black southern folk musicians they eventually did.[24]

If record executives reacted in alarm to the sudden ascendancy of radio, many of their established recording artists felt the same way. In the mid-1920s, radio and phonograph were commonly perceived in zero-sum competition wherein the advance of one medium happened at the expense of the other. Because of this, many successfully recorded singers and musicians of the era simply did not see how radio exposure could further their careers. A noteworthy example is early recording star Vernon Dalhart. In 1924 Dalhart was the first to record a million-selling hillbilly disc, "Prisoner's Song" coupled with "Wreck of the Old '97." Dalhart had earlier gained notoriety as a "light opera tenor" with Edison, singing hallmarks like "I'm Waiting for You, Liza Jane," and "Rock-a-Bye Your Baby with a Dixie Melody."[25] He was also a key player in Edison company's "tone-testing" tours, where audiences would gather in a local music store to hear a record and then to witness the artist sing the same song live, thus experiencing firsthand the lifelike Edison sound.[26] These tours helped establish Dalhart's reputation. Following the unprecedented success of his first hillbilly recording in 1924, Dalhart recorded hillbilly music for the rest of his career. In 1925 he switched from Edison to Victor, convincing them to rerecord his 1924 hits; in the meantime, Edison continued to reissue Dalhart recordings until the company folded in 1929.

Despite his watershed contribution to the history of hillbilly music, Dalhart is relegated to its back pages. Although his critical obsolescence resonates with stereotypes and prejudices about the measure of a genuine hillbilly, Dalhart is popularly forgotten simply because he lost popularity. More specifically, he lost his audience when he failed to make the transition to radio rather than recording studios and furniture shops. Not only did he neglect radio's promotional opportunities but his singing style—full-throated and well-suited to a vaudeville stage—sounded old-fashioned to a radio aesthetic.[27] It took younger pioneers like Jimmie Rodgers to establish radio performance as a prerequisite to professional success. While Dalhart was toted home on thick discs of shellac, his successor floated the airwaves. Rodgers embraced the two media at once, securing himself a legacy by both yodeling on records and guitar-picking his way into every home blessed with a radio.[28] Thus, Rodgers earned the epithet "Father of Country Music" not because he was the pioneer of a folk music form, but because Rodgers mastered both an older medium and the medium that supplanted it. With one foot in the record market and the other straddled into radio, Rodgers set the precedent of the media-dexterous pop star, even to the point of filming an inchoate music video.[29]

By the 1930s, local radio broadcasts like the ones that began Rodgers's career became the prime venue for unsung hillbilly musicians to further their careers. Phonograph recording was losing its prominence in the world of entertainment, and the field recordings that sparked the commercial country music industry became less common. Nashville was not yet the music's commercial center or the guiding star for its young performers. Small radio broadcasting stations all over drew ambitious young hopefuls with dreams of following in the "singing brakeman's" footsteps. The immediacy and vitality of this newer medium promised a fast path to notoriety like nothing before it, and the migration of young singers and players to radio filled country music's earliest stable of talent. In this way, Shreveport's station KWKH began to be an influential musical force, drawing hillbilly musicians from East Texas, Arkansas, and much of Louisiana during the 1930s. But its story begins outside the context of country music, with the peculiar legacy of W. K. Henderson.

KWKH's formation during the mid-1920s provides both a local case study for the emergence of independent radio and a curious example of how personality and circumstance can congeal into a history-making gestalt. Radio first came to northwest Louisiana in 1922, when the Elliot Electric Company hired aspiring radio engineer William E. Antony to construct a broadcast station in order to stimulate receiver sales. The Department of Commerce quickly closed Antony's first effort, the 10-watt experimental station he called WAAG, due to the lack of a licensed operator.[30] Holding down his day job at AT&T (where he picked up much of his knowledge about running a transmitter), Antony acquired a license, reopened, and for a short period, operated the station alone at night, when the broadcasts were most audible. His programming consisted mostly of chat about the weather, recent events read directly from the local paper, and his own phonograph records played near the microphone.

The next year, retailer W. G. Patterson built the 100-watt WGAQ and enlisted Antony as engineer. Patterson hoped his station would bring in customers to his recently opened store that sold, among other things, radios and crystal receiver kits. This station broadcast one hour every night, occasionally featuring live music in the form of a local piano prodigy or singing group. Soon finding himself in unanticipated financial trouble, Patterson sold interests in WGAQ to other entrepreneurs: W. K. Henderson, owner of the Iron Works and Supply Company; John D. Ewing, associate editor of the Shreveport *Times* newspaper; and Jack Tullos and Sam Weiner, owners of the Youree Hotel in downtown Shreveport, where the WGAQ studio relocated.[31] From this new locale, the station increased its use of live musicians.

In late 1924 Henderson bought controlling interests in the station and moved it to his country home at Kennonwood, 18 miles outside Shreveport.[32] He purchased the self-referential call letters KWKH from a Georgia station for $250 and hired Bill Antony to build a new transmitter.[33] Henderson funded the station himself, with no advertising in the early years. He went on air in the evenings, playing records from his varied personal collection of over 6,000 discs, usually by audience request, over the Brunswick players that Antony reworked to feed directly into the transmitter instead of through an amplifier in front of a microphone. Eventually, Henderson published catalogs of his records so that listeners could request tunes by number.[34] Demand for his broadcasts grew and, by 1926, he hired Stedman Gunning, a young man who already worked as an office runner at the Iron Works, to take up residence at Kennonwood and work nights as disc jockey and radio engineer.

Besides music, Henderson filled the region's airwaves with impassioned rants about the matters that weighed heavily upon him. He erected broadcasting setups at his Iron Works office, in his living room, and beside his bed so that he could interrupt the music whenever he felt moved, which was often, introducing his soliloquies with the signature greeting: "Hello, world, doggone you. This is KWKH in Shreveport, Lou-ee-isiana, and it's W. K. Henderson talkin' to you."[35] For years, Gunning announced "KWKH: Kill Worry, Keep Health" between phonograph records, never knowing when Henderson would burst into the room and launch into one of his harangues. During the Great Depression, Gunning and other KWKH employees resided at Kennonwood, working for a year and a half in 1931–32 in exchange for room and board.[36]

KWKH's reputation spread not only because of Henderson's audacious personality but because of the broad coverage of its signal. During the late 1920s and early 1930s, the only limiting force on a radio station's airwaves was the wattage capacity of its transmitters, and this could be boosted by the antenna installed at the transmitter's top. Gunning once recalled the effect of Henderson's setup:

> At that time, KWKH had what we call the flattop antenna—it wasn't like the vertical radiators that came into use in the early thirties. It would put out an awful strong signal for a longer distance, but have a close-in skip distance before the skywaves came back down. We'd pour into Baton Rouge, New Orleans, south Louisiana like a local.[37]

Thus, Henderson attracted a large audience, out of proportion to the size of Shreveport, and by 1930 his station earned the *Radio Digest* "popularity award" for the South. According to Gunning, "due to that type of antenna, when Mr. Will [Henderson] sold it, we were getting mail from Europe—France, England, Switzerland, Germany, Italy."[38]

Henderson's personal crusades drew an enormous response from listeners. One of his most popular was the anti-chain store campaign. To bolster this effort, Henderson formed an association of independent businessmen, the Merchants' Minute Men of America (renamed later that year the Modern Minute Men) in early 1930. Members paid dues of $12 per year to help counter the influence of corporate chain retail stores. By September of the first year, the organization's membership was 32,000 strong.[39] Association-funded agents, working on commission, traveled and enlisted more and more members. Henderson charged these representatives with another mission: to enter chain stores, purchase five-pound sacks of flour or sugar, and weigh them. If the goods weighed less than advertised, Henderson railed against the store on the air, reportedly supplying listeners with the name, address, and telephone number of the offending storeowner.[40] In his nightly obloquies, Henderson then admonished his listeners:

> I'll tell you what I'm doing,—I'm exposing the short weight trickery of these contemptible daylight burglars, the Chain stores [*sic*]. I'm teaching the people that it takes sixteen ounces to make a pound. Wake up, people! Open your eyes! Even a puppy has its eyes open when it's nine days old. You ought to have enough sense in your *heel* to know that you can't give your money to outside chains and at the same time, keep it at home. Hello, World. It's W. K. Henderson talkin' to you and I'm not afraid of anything but pneumonia.[41]

Louisiana broadcast historian Pusateri reports that at the peak of his popularity Henderson received "an incredible figure of 20,000–30,000 letters per day" and that at the height of the Minute Men operation, KWKH employed as many as sixty young women to process thousands of daily letters with money "placed in barrels in the office until such time as they were full enough to be hauled to the bank."[42] Gunning confirmed this quantity of feedback from KWKH listeners, recalling a single broadcast that elicited 28,000 pieces of mail.[43] Precise documentation of the scale of Henderson's daily communications during the era is impossible due to a fire at Kennonwood during the late 1950s. It is clear, however, that a great many people found him both evocative and persuasive.

Advertisement gradually found a place on the KWKH frequency, but limited mainly to products in which Henderson held a financial stake. For example, Hello World Coffee, which Henderson began selling over the air in 1928, was one of his most popular items, priced at an extravagant dollar per pound at a time when the average grocery store per-pound price was eight cents. Henderson peddled other items on occasion, including a book, *The Life of W. K. Henderson*, Hello World Syrup, carved ivory elephants, Bibles covered with olive wood from Palestine, pecan trees, patent medicines, life insurance, real estate, and oil wells.[44] He also used his airwaves to support election candidates, for example, for the notorious Louisiana politico, Huey P. Long, for whom Henderson raised $10,000 during his initial stab at the governorship.[45] For his part, Long frequently broadcast from the station and appeared in support of Henderson's Merchants' Minute Men convention that in 1930 attracted 1,000 delegates to Shreveport from forty states[46] (fig. 4.1).

Henderson's talks eventually reverberated all the way to Washington, D.C., where U.S. Senator Clarence Dill publicly denounced his peppery broadcasts as a "disgrace to this country." Adversarial as ever, Henderson

Fig. 4.1 W. K. Henderson at the microphone. Noel
Memorial Library Archives, LSU in Shreveport.

minced no words in his on-air response to the Senator: "Hell! I have to
cuss. My vocabulary is limited and I can't express myself unless I do."[47]
Henderson's name was bandied in Washington more than once during the
several battles he faced in his relatively brief radio career. In some of these
he was quite successful. For example, he gave strong voice to the popular
outcry for equal treatment of southern stations by the FRC, resulting in the
Davis Amendment in 1928 that specified forty frequencies to remain clear
of interference and divided these clear channels equally among five regions of the country.[48] Despite this victory, Henderson remained defiant of
the FRC, a stance that nearly brought him trial in a federal court. In response to his persistent disregard for FRC-prescribed wattage limits for
KWKH, "the commission recommended to the Justice Department the
criminal prosecution of Henderson for 'illegal operation' of a broadcast
station, specifically the use of 'excessive power' on more than forty occasions in June and July alone."[49] The attorney general never pursued the
charges, and Pusateri suggests that the hesitancy probably resulted from
Henderson's popularity and the fear of "political backlash against the Republican dominated commission in an election year."[50]

Henderson's most dramatic triumph began in 1929, when Oklahoma oil
tycoon W. G. Skelly charged that KWKH was not serving the public. Skelly
wished to appropriate Henderson's frequency for his Tulsa station KVOO.
In formulating his argument against KWKH, he appealed to the recently
formulated, and characteristically nebulous, bureaucratic language of the

FRC criteria for license renewal: "public interest, convenience, or necessity." As the struggle heated up, Henderson's detractors in the trade journal *Radio Digest* called the rabble-rouser "unfit" and "uncouth," in part because they claimed over two-thirds of his programming was records (thus, intimating a larger issue that would heat up over the next decade).[51] Henderson launched a campaign for public support of his station, encouraging listeners to tear out the pre-written testimonies that appeared in newspapers across the South declaring KWKH their "favorite station." The demagogue encouraged his listeners to sign the document, get it notarized, and mail it to Kennonwood. The response was enormous. Some 163,000 affidavits poured in.[52] Before making the trip to D.C. for a hearing on Skelly's contention, Henderson announced an itinerary of stops along the way. His supporters flocked to the brass band hoopla, rallying behind Henderson's homespun banner of populist media. Armed with the evidence of support, Henderson delivered a *coup de maître* in the hearing room of the Federal Radio Commission, wherein he proved his station to be, according to commission guidelines, "in the public convenience."

W. K. Henderson belongs to the transitional period between early radio's free-form experimentation and autocratic entrepreneurship to government-regulated formalization and network proliferation. But he was not a lone, liminal figure, nor was he the only independent radio operator to attract attention from the U.S. government. While Henderson crowed politics and peddled coffee, others saw radio as a natural extension of the old medicine show. Dr. John R. Brinkley, the "goat-gland man," whose unique transplant procedure was touted to relieve prostate troubles, and Dr. Norman Baker, who claimed to have found a cure for cancer, were both wealthy businessmen (neither of whom were licensed by the AMA) whose success depended on their radio personalities. Increased government regulations during the 1930s pushed both of these men south to open "border stations" across the Rio Grande from Texas. Their stations stood just beyond the jurisdictional reach of the U.S. government, but with antennae aimed back toward the Lone Star state, reaching all the way to Canada. XERA, XENT, and other border stations vexed radio officialdom in the United States at the same time they played a critical role in exposing new audiences to country music. With the unrestricted wattage available in Mexico, hillbilly music blasted from these mega-watt dynamos in between monologues from savvy hucksters who dazzled listeners with the latest vial of "snake oil" or jar of liniment.

The story of the two most infamous Texas-border mountebanks begins in the Midwest. Brinkley and Baker both used the airwaves to advertise their curatives. Brinkley purchased his medical credentials for $100 from a "diploma mill" in Kansas City and enjoyed a brisk business in his wide range of patent medicines, identified only by number.[53] Sufferers could write a letter describing their ailments and then listen for Brinkley's advice over the airwaves. While his medicines brought steady income, Brinkley's greatest success was with a surgical procedure for male impotency that involved transplanting part of a goat testicle into a man's scrotum. The afflicted traveled from all over the country to Brinkley's Kansas sanitorium.[54] Baker, who boasted similarly dubious credentials, claimed to cure cancer at his equally lucrative Iowa hospital.

The activities of both quacks coincided with a general increase of government interest in the legitimacy of manufacturers' claims to consumers. For example, the American Tobacco company spent $19 million in 1931 advertising the ability of Lucky Strike cigarettes to maintain womanly figures and soothe sore throats.[55] Such specious claims led to a 1933 Food and Drug Administration bill to require that both product package and advertisement include precise information about the contents. Ad agencies vehemently assailed the proposed law and succeeded in winning exception for advertisements but not for packaging. This watershed attention to market regulation from federal officials was, in part, precipitated by Brinkley and Baker.

In 1930, the same year *Radio Digest* magazine reported Brinkley's KFKB the most popular radio station in the United States, the FRC denied his license renewal.[56] The undaunted humbug moved to Del Rio, Texas, in 1931 and began broadcasting over station XER (XERA after 1935) across the Mexican border in Villa Acuña. When the U.S. government succeeded in pressuring Mexican officials to deny Brinkley a visa to cross the border, he simply funded construction of a telephone wire for transmission and broadcast by remote from Del Rio. When new regulations prohibited remote broadcasts by an American in a foreign country, Brinkley began recording his promises of impotence relief via Toggenburg goat glands onto electrical transcription discs and sending them across the border for later broadcast. Transcriptions like the ones used by Brinkley originally developed as a convenience to performers, allowing them to travel long distances to gigs by pre-recording the daily shows they would otherwise miss. Similar to a phonograph record but larger, these acetate and aluminum discs required special equipment to play back. Border stations eventually produced huge numbers of transcriptions of hillbilly performers like Rodgers and the Carter Family. Few of them survive, however, as they were discovered to be equally useful as long-lasting shingles for nearby homes.

Following Brinkley's Del Rio precedent, Norman Baker built radio station XENT in 1933 across the border from Laredo, Texas, where he touted his cure for cancer. Other entrepreneurs followed suit, opening border stations across from towns in Texas and southern California. The United States pressured Mexico to stop the stations, but met with resistance. Mexico and Cuba had been snubbed earlier when the United States and Canada divided the broadcasting radio wave band between themselves, leaving no clear channels for the rest of North America.[57] While the United States was interested in counteracting fraud, it was more interested in regulating outsized signals. With the Mexican stations operating at 100-, 150-, or even 250-kilowatts of power, some stations in the United States, where the legal limit was 50 kilowatts, received interference or were blocked out entirely.[58] Following the International Radio Conference of 1932, the Mexican press was vocal about what it perceived as "imperialistic aerial designs" on the part of the United States.[59] After years of disagreement, the North American Regional Broadcast Agreement in 1941 finally put an end to the border mega-stations and Mexican *federales* seized XERA in 1942. Five years later, friends of Brinkley and his partners resurrected the station as XERF and began broadcasting over a more modest 50-kilowatt transmitter.

Border radio remained a softer but still significant presence in the United States well into the 1960s, when Wolfman Jack spun late-night rhythm-and-blues records and howled his way into American pop culture from Rosarita Beach in Baja California. During their rogue years of the 1930s, however, the free form, great power, and experimental nature of border radio played a key role in the national growth of country music, since among ads for hair dyes, laxatives, baby chickens, and scrotum surgery, and amid the evangelical eschatology and numerological auguries, border stations featured plenty of hillbilly music. Thus, throughout the United States and into Canada, the "X-stations" laid the foundation for country music's widespread popularity in the 1940s and beyond.[60] KWKH and W. K. Henderson belonged to the same era as Brinkley and Baker. Henderson was a colorful, if less medically dangerous, icon of the age of radio as "a wide-open free-for-all" and, like the others, he offset his radio sales and self-promotions with the music of pickers and fiddlers.[61]

In contrast to the border stations, most of the hillbilly music for which KWKH is most famous broadcast live, rather than by transcription, into the 1950s. The pioneer for KWKH's hillbilly music legacy was Jimmie Davis, who began performing *The Jimmie Show* from 8:00 to 9:00 on Friday nights in 1927.[62] Davis's show reportedly drew thousands of letters from listeners and, thus, launched KWKH's role in broadcasting the seeds of hillbilly music, a sound that would sprout into modern country music (fig. 4.2).

Born on 11 September 1902 near the small north Louisiana town of Beech Springs, James Houston Davis eventually won fame as a country performer and songwriter, movie star, and twice-elected governor of Louisiana. He grew up inundated with the diverse sounds of the region: the sentimental parlor songs of the late nineteenth and early twentieth centuries, the white string music and black blues songs of the red clay, piney north Louisiana backwoods, and the Baptist revival hymns and spirituals from the evangelical denominations ubiquitous in the Bible Belt. As a young man, Davis pursued education with a resolve unusual for his time and place, becoming the first male in his small town to earn a high school diploma; he went on to earn a Master of Arts in Education at Louisiana State University in Baton Rouge.[63]

In 1927 Davis moved to Shreveport where he began teaching at Dodd College, a Baptist school for women. He also started playing around town on the second-hand guitar he had bought during his college days and singing, which he had also done in a quartet and as a member of the college glee club. In this musical capacity, W. K. Henderson approached Davis about putting him on the air. Henderson also may already have had Davis in mind for his small-scale record labels, Hello World and Doggone Records, another sideline interest for the indomitable businessman. Over

Fig. 4.2 Jimmie Davis reads stacks of his mail at the KWKH studios. Louisiana Hayride Archives—J. Kent.

KWKH, *The Jimmie Show* featured Davis most often accompanied by a pianist from nearby Mansfield, Louisiana, James Enloe. Davis and Enloe were not the first live musicians on Henderson's station. Other 1920s live performers included the Sawyer Sisters, a ukulele-vocal duet; the Duncan Sisters, a similar duo; and the Newman Brothers, a trio who performed pop, novelty, and traditional songs from 1928 to 1934.[64] Another group, a seven-piece family string band, known as the Taylor-Griggs Melody Makers, began KWKH's first daily live morning show and played for the political campaign of Al Smith (Herbert Hoover's Democratic opponent for president in 1928). None of these performers gained the notoriety of Davis and subsequent KWKH musicians, but they contributed to the station's growing link with hillbilly music.

During the late 1920s, Davis made several recordings for Henderson's Doggone label with Enloe on piano at a Chicago studio.[65] These included tunes like "You'd Rather Forget than Forgive," stiffly crooned with a four-square parlor piano accompaniment in a formal, reserved style. It also included the much looser "Way Out on the Mountain," which Jimmie Rodgers had recorded earlier that year. In contrast to Rodgers's guitar and voice arrangement, Davis delivers his piano-accompanied version in a faster, more jaunty tempo and with humor inflected in his delivery of phrases like "the buffalo lows." In contrast to the sentimental tone of "You'd Rather Forget," Davis delivers "Way Out on the Mountain" with a relaxed, full voice, enjoying the breadth of his range from a pleasant baritone to a light and flexible yodeling falsetto.

In 1929 Davis signed on with Victor Records, a company with whom he recorded until 1934 when he switched to the newly formed Decca Records of America. The Victor recordings contain a smattering of sacred and sentimental tunes, as well as a set of sometimes risqué and often ribald country blues.[66] Recordings from two sessions, in Charlotte, North Carolina, on 26–28 May 1931, and in Dallas on 6–8 February 1932 stand out as fascinating examples of the interaction between black and white music and musicians as a vital feature of southern practice. Both of these sessions included collaborations with African-American guitarists Ed Schaffer and Oscar "Buddy" Woods, and demonstrate that the line between white and black southern musical cultures was a dotted one, fluidly crossed by all three musicians in these recordings. Particularly noteworthy is the tune "Saturday Night Stroll," on which Davis sings a duet with Woods, who takes the lead vocals during a portion of the performance.[67] In "Davis' Salty Dog," Woods and Davis play off one another in the studio, with Woods encouraging soloists and acting as a chorus to Davis's lead.

From these early sessions, Davis went on to record for six decades. Fully cognizant of radio's potential for promoting record sales, Davis continued to perform live music on KWKH for years, albeit intermittently, with expanded personnel. For example, a Shreveport *Times* photo dated 22 November 1936, announced a new series of Sunday afternoon programs: *Jimmie Davis and His Cowboy Pioneers* at 4:45 p.m.; besides Davis, the band included seven other members. During that same year, Davis appeared in a daily half-hour show from 4:45 to 5:15 p.m. during the weekdays. In the meantime, he pursued politics. In 1930 Davis became clerk of court for a local criminal judge, David B. Samuel. He served this post for eight years, and then won the office of Shreveport Public Safety Commissioner in 1938. All the while building political momentum, Davis continued making Decca recordings and performing on radio, and he even made a handful of Hollywood westerns. In February 1940 he recorded "You Are My Sunshine" in New York with a six-piece Western swing ensemble that included Shreveport musicians Leon Chappelear on guitar, Charles Mitchell on steel, and trumpeter Sleepy Brown. Covered famously by Gene Autry and Bing Crosby in 1941, "Sunshine" propelled Davis into the echelon of inimitable songwriting; the tune would become Louisiana's state anthem and one of the most easily and widely recognized melodies ever put to record.[68] The popularity of the song, and Davis's association with it, helped him win a seat on the Louisiana Public Service Commission in 1942 and enter the governor's race in 1944 (fig. 4.3).

Davis won the election easily, campaigning "for Peace, Harmony, and Progress" with such an egalitarian air that a billboard in Shreveport was strewn with graffiti, adding Lena Horne and Louis Armstrong to the ticket.[69] Davis then served four years, continuing to record and make movies. He again served as governor from 1960 to 1964. He won this sec-

Fig. 4.3 Jimmie Davis at the KWKH studios in 1942.
Louisiana Hayride Archives—J. Kent.

ond term with more difficulty (as segregationists ranted "Can Jimmie Davis be for segregation in Louisiana when he operated an integrated honky-tonk in Louisiana?") and endured far more trying politics vis-à-vis the civil rights movement. Even though Davis tacitly supported the southern segregationist regime at the dawn of the civil rights movement, the racial openness he demonstrated as a musician carried over into his political persona, making him one of the most flexible centrist governors the state has seen.[70] While most well known for his legacy of gospel as well as country classics like "You Are My Sunshine" and "Nobody's Darlin' But Mine," Davis's early years at KWKH left indelible marks on the histories of country music recording and live country broadcasts. Embracing radio at a critical juncture of his career, Davis belongs to the forward-looking generation of Jimmie Rodgers and other hillbilly greats. And Davis's presence at KWKH beginning in the late 1920s inaugurated the station's future influence in country music.

Henderson himself, on the other hand, did not fare as well. With the onset of the Great Depression, his finances strained to the breaking point and he was forced to sell the station. In the spring of 1933, Sam D. Hunter, an oil man who headed the newly formed International Broadcasting Company, bought KWKH. Hunter owned the station for only two years, during which hillbilly music suffered. Hunter affiliated with the CBS network in 1934, and for the next year and a half the station favored national programs over those produced locally, with more than two-thirds of its broadcasts from the network feed.[71] KWKH's network dependence during the Hunter years typified the developing radio industry. As radio gained popularity, so grew the networks, which helped fill the demand for professional entertainment on the airwaves. Network domination led to greater standardization of radio, further development of industry accountability, and imposition of regulation both by the federal government and from within the industry itself. The 1937 publication of the inter-industry pamphlet "Standards of Practice for Radio Broadcasters" marks the definitive end of the radio era of Henderson, Brinkley, and Baker. Its guidelines not only include concrete advice (for example, urging broadcasters to avoid "the advertising of fortune-telling, occultism, spiritualism, astrology," etc.) but also outline more ambiguous parameters for radio material to meet "accepted standards of good taste" and for programs to promote "spiritual harmony and understanding of mankind."[72]

KWKH's ties to network norms loosened in 1935, when John Ewing purchased the station from Hunter. Ewing, one of Henderson's original mid-1920s partners, had since become editor and publisher of the Shreveport *Times*. Ewing also owned another local station, KTBS, and, as such, his business actions mirrored a nationwide burgeoning of newspaper-owned stations. While this trend alarmed government officials at the time, most notably Franklin Roosevelt, it nevertheless grew to the point that "by 1940 more than one-third of all stations were owned or controlled by newspapers."[73] In the case of KWKH, the newspaper connection amounted to greater freedom for program directors, since the owners viewed the station as a sideline to their main business and largely kept distance from the details of its daily operation.

The first broadcast of the station under Ewing's ownership occurred on New Year's Day in 1936 and included three fifteen-minute news segments and a local man reminiscing on "battles of the Rainbow Division of the US Army during World War I."[74] The station expanded rapidly and, by August of the first year, moved to larger office spaces in the Commercial National Bank building in downtown Shreveport. For the remainder of the 1930s, live country music fit into regular daily programming and included the Lone Star Cowboys, the Sunshine Boys, and the Paradise Entertainers. While steadily gaining prominence over the late 1930s, country music was only one component in an eclectic lineup of local pianists, parlor singers, guitarists, and front porch string bands. Religious programs aired from Saint Mark's Episcopal Church and from the First Baptist Church every Sunday morning and Sunday night, respectively.[75] The station still aired network programs, including comedy shows, dramatic serials, news, live sports commentary, and popular and orchestral music. The variety in radio program schedules, so different from format radio of today, remained the norm on KWKH until the late 1950s. This diverse mix of entertainment contributed to the growing popularity of country music because it helped plant seeds of interest in audiences who otherwise would have paid little attention to the music.

When the Federal Communications Commission, successor after 1934 to the FRC, bumped the station's power up to 50,000 watts in 1939, Shreveport became the smallest community in the nation to house a station of maximum power.[76] So it was that by the beginning of the 1940s Shreveport was poised to exert significant influence in the country music industry. Nashville had yet to become the mecca of country music, though WSM's *Grand Ole Opry* picked up a powerful sponsor that year, which increased the status and influence of the original radio barn dance beyond its competitors. Without the weekly half-hour broadcast on NBC, paid for by the R. J. Reynolds Tobacco Company, the *Grand Ole Opry* and its "Prince Albert" portion of the show might not be the American institution it is today.[77] Still, at that time, Shreveport had the means to compete: caches of talent, fortuitous location, and a muscular radio signal gave it the ability to carve a niche in the hillbilly music business. By 1939 the KWKH staff listed twenty-eight country music acts.[78]

Among these was a group known as the Lone Star Cowboys, who played a critical part in KWKH's deepening connection to country music during the 1930s and were active in several of the live variety shows that preceded the *Louisiana Hayride*. The Lone Star Cowboys first came to Shreveport in 1930, already experienced entertainers in east Texas cafes and taverns, and on nearby Tyler station KGKB. The heart of the group, brothers Bob and Joe Shelton, began performing as a duet in Longview, Texas in the late 1920s.[79] They moved to Tyler, where they met guitarist Leon Chappelear and formed a trio. W. K. Henderson hired them for a regular 8:30 a.m. morning show, immediately following Henderson's scheduled daily polemic. The Lone Star Cowboys gained an enormous following, pursuing the exhausting performance schedule typical of hillbilly musicians of the era.

Performers like the Sheltons kept a rigorous daily routine that remained common in the next generation of country performers. Often, they appeared early in the day on a live fifteen- to thirty-minute program, announced where they would perform that night, then drove to one of the many small communities in the station's listening area. There, they played in a school gymnasium, church auditorium, ballpark, or sometimes simply an open field, only to return to the station in time for the following morning's broadcast. This lifestyle continued to be the norm for professional country musicians into the 1950s. Much more than record sales or radio sponsorship, live performances in these rural communities were the bread and butter for country musicians for several decades, and listeners traveled for miles to hear their favorite radio performers. As KWKH's transmitter power increased, schedules of live performances became even more grueling for musicians, who ideally desired to build audiences in the farthest reaches of the station's listening territory.

Since a station's broadcast area could easily become saturated, musicians moved frequently from one territory to another. Thus, Bob and Joe Shelton led an itinerant lifestyle typical of the era's country musicians and spent intermittent periods away from Shreveport during the 1930s. In 1933 they left KWKH to join one of the last vestiges of a bygone era, the Harley Sadler Tent Show, then moved to WSB in Atlanta, WWL in New Orleans, and finally back to KWKH in 1935. This time they brought with them Hoke and Paul Rice, who remained with KWKH for years, eventually befriending Jimmie Davis and providing musical support for his political aspirations. The Sheltons left KWKH for WFAA in Dallas in 1936 and returned again to Shreveport in 1939. After 1940 they went back to WFAA, which remained their home base for most of their career. Their sometimes partner Chappelear remained in Shreveport all the while, continuing to use the name Lone Star Cowboys, even after severe injuries in a car accident in 1935 slowed down his musical career.

Despite their ramblings, the Sheltons' association with KWKH remained strong, and they maintained a large regional following. Musically, they reflect the uniqueness of the region's musical sensibilities. As music scholar Ivan Tribe suggests, their sound contrasts with many other 1930s brother duets by pointing more toward later honky-tonk style than toward bluegrass. In addition to their own recording of the Sheiks's earlier hit, "I'm Sitting on Top of the World" with Curly Fox on fiddle, their best-known tunes today, "Deep Ellum Blues" and "Just Because," attest to the cross-section of hillbilly, western, blues, gospel, and sentimental ballads that influenced country musicians of the region. Like Jimmie Davis, the Sheltons understood radio as a matter of course for professional success, and their popularity and plethora of recordings through 1941 compare with that of Davis.[80]

In addition to their music, the Sheltons are furthermore significant because in 1936 they hosted a live weekly Sunday afternoon talent show on KWKH, which was one of the precursors to the *Louisiana Hayride*. It was called the *Hillbilly Amateur Show*, and it attracted audiences so large that the show moved from the Washington-Youree Hotel to the auditorium at City Hall, where it drew capacity crowds of 1,200 and reportedly turned away many more.[81] Both country music and white gospel groups performed on the show, including the Blackwood Brothers during a brief association in 1939 when they came to the attention of the era's biggest name in southern gospel music, V. O. Stamps of the Stamps-Baxter publishing house. Most critically, it fueled the steady popularity of live country music and gospel on KWKH, building an audience and preparing the way for the *Louisiana Hayride*. As one writer for *On the Level*, the KWKH newsletter, noted in 1936: "We've watched the success of hillbilly musical organizations that 'book' out from KWKH. Using KWKH as their sole source of publicity, these acts have played to several hundred men, women, and children in churches or schools that are miles from the nearest town."[82] KWKH's identification with country music thus continued to gain momentum.

The *Hillbilly Amateur Show* ran until it was replaced in 1940 by another weekly KWKH variety show, the *Saturday Night Roundup*, which featured the Rice Brothers and as many as twenty-five other acts on a given week.[83] World War II stalled this enterprise in media res, but country music on KWKH picked up after 1945 and led to the *Louisiana Hayride*, an eventual staging ground for stardom. The immediate effects of World War II on Shreveport radio were the same ones felt everywhere, namely, the void of performers left behind by musicians-turned-soldiers. This accelerated the prominence of disc jockey shows, a programming option that local stations like KWKH embraced from their beginnings. But the cultural upheaval on a national level wrought by World War II extended far deeper than format changes.

Before its end, the cataclysmic World War II both directly and indirectly shaped the future of American popular culture from New York to Shreveport. Some of these effects contributed specifically to the conditions for the *Louisiana Hayride*. For one thing, country music both during and after the war enjoyed an unprecedented boom in popularity. Performers like Jimmie Davis appeared in Hollywood movies, including *Riding through Nevada, Frontier Fury, Cyclone Prairie Ramblers,* and *Louisiana*, which was loosely based on his life. For movie audiences on the home front, Gene Autry continued to epitomize the Hollywood singing cowboy. Roy Acuff made several motion pictures during the early 1940s, including *Hi Neighbor, My Darling Clementine, Cowboy Canteen,* and *Night Train to Memphis.*[84] In 1942 Acuff and songwriter Fred Rose formed Acuff-Rose Publishing Company in Nashville, the first music publishing house devoted exclusively to country music. In fact, Roy Acuff won such currency in U.S. pop culture that Japanese soldiers on the attack on Okinawa yelled "To hell with Roosevelt! To hell with Babe Ruth! To hell with Roy Acuff!"[85]

Meanwhile in the barracks, many soldiers intuitively linked the traditional country strains with the melancholy of their peculiarly American homesickness. Men who might never have been exposed to country music returned home from the war with a developed taste and an appetite for more. This exposure happened as early as basic training, when many soldiers from above the Mason-Dixon line were trained in the South.[86] Armed Forces Radio Services—a worldwide system of radio stations for troops abroad—was a more uniform way soldiers from all over the country were exposed to their fellow soldiers' music. It began in mid-1942, in part stimulated by makeshift stations constructed by troops based in Kodiak and Nome, Alaska.[87] It was also motivated by the realization that U.S. troops in the Pacific and in Europe were tuning in to Tokyo Rose and Axis Sally, enemy vixens who mixed swing music with sexy subterfuge.[88] As the Armed Forces Radio Service headquarters in Los Angeles controlled most of the disc-pressing plants in the United States, it shipped programs transcribed on vinyl discs to more than 800 stations every week.[89] Frank Page, later an announcer on the *Louisiana Hayride* and the show's producer for its last several years, hosted shows on Armed Forces Radio at several stations during World War II; at his final station in Berlin, he hosted the live country show *El Rancho Berlin* and a call-in request program "You Pick'em."[90]

Shows like Page's *El Rancho Berlin* helped to develop the sound and style of country music by bringing together musicians from a variety of backgrounds to play, sing, and, as a matter of course, exchange sometimes disparate musical ideas. *Hayride* bassist and music businessman Tillman Franks, for example, participated in such musical exchange while stationed on Saipan. He recalls gathering a group of musicians and approaching the manager of the Armed Services Radio Station, the Voice of America, about hosting a weekly country music show:

> I went around to all the different outfits on Saipan, finding people that could play. And I listened to them. And I got some together and I went down and got Jim Moore—he was in charge of the Armed Forces Radio Station there—and I told him that we wanted to do a program if he'd put us on once a week 'cause we needed to have some country music on. . . . We did real good. And we got real good [at playing]. I went around and got me some better musicians and they started putting us on three days a week in Saipan—Monday, Wednesday, and Friday. When they'd come on the air at 5:00 in the afternoon, we'd open up the show. And I got tremendous mail from Guam and Tinian and all those Pacific islands.[91]

Franks recalls that his most remarkable fellow band member was Pete Seeger, who sang and played banjo with the group.

Another Shreveport musician-turned-wartime-musical-envoy was trumpeter Sleepy Brown. Three months after his basic training, Brown first got to play as a soldier in Utah where he was a member of the 408th Army Air Force Band, which featured an eighteen-piece dance orchestra. Interest in flight school motivated Brown to request a transfer to the 63rd air service group, with which he served a tour of duty in the Pacific. At the request of his commanding officer, Brown began to give nightly twenty-minute trumpet concerts while stationed at Nadzab, New Guinea. He also played "Taps" at the first memorial for an American casualty after the U.S. arrival in Japan.[92]

Future *Hayride* pianist and North Louisiana native Harland H. "Sonny" Harville honed his musical chops as a GI as well. Harville later played piano in the *Louisiana Hayride* staff band and with singer Slim Whitman, as well as banjo and guitar with Tex Grimsley and the Texas Showboys. Born in 1921 in Vivian, near Shreveport, he was playing banjo on radio station WJLS in Beckley, West Virginia, with fellow Shreveport natives Tex and Cliff Grimsley, when he joined the Army in 1942. Harville was stationed in New Guinea with the 339th engineers, whose commanders decided to form a big band:

> They looked through our papers that showed what we did before we came there and . . . I was a musician. . . . But they were looking for a

bass player and . . . so they asked me if I could play bass. And I said, "Yeah." Although I'd never played bass before, I had guitar. And the four strings on a bass are like the top four on the guitar, so I knew that I could play bass. So anyhow, we formed a fourteen-piece orchestra.[93]

The rhythm section, along with the clarinet and saxophone players, made up the nucleus of the band. Because it was logistically difficult to rehearse the large group, comprised of members from several different companies, the big band was eventually pared down to its five core members and transferred to I Corps Headquarters. There they became the I Corps Five and roomed together in a tent dubbed the "Tempo Teepee."[94] The five members doubled as the I Corps Drum and Bugle Marching Band, with Harville playing the snare drum. Besides entertaining troops through live performances in dining rooms, hospitals, officers clubs, and on board ships, the I Corps Five performed regular live broadcasts on local signals in New Guinea and over the Armed Forces Network out of Japan.[95]

When Franks, Brown, Harville, and other musicians from the area returned from their military service, they did so with a short history of intensely steady gigs and increased mastery of their instruments, the likes of which can only be accomplished through a regimen of performance. With experience and ability came a heightened sense of possibility. The Army gave Franks his first taste of singing and playing behind a radio microphone, and instilled in him a lifetime passion for music performance. Brown returned to join Jimmie Davis's Sunshine band, with whom he toured and played an extended stint at the Stables, a Palm Springs nightclub Davis purchased in 1948.[96] As a result of having come in contact with musicians from throughout the nation, Franks, Brown, and others returned home to Shreveport with deepened ambition and a clear understanding of the potential of radio for their careers as country musicians. They were sure of their audience, as they had seen service men from throughout the States moved and enthused about their music. After the war, this groundswell of interest grew into a populous, eager audience for live country music radio shows during the late 1940s and after.

Besides the immediate human realities of fighting World War II, other changes in radio broadcasting stemmed directly from the war. Sometimes called radio's "Golden Age," the early 1940s saw historic broadcasts of front line eyewitness accounts by Edward R. Murrow, Eric Sevareid, and others. Symphonic performances as well as the artistic, poetic, and theatrical productions that began in the late 1930s as unsponsored programming continued to become both more frequent and more elaborate with the wartime flowering of sponsorship. While some sponsors sought the prestige associated with certain programs, many attached themselves to whatever shows they could in an atmosphere of intense competition for buying radio time. Radio as a business, then, flourished during the war. With markets closed on the war-torn European front, the American consumer industry turned marketing money exclusively toward home. Print media was unable to absorb the extra business that came their way because of space limitations due mainly to a wartime paper shortage. There was, however, no scarcity of airwaves. Radio advertisement sales—and, thus, the industry itself—boomed during the war as never before.[97]

When Congress deemed advertising a tax-deductible expense in 1942, it gave further incentive for this trend. Companies spent money on radio advertising both to avoid draconian taxes on wartime profits, as high as 90 percent, and to keep their company name current in the consumer mind. As a result, sponsored time on the networks doubled over the course of the war and eventually took over completely. When postwar radio entered the age of the disc jockey, the notion of unsponsored "sustaining programming" lost its meaning.[98] All programming was commercially sponsored, since advertisements aired between records throughout the day. In this way, both the increase in radio business and the decrease in live network programs grew from the realities of World War II.

In contrast to the networks, local radio programmers had long realized the obvious advantage of hiring a disc jockey over paying a stable of musicians. From its very start, for instance, KWKH engineers broadcast phoned-in requests for songs on phonograph discs from Henderson's personal stash. Many early local stations used phonograph records despite the obstacle imposed by the FCC that recordings must be constantly announced as such; the FCC relaxed the requirement some in 1940, reducing identifications to one per half hour, with the wording left to the individual announcer.[99] The networks, on the other hand, forbade the use of recorded material other than sound effects, partly under pressure from musicians' organizations to eschew phonograph records. The recording taboo dated back to the 1930s, when many discs bore the label "Not Licensed for Radio Broadcast" in order to protect the "exclusivity" clause in network-performer contracts. This injunction began breaking down after a 1940 lawsuit involving bandleader Paul Whiteman concluded with the court determination that, once purchased, phonograph records could be used and broadcast freely. The war further eroded the restriction when, beginning in 1943, network news reporters used wire recorders to capture their eyewitness accounts of events on the Italian front. Not only did these precursors to magnetic tape allow reporters to move unobtrusively into the middle of the action but recordings made on them were easily censored for broadcast.[100]

Meanwhile, other legal struggles ensued between radio broadcasters, record companies, and the musicians and songwriters who supplied them with material. Several of these coincided with the war years and held critical consequences for popular music in general. The most dramatic skirmish occurred at the height of a feud between the National Association of Broadcasters (NAB) and its long-standing adversary, the American Society of Composers, Authors, and Publishers (ASCAP). As the eminent music licensing monopoly, ASCAP foresaw the trend and announced its intent to sharply increase its fees for records broadcast over radio. In response, the NAB formed a competing music licensing organization, Broadcast Music, Incorporated (BMI), which rapidly gained a foothold. Record studios and many radio stations kept a moratorium on ASCAP-licensed music throughout the dispute. With the exception of public domain tunes, stores of older ASCAP-licensed music remained absent from the airwaves and sound booths, a void that altered the future trajectories of hillbilly and other roots genres. For their part, the networks whittled their music offerings to almost nothing, and expanded drama, news, and other types of programming. A further boon to BMI was its ability to draw younger songwriters, who were dissatisfied with ASCAP's hierarchical system for dispersing copyright fees.[101] Furthermore, ASCAP's traditional focus on classical and popular composers meant that otherwise neglected songwriters within genres of blues, country, and other roots music joined BMI. As a result, most hillbilly music, as well as blues and rhythm-and-blues of the 1940s, would be licensed by the newer agency. When Acuff-Rose joined BMI, it sealed the success of the fledgling organization and clinched its association with traditions previously excluded by ASCAP.

Record companies, in the meantime, contended with the American Federation of Musicians (AFM) over the rights of performing musicians to royalties for records aired publicly over radio and jukeboxes. Citing these trends as threats to the livelihood of professional musicians, AFM President James Caesar Petrillo ordered his members to stop making records in August of 1942. The three major record producers held out against the AFM for over a year, until September 1943, when Decca caved and signed an agreement. RCA-Victor and Columbia followed the next winter. All three companies agreed to establish a fund for unemployed musicians.[102] Shortly after the AFM ban lifted, World War II ended, supplies of vinylite and shellac again became plentiful, and recording went into full swing. In the context of Shreveport, the AFM ban lay the groundwork for the financial rights of musicians, including country musicians who made their living playing on radio shows like the *Hayride*.

A keystone legal battle for the national networks included even more direct ramifications for broadcasting in Shreveport. In 1941 the FCC concluded its three-year investigation of "chain" broadcasting by ordering NBC to divest itself of one of its two networks. But it extended its ruling further, and limited ownership by a single licensee to one radio station per market area, of which there were eight nationwide.[103] The Supreme Court upheld the FCC decrees in 1943 and made them law. As a result, the Ewing family, who owned KWKH and KTBS in Shreveport, traded with another company, acquiring KTHS in Little Rock, Arkansas, in exchange for KTBS. The Arkansas station would later broadcast the *Louisiana Hayride* over its own 50-kilowatt transmitter, further stretching the powerful reach of the Shreveport barn dance.

The prosperity radio enjoyed during World War II would have been cut short much sooner were it not for the vagaries in the development of both television and FM radio, both of which would shake the long-held security of AM radio. Since the mid-1930s, the two not-yet-established media technologies contended over the allocation of spectrum frequencies. Shortly after the war, the FCC rendered a critical decision in that struggle when in 1945 it decided to move the assigned FM frequencies to the upper end of the spectrum, rendering all pre-war FM receivers completely useless. Those who had placed hopes in FM as the future of radio argued that the decision would set industry back years and cost $75 million to convert.[104] For television, this victory alleviated the blow that World War II represented. Still in its infancy when the United States entered the war in 1941, with twenty-three television stations offering minimal broadcasts in a handful of major cities, programming was first cut and then frozen completely. Only six stations survived the war moratorium, and these provided programming to only about 10,000 sets.[105] The 1945 FCC ruling opened up spectrum space and insured at least a temporary check on radio's growth. The stasis also allowed extant AM stations, including KWKH, to continue operating on stable financial ground.

The major networks actually planned to sacrifice radio on the altar of television. Network executives imagined that the inevitable profit losses in television's first few years, estimated at $8 million in an NBC research department memo from 1946, could be defrayed by radio profits, with the added benefit of millions saved in income taxes.[106] This gave impetus to further cut expenses in the form of the "sustaining programs" now looked upon as the fruits of radio's Golden Age to make room for more daytime serials and other low-overhead, high-profit fare.[107] Further industry delays, network competition, and more international conflict prolonged the temporary vitality of AM radio during a period that was critical for the introduction of the *Louisiana Hayride*. Perpetual infighting over the development of color between television's major commercial players, RCA-NBC and CBS, delayed its progress. Another factor that protracted radio's viability came late in 1948 when the FCC again stopped issuing television licenses. This was initially due to continuing signal interference, but the Korean War extended the freeze until 1952.

In the meantime, 108 scattered television stations were on the air. Twenty-four cities had more than one station; only in Los Angeles and New York, each with seven stations, was the potential audience size apparent to broadcasters and program sponsors.[108] Throughout the radio industry, many of its diehards saw television as a novel excitement, but no real threat to the entrenched traditions of their medium.[109] When the FCC lifted its licensing suspension in 1952, television dealt a blow to its established rival. The new medium shook the fiscal foundations of the old, as advertisers began scuttling dollars away from radio to television. Fascinated audiences increasingly spent their evenings in the glow of the cathode ray rather than the hum of the amplifier tube. The networks themselves shifted their financial and creative energies to the more lucrative television medium, leaving their radio affiliates with a void of both funds and programs.

As radio station owners scrambled to survive, they developed new approaches to filling airtime, paying for it, and finding audiences. Within a few years, the radio enterprise was overhauled. It became a medium dependent mostly on local advertising, with programming dominated by disc jockeys who played records and prattled varieties of lively banter between songs. Local news, promotional prize giveaways, and gimmicks became protocol. Radio stations soon moved away from attempting broad appeal to specializing music, ads, and deejay patter to a particular group, or "market." Thus, the era of format radio was born.[110] As stations began to rely more and more on disc jockey shows, which cut costs dramatically and were popular with listeners, locally produced live shows like the *Louisiana Hayride*, gained the increasing status of a rarity. During the years of the FCC television freeze—an artificial calm before the storm—the *Hayride* had won an audience and a reputation upon which it rode comfortably for most of the 1950s. Even after the freeze lifted, television made its way only slowly to Shreveport, which was the largest market in the country to be without a television station[111]when its first license was granted in 1952; and newspaper listings of programs did not appear until August of 1953.[111]

The delay of television was only one factor among many that made Shreveport, 1948, the right time and place for the *Louisiana Hayride* to assert a far-reaching influence over the next decade. But the *Hayride* did not emerge from a vacuum, as recordings and broadcasts by musicians like the Sheltons and Davis in the 1920s and 1930s bear out. The *Hayride's* story is about the convergence of rich history, fortuitous timing, and motivated individuals with a broad sense of possibilities. In an industry once typified by the practices of national networks, the live music on local stations like KWKH during the postwar decade now played the central role in extending radio's legacy as a medium of unparalleled immediacy and personal intimacy. And, in the case of the *Hayride*, that role included the communication of a powerful element of regional character in Shreveport, so long a crossroads culture. Now the *Hayride* occupied the point of intersection for music from all around the region: from the ports and prairie swamps to the south, from the piney forests and dry plains to the west, from the backwood hills to the north, and from the red clay cotton farms in the hinterland. On the Shreveport stage, accordion met cowboy guitar, swing fiddles met rapturous hymn-singing. Shreveport's advantageous situation amidst a variety of musical and cultural influences shaped the receptivity of the area's audiences to a broad range of musical styles, while also making it possible to project those styles to the rest of the nation.

5

⌒⌒⌒⌒⌒

Country Music Crossroads

That show wasn't produced, it just happened.
—Bob Sullivan, KWKH radio engineer, 1949–59

When the *Louisiana Hayride* began, country music reached a larger audience than ever, not only in the South but throughout the nation. World War II in part catalyzed country music's ascent, especially in the mingling of people from all regions of the nation during military training and service abroad. This cultural cross-pollination was also fertilized at home by the migration of rural dwellers to metropolises like Washington, D.C., Detroit, Chicago, and Cincinnati for employment in the now-booming war industry. The success of BMI as a licensing organization in competition with the older, more established ASCAP further broadened the market. Even the AFM recording ban hoisted country music to the extent that many hillbilly performers did not belong to the union, so were free to make recordings. Still, wartime rationing imposed limits on the use of gasoline, rubber, and shellac. Once the war ended and shellac was again plentiful, record companies fed the emergent demand for country music with releases on more than sixty-five different labels.

Radio stations tapped into the booming demand for country music just as the postwar radio industry itself mushroomed, naive to the impending upheaval to come with television. In 1946 alone, 500 new radio stations went on air in the United States with 400 more to begin broadcasting the next year.[1] Country music figured heavily on the airwaves and, in the next few years, at least 650 radio stations jumped on the bandwagon to feature live country music shows.[2] KWKH had long broadcast live country music, so when musicians like Tillman Franks returned home to Shreveport from World War II service, they naturally gravitated toward the station's powerful signal in their determination to make a professional living in country music.

Franks would play a prominent role in many aspects of the *Louisiana Hayride*, alternately entertaining, managing, booking, songwriting, and even teaching guitar to later famous players. His experiences on local radio during the late 1940s prepared him for the challenges of the chang-

Fig. 5.1 Harmie Smith and band at KWKH studios, including Tillman Franks on bass. Louisiana Hayride Archives—J. Kent.

ing country music business. Immediately after the war, Franks returned to Shreveport and began playing bass with country bands on morning radio shows, writing songs, teaching guitar lessons, and acting as booking agent for local musicians. He endured a hardscrabble existence not uncommon for country players of the era. But Franks felt his big break came when a Sears salesman living in a garage apartment behind his brother told him about an opening for a bassist on a twice daily KWKH radio show with bandleader Harmie Smith. The salesman, future country chart topper Webb Pierce, already played guitar, along with electric guitarist Owen Perry, for Smith's band, the Ozark Mountaineers. Franks joined Harmie Smith, and remained even after Pierce and Perry were replaced by notables Buddy Attaway and Claude King (fig. 5.1).

Smith's show typified the daily live country music on KWKH during the late 1940s and early 1950s. His spots lasted fifteen minutes, with performances loosely structured according to the bandleader's direction. Band members huddled around one or two mikes, joking, swapping stories, and generally "shooting the bull" between numbers. Country shows, in particular, were popular with sponsors who found the salt-of-the-earth personae of country radio musicians imbued their products with a cornpone authenticity. The major local sponsors of KWKH live country music programs during the *Hayride* era included Johnny Fair Syrup, Southern Maid donuts, Martha White flour, Harbuck & Womack Sporting Goods, and a company that sold baby chicks by the dozen.

In the spontaneous context of Smith's daily show, Franks developed a shtick as an entertainer that fit the country music convention of the comedic bass player. On broadcasts, Harmie Smith gave Franks the nickname "Radar" and played up the fact that he was the only band member who never sang solos. According to Franks, this routine caught the radio audience's fancy:

> People began to write in asking when Radar was going to sing a song. . . . Harmie said, "When we get 5000 letters we'll let him sing." Little towns around would have everyone around sign a petition. He had so many. Really, it was unreal—I got baskets of mail. So he said, "Well, now you're going to sing." . . . So I got with Buddy and Claude and I rehearsed this song:
>
> > 'As through this world, I roam along
> > Friends all ask me to sing a song
> > And when I ask what shall I sing
> > They say, "Radar, sing anything."
> > I thank you friends for your request
> > And so I've tried and I've done my best.
> > Should it not sound so good,
> > It'll sound better than Harmie would.'
>
> People would write in wanting to book and say, "We'll book you, providing Radar sings."[3]

During the era when the banter between Smith and Radar drew stacks of postcards and letters, radio brought a sense of personal and intimate connection to a community like the one surrounding Shreveport. For performers, the looseness of the daily live format offered leeway to develop a breadth of skills. With the Ozark Mountaineers, for example, Franks began to understand the process of constructing an entertainment personality, an insight he later applied to jobs as manager for country musicians Webb Pierce, Johnny Horton, David Houston, and Claude King. But while these radio jobs offered a laboratory for an aspiring musician like Franks, they represented only the most tenuous security. During his time with the Ozark Mountaineers, Franks necessarily supplemented his income with a stint on the Shreveport Police Department.[4]

In the meantime, two musicians from Little Rock, Arkansas, Les Gibbs and Dick Hart, contacted Franks about starting a band. They invited him, steel guitar player Felton Pruitt, and fiddle player Dobber Johnson, both of whom were in their teens, to move to Little Rock for a morning program on KERK, *The Arkansas Travelers*. The sponsor was Sunway Vitamins, and Hart guaranteed Franks and the other band members $40 per week. As Franks recalls, there were many similarities between the old job and the new: "I was the comedian and the bass player and they called me either

'Radar' or 'Peach Seed Jones.' I played comedy and bass fiddle. And we were starving to death."[5] Hart never put his financial promise in writing and the $40 per week guarantee soon fell through. Within a couple of months, Franks, Pruitt, and Johnson returned to Shreveport.

Franks had another reason to return. While still in Little Rock, he had been invited by Johnnie Bailes to play bass with the Bailes Brothers. The Bailes Brothers in their original foursome already had found success as performers on the *Grand Ole Opry* at WSM in Nashville before they moved to Shreveport's KWKH. According to Homer Bailes, the group had been fired from the *Opry* when a former girlfriend of Johnnie Bailes committed suicide. Known for strict concern for the public perception of its stars, the *Opry* would not tolerate negative publicity, thus the dismissal of the Bailes Brothers. To protest their summary dismissal, WSM artist services manager Dean Upson quit and moved with the Baileses to Shreveport, where he had heard KWKH had ambition to start a weekly barn dance variety show along the lines of the *Grand Ole Opry*.[6]

The Bailes Brothers arrived in Shreveport during December 1946, following Upson who had taken a position as KWKH sales manager. Not long after, guitarist Walter left to become a preacher, playing only occasionally with his brothers thereafter. Shot Jackson joined the group on steel guitar. Ernest Ferguson, the mandolin player who had come with the group to Shreveport from Nashville, left in 1947 and was replaced by Clyde Baum. Kyle Bailes quit playing bass, although he stayed on as manager for a while. Homer Bailes still played fiddle with the group. It was at that time in 1947 that Franks became bass player. With their daily *Martha White Time* morning radio show, the Bailes Brothers with Tillman Franks did well at KWKH.

Bailes offered Franks $45 per week, plus $15 each for as many "whiskey and devil songs" (that is, gospel songs denouncing both) the bassist could pen in the few weeks before an upcoming Columbia recording session. In line with a common practice of the era, the per-song pay included the stipulation that Bailes would own the rights, and therefore any future royalties, for the song. Franks wrote "You Can't Go Halfway and Get In," "Has the Devil Got a Mortgage on You?" and "Sinner, Kneel Down and Pray." All three were recorded for Columbia in Nashville on 21 December 1947, with Art Satherley as producer.[7] By late 1949 personal differences between Johnnie and Homer caused them to disband. Homer became a preacher and Johnnie joined musician Dalton Henderson on Shreveport station KTBS. Before then, however, the Bailes Brothers brought their experience as seasoned entertainers to KWKH's *Louisiana Hayride*, where they were one of the founding acts during the show's first year (fig. 5.2).

Several stories exist about who originated the idea of the *Louisiana Hayride*. According to Homer Bailes, the owners of KWKH contacted Dean Upson in Nashville about hoping to start a show modeled after WSM's *Grand Ole Opry*. In other words, Upson and the Bailes Brothers left Tennessee with the specific intention of creating a music-variety barn dance. Homer recalled convincing his brothers that their southeastern

Fig. 5.2 Homer and Johnnie Bailes at the KWKH studios. Louisiana Hayride Archives—J. Kent.

mountain country sound would be fresh in the Shreveport region: "I said, 'I was down there . . . in Louisiana in the Army. There isn't any country music down there.' . . . The Shelton Brothers were here and the Western music, but what we call hard country just wasn't around. I said, 'It would be a brand new thing, be commercial, and it would sell like wildfire.'"[8] The youngest Bailes brother was right about the group's potential appeal. Their act consistently sold out auditoriums, churches, and ball fields where audience members occasionally arrived in ox carts.

Unlike many country and western acts, the Bailes brothers built their repertoire almost exclusively on sacred and gospel songs, with an occasional lovelorn "heart song." They advertised their shows as appropriate for the whole family. Raised in West Virginia as sons of a Baptist preacher, Homer and his brothers grew up playing stringed instruments in country churches in the area and singing harmony. While sacred songs and a clean image were certainly part of their heritage, they emphasized this aspect of their show for its commercial appeal. As Homer explained, "We played a lot of churches and we tried to keep the show clean and wouldn't insult anybody. A man could come and could bring his wife or his mother or his child. We tried to keep it that kind of thing. A lot of hillbillies we know told some pretty rough stories."[9]

At times, the wholesome image of the Baileses opened doors that were otherwise closed to country music acts. Homer recounted the rebuff they received from the school principal, who was also a preacher, in Robeline, Louisiana, when they tried to book into the auditorium: "We wouldn't have you here—you'd insult all the women and all the children, tell dirty jokes. We wouldn't have a hillbilly show here." Johnnie managed to parlay the brothers' Baptist heritage into a change of heart for the principal and a paid gig for the band. As Homer, now a Methodist preacher himself, reflected years later:

> He had a hillbilly show before he knew it. He didn't know we was [*sic*] just an ornery bunch of boys—we were talking about the show, not about how great we were. And he got up and told everybody how great we were that night and kind of embarrassed us because we just weren't that nice a people. We just didn't put on bad shows.[10]

All the while building a following in rural towns throughout the Shreveport region, the Bailes brothers with Upson auditioned talent for the upcoming live radio show. According to Homer Bailes, the four brothers and Upson conceived of the show and enlisted as its emcee KWKH program director Horace Logan.

Logan contends that he first envisioned the *Hayride* taking up the mantle of KWKH's *Saturday Night Roundup*, which began in 1940.[11] Logan had been employed by KWKH since 1933, while still in high school. He moved from position of errand boy, news runner, and handyman to that of full-time announcer by 1939. He became emcee for the *Roundup*, where he remained until he was drafted into military service in 1942. The wartime absence of personnel ended the *Saturday Night Roundup*, and when Logan returned to Shreveport after military service, he opened a gun repair shop. But the airwaves beckoned his return. In early 1947, he accepted the position of program director at KWKH. According to Logan's memoirs of the *Hayride* era, the notion of a live Saturday night barn dance show was on his mind when he returned to the station, although a publicity essay written by him in the late 1950s includes the statement, "Though I didn't start it, I soon became producer of the 'Hayride' and was in charge of all talent."[12]

Another key player in the *Hayride*'s beginning was station manager Henry Clay. Although he had little experience in radio, Clay took the job offer by John Ewing in 1946 shortly after he married Ewing's daughter. His involvement in many business aspects of running the *Louisiana Hayride* grew as the show's profitability increased.[13] Logan discredits the idea that Clay held any genuine passion for the music, claiming in his memoir to have fought him every step for the show's financial backing. Louisiana music scholar Steven Tucker, however, makes a convincing case for Clay's enthusiasm for country music and his significant role in the development of the *Hayride* idea.

In all likelihood, the Baileses, Upson, Logan, and Clay were each involved on some level with the early efforts to put the show together. Logan's involvement in the *Saturday Night Roundup* certainly supports his claim of being instrumental in its more famous descendant. Besides serving as an emcee, Logan soon took over *Hayride* production when Upson left the station. That role quickly became a full-time job, at which time Frank Page took over as KWKH program director. Both Upson and the Baileses would have had more personal contacts, most useful in early efforts to draw talent to Shreveport. Because of his previous employment with the *Grand Ole Opry*, Upson also would have had more practical experience with the logistics of producing a weekly barn dance program, while Clay was ultimately responsible for approving ideas and funding the show's operation.[14]

However it got started, the *Louisiana Hayride* made its initial broadcast on 3 April 1948 from Shreveport's Municipal Auditorium. Roy Acuff, who had been associated with the *Grand Ole Opry* since 1938, came to Shreveport two weeks before and performed a Saturday night program at the Municipal. In fact, he originated his national network program from Shreveport, featuring the Bailes Brothers as guest performers. Acuff's Shreveport show broadcast over the Universal network, an independent chain of twenty-five stations of which KWKH was a part, thus drawing national eyes on the Shreveport station. Acuff's cameo, most likely the result of his personal friendship with the Bailes brothers, gave the *Hayride* an auspicious boost enjoyed by no other radio barn dance program of the era.[15] After that, the *Louisiana Hayride* became a regular feature on KWKH's Saturday night broadcasts.

Regardless of who initiated the idea in Shreveport, the notion of a radio barn dance was not new. The *Louisiana Hayride* was one among many radio shows devoted to live Saturday night country performance, each of which followed a basic format of alternating comedy bits, country songs about drinking or loving, advertisements, and gospel tunes. All of these shows existed somewhat in the shadow of the first and most famous of the type, the *Grand Ole Opry*. But unlike others, the *Hayride* stood out as a lightning rod for talent that would become iconic of the era. Only the *Opry*, established in 1925 on Nashville's WSM, claims more centrality in the history of country music and the number of key players who graced its stage—a status largely due to the amassing music industry that pushed Nashville to become the epicenter of the commercial country music business. Even without the benefit of supporting industry, the *Hayride* asserted a strong voice in the directions of commercial country music during the postwar decade.

During this period, Shreveport's KWKH showcased a wide array of stylists from yodelers to Cajun fiddlers, from crooners to honky-tonkers, from string bands to gospel quartets in direct reflection of the city's historical situation at a regional crossroads. Timing and circumstance pushed the *Hayride's* significance even further. At the same time the *Louisiana Hayride* expanded country music's scope, style, and audience, it served as a training ground for seminal rockabilly players—the pioneers of rock-and-roll. Only the *Hayride* boasts the singular historic claim to have launched, from the same stage, both modern country as well as rock-and-roll. Understanding how that came to be requires first an examination of the show's distinct spirit, operation, and first stable of talent.

In some ways akin to the eclecticism of tent shows and vaudeville, not to mention the unpredictable nature of early radio, onstage variety was the modus operandi for producer Horace Logan. In pursuit of this aim, he added audience participation segments like "Beat the Band," where contestants guessed the songs played by the *Hayride* staff band, known as the "Lump Lump Boys" for these occasions. Logan frequently rotated performers, scheduling them for only one or two songs in a row, and alternated four different announcers for each hour-long segment.[16] During the watershed decade from 1948 until 1958, eight different announcers filled these positions: Logan, Ray Bartlett, Norm Bale, Bill Cudabac, Frank Page, Hi Roberts, Jeff Dale, and country music star Jim Reeves (fig. 5.3).

As a result, the *Hayride* kept a quick pace. Onstage, the show appeared at the smooth command of its cadre of professional announcers, in contrast to the *Opry*, which emphasized its image as a casual get-together of pickers and singers. On the *Opry*, cast members sometimes wandered across the stage during songs or even chatted softly behind performers. Stars like Roy Acuff might linger at the microphone as long as half an hour. As *Hayride* announcer Frank Page put it, "the Opry was loose as a goose."[17] By all appearances, *Opry* artists themselves directed the flexible pace and overall mood of the show, whereas the *Hayride* depended on its staff of announcers, who enjoyed a good deal of latitude in carrying through these elements. As Page recalls, producer Logan "would give me a list of talent. And then I would sit down and plan out who was to appear where and why and for what sponsor and then designate what announcer."[18] As a result, the artists "knew where they were going to be and how many songs they were going to do. And Logan in the beginning would only allow them to do two songs at a time. And so they, as he always said, had to give their best shot when they came out—and usually do their record, if they had one."[19]

If the *Hayride* came across as a tight ship in contrast to the *Opry's* projection of a less formal atmosphere, the backstage picture reversed. The spontaneous image of the *Opry* differed from the reality of its behind-the-scenes machinations just as much as the bucolic, sometimes rube, personae of its artists contrasted with their skilled professionalism. The NBC portion of the *Opry* was rehearsed so completely that, as music writer Colin Escott said, "every word, every wordless gooberism was scripted."[20] The *Hayride*, on the other hand, came together each week based on the outline of musicians, slots, and sponsors. "There was no rehearsal, everybody just showed up," recalls Bob Sullivan, who missed only a handful of Saturday nights operating the board alongside chief engineer Jack Jones. With the exception of the Maddox Brothers and Rose, who changed costumes each time they reappeared, "everybody showed up to the show dressed like they were going on stage."[21] More punctilious organization ruled the portion broadcast, beginning in 1948, over a regional network and later over a national network. However, for the most part, in Sullivan's words, "that show wasn't produced, it just happened."[22]

Reports by musicians who took the stage in its earliest days certainly support Sullivan's depiction of the *Hayride* as a kind of weekly happening. When the show first aired, no arrangement existed for the performers even to be paid. They agreed to appear simply for the exposure, expecting a cut

Fig. 5.3 *Hayride* announcers Frank Page, Horace Logan, Hi Roberts, and Jim Reeves. Louisiana Hayride Archives—J. Kent.

of only the profits, if there were any. One of these early performers was pianist Sonny Harville, who played with Tex Grimsley and the Texas Showboys from the first *Hayride* in April 1948 and later performed and recorded with Slim Whitman. As Harville recalled, "It was advertising, that's all the pay we got. When the *Hayride* started, I guess for six months to a year, nobody got paid. . . . But the acts did it for the advertising so they could go out. Some of them had records—they could plug their records, you know. Others of us that didn't have records, we could go out and play show dates."[23] Announcer Frank Page confirmed Harville's recollection that "the way they made their money was by appearances in Texas and southern Arkansas, and Mississippi. They didn't make anything appearing on the Hayride. . . . So they made their money by the appearances during the week and then came back in for the Saturday show."[24]

Before long, after the show proved successful and under pressure from the local musician's union, the *Louisiana Hayride* adopted the *Opry*'s policy of paying most of its performers according to union scale. A band-leader made $18 per show, and his or her band members received $12. If the band consisted of five or more members, then the featured artist qualified for the higher bandleader pay of $24.[25] This salary was decent for an up-and-coming young musician; however, as performers gained popularity, the *Hayride* reputation retained them more than the financial compensation. After all, in-demand performers could easily earn several times the *Hayride* money at a Saturday night booking. But the *Hayride* offered exposure—immeasurable in financial terms—that was essential to achieving and sustaining popularity in the still-golden era of wireless, and a key to obtaining record contracts and the coveted invitation to Nashville. Frank Page described the wide coverage of the KWKH signal, which benefited both from its maximum wattage capacity and from the AM radio phenomenon known as "skip." With the combination of these forces, the KWKH signal reached far and wide even before the *Louisiana Hayride* began. As Page recalled years later:

> We covered about twenty-eight states at night. And our skip goes out all over the world. We still get letters from Honolulu, Venezuela, Australia, Guam, wherever. A week doesn't go by that we won't hear from somebody way off somewhere. During the war, aboard ship they would pick up KWKH out in the Pacific, and they'd turn it on all the speakers on the ship and everybody from this part of the world was really excited about it.[26]

Once the *Hayride* began, the powerful frequency positioned Shreveport to draw musical talent from many directions toward the promise of financial success just as the Red River lured diverse travelers and settlers to its banks a century before. The station's reputation and coverage continued to expand over the course of the 1950s. As Page put it, "We almost had a national show."[27]

The strong signal alone did not account for the country music legacy of the *Louisiana Hayride*. Several other factors converged to create in Shreveport a dynamic forum for what seemed for a while to be an endless cavalcade of unique talent. Among these was a well-timed early association with an Alabama bandleader destined to become country music's most stellar songwriter and one of its most charismatic performers. In August 1948, the *Hayride* introduced Hank Williams to a broad radio audience. Following the phenomenal success of his first major hit, "Lovesick Blues," Williams began his intense and legendary career of hallmark recordings with MGM. By the next year, in latter 1949, he had moved to the *Opry* and proved a contagious pop sensation when his debut there won him a coveted spot in the NBC Prince Albert portion the next week.[28]

"Lovesick Blues" christened both Williams's rise to fame and the *Hayride*'s rise to prominence. In the context of the rich musical heritage of northwest Louisiana, the song's mixed lineage seems only appropriate. Penned by Tin Pan Alley lyricist Irving Mills and composer Cliff Friend,

"Lovesick Blues" was recorded several times over by blues singers like Bertha Chippie Hill (1927), as well as by vaudevillian Emmett Miller (1925 and 1928, the latter backed by jazz musicians) and hillbilly singer Rex Griffin (1939), both Williams's direct yodeling predecessors.[29] Noting the song's crazy quilt lineage, music writer Nick Tosches mused: "There are those who would not hear it was written by a Jew from Russia [Mills], that it was midwifed by a redneck jazz singer [Miller] who would have been puked off the Opry."[30] "Lovesick Blues" found an enthusiastic audience at the *Hayride*, where the song's hodgepodge pedigree fit the gumbo demography of Louisiana in general and Shreveport in particular, both longtime crossroads of cultural impulses from every direction, both black and white. Williams's own musical voice formed out of a similar context, during his youth spent soaking up the sounds of black and white musicians in deep southern Alabama, iconized in the oft-told story of his tutelage under African-American guitarist Rufus "Tee Tot" Payne. Williams's musical persona came across well in Shreveport.

"Lovesick Blues" indelibly marked both singer and barn dance. Were it not for KWKH's promotion of the song and the *Hayride* audience's receptivity to it, Williams's version of the Tin Pan Alley number may never have become one of country music's quintessential recordings. In fact, the overwhelming response to the song in Shreveport likely fueled Williams's determination to record it over the objections of his producer Fred Rose, who found it unsuitable.[31] The *Hayride* exposure given "Lovesick Blues" sparked sales of over 48,000 copies in seventeen days, and, by 7 May 1949, it had reached number one on the country chart.[32] The *Hayride* spotlight galvanized not only the success of "Lovesick Blues" but also the career of Williams, who would forever take country music's first chair, despite (or perhaps because of) a career abbreviated by his tragic death on New Year's Day 1953.[33] In turn, the notoriety of Williams and his "Lovesick Blues," and the fact that both were introduced to a national audience from Shreveport, lent the *Louisiana Hayride* an almost premature patina of prestige (fig. 5.4).

Williams absorbed musical sounds wherever he went and, in that way, epitomized the dynamism of southern roots music evident throughout its history, from Jimmie Davis to Jimmie Rodgers, from Leadbelly to the Mississippi Sheiks and so on. The song "Lovesick Blues" represents the process of exchange that took place across the often artificial barriers between genres of music and performers. The introduction of "Lovesick Blues" in Shreveport also reflects the river city's historical situation as a meeting ground, demographically and culturally. Situated in the state of Louisiana, itself broadly characterized by a motley assortment of ethnicity, race, and culture, it makes sense that the *Hayride* created a stage for sounds from southern Louisiana to eventually find a national audience. With its own distinct mix of French, Spanish, Anglo, and West African cultural strains, southern Louisiana was even more well known for its comfort with musical hybrids than its neighbors to the north. In a manner perhaps appropriate to the roundabout pathways of musical exchange, Hank Williams

Fig. 5.4 Hank Williams, wife Audrey, and band at KWKH studios.
Louisiana Hayride Archives—J. Kent.

figures prominently in the story of how Cajun sounds found their way
north to the *Hayride*.

Although far from native to the region, Williams long had harbored a
deep affection for Cajun culture and, even before his exposure on the
Louisiana Hayride, southern Louisiana audiences appreciated his music,
especially raucous numbers like "Move It On Over" and "Honky Tonkin'."
Eminent *Hayride* Cajun Jimmy C. Newman commented on Williams's appeal in south Louisiana: "With Cajun people, he hit. He was telling it the
way it was, you know, and the Cajun people love that real sincere story in
a song."[34] Williams's tribute to the musical sounds of the southern part of
the state, in fact, came to national attention only after he had left Louisiana for the *Opry*. When Williams released "Jambalaya (on the Bayou)" in
1952, it quickly became a nationwide hit and a perennial favorite with
Cajun audiences. The song claimed authentic Cajun roots, since it adapted
the 1946 Cajun melody "Gran Texas" by Chuck Guillory. Williams then
wrote lyrics with boogie pianist Moon Mullican. "Jambalaya" was a port-
manteau of French and English lyrics set to a laid-back groove that evokes
the squeezebox, intended to retain the spirit and spice of Cajun music
while remaining palatable to mainstream country tastes.

"Jambalaya" had recently reached the top chart position when Williams
returned to the *Hayride* to perform it at his "homecoming" in the fall of
1952, after having been fired from the *Opry*. A live recording of this performance, released on CD as part of a series preserving memorable *Hayride*

moments, allows the closest possible contemporary stance on this historic performance only a few months before Williams's death. In the *Hayride* recording, a tinkling piano, reminiscent of an old-West barroom weaves in and out of the steel guitar punctuation and solo fiddle breaks that carried the song's commercial release.[35] Some of the experience for the home radio audience remains in the recording, as periodic outbursts of applause occur in mid-verse or mid-break, seemingly disassociated with the musical performance in progress. In the days of live radio, these moments were a calculable source of exhilaration for home listeners, who could only imagine the reasons for it. Microphones placed among the live audience enabled an astute audio engineer to crank up the levels during these explosions of enthusiasm, as clearly happens in "Jambalaya." Following the song, emcee Horace Logan announces that "the old lonesome Drifting Cowboy is coming home again" and will be in Shreveport "every Saturday night for a long time to come." While his appearances on the *Louisiana Hayride* continued only a few months more, "Jambalaya" lived on. It not only set a precedent for Cajun music on the *Hayride*. The song became immensely popular and was soon recorded with great success by Jo Stafford, and eventually by artists as divergent as Fats Domino and John Fogerty. Thus, in addition to bringing a sense of Cajun aesthetics to wider attention, Williams drives forward the breakdown of commercial markers separating popular music as such from roots genres of white country and black rhythm-and-blues.

The immense crossover popularity of "Jambalaya" was not an isolated phenomenon in Williams's career. Beginning with the release of "Cold, Cold Heart" in February 1951, he blazed trails into mainstream pop music culture to an extent achieved by no previous country songwriter. Again, Williams's success bears directly on qualities of the *Hayride* that set the show apart from its peers. Beginning with Williams, KWKH exhibited a willingness to take risks that paid off time and time again as one innovative performer after another distinguished its stage. In the case of Williams, as his son Hank Jr. once suggested, without this inclination on the part of the station, Williams might not have created the lasting inroads and iconic pop legend for which he is hallowed.[36] "Cold, Cold Heart" bent the ear of musicians of every stripe when in May 1951, crooner Tony Bennett, who had yet to chart a hit, covered it and earned his first number one single. Other singers soon followed Bennett's lead, including the Fontaine Sisters and Perry Como, Louis Armstrong and Eileen Wilson, Tony Fontane and Dinah Washington, and Kay Starr.[37] "Cold, Cold Heart," in fact, garnered such pop capital that it maintains its staying power, appearing on the 2002 Grammy Album of the Year, *come away with me,* by light jazz songstress Norah Jones.[38]

Following his death at age 29, Williams became one of the legendary figures of U.S. popular music, hallowed as a songwriter of rare, poetic genius and a performer of uncanny personal magnetism. In his initial ten-month-long *Hayride* stint, Williams effectively set a pattern followed by many future country music luminaries: he came to Shreveport, won an enthusiastic regional following, honed his performance style through radio shows and numerous personal appearances, released one or two records that sold well and gained national attention, and shortly thereafter, left for Nashville.[39] This pattern unfolded alongside transformations in the business of country music that occurred as quickly as the upheavals of the larger postwar society. Amid these changes, KWKH beckoned musicians, both the experienced and the untried, to follow the flow of modern country music's first water. Most notably among these, Kitty Wells represents how Shreveport nurtured the era's most distinctive country performers.

Johnnie Wright and Jack Anglin, performing as Johnnie and Jack and the Tennessee Mountain Boys—including Johnnie's wife, Kitty Wells, as a vocalist—first came to KWKH before Williams in January 1948. They left for a short period only to return in Williams's wake, after which point Wells also joined the pantheon of country music demigods. Like the Bailes brothers, Johnnie and Jack had enjoyed a stint on the *Grand Ole Opry*, which they left to become one of the original acts on the *Hayride*. Johnnie Wright recalled that Johnnie and Jack were working at the *Opry* as guests but not members during a time when Kitty had stopped performing to care for their three children. KWKH's reputation as a lucrative base for country musicians first drew them to Shreveport. As Wright explained:

> We had heard about people down here, Harmie Smith, Curley Williams and the Georgia Peach Pickers . . . so we decided to come down here and see if we could get on. . . . And Horace Logan, I guess he was the program director at that time, and Horace heard us sing as Johnnie and Jack and Kitty and so that's the way we got on. . . . We all went to work on KWKH and the Bailes brothers and us worked auditoriums and school houses together. We teamed up. . . . That's the way we started and we did real well in places in Louisiana and Texas.[40]

While performing in Shreveport the duo had their first hits: "Poison Love" and "Crying Heart Blues," followed by "What about You" and "Ashes of Love."[41] Kitty Wells worked for a brief time as a disc jockey, known as the "Little Rag Doll" for the quilt pieces she sold during a daily half-hour program.[42] In September 1950 they left Shreveport for a time and performed at stations in Tennessee, North Carolina, and Georgia.[43] Throughout their interrupted tenure at KWKH, Johnnie and Jack regularly featured Wells as a vocalist and she made an unsuccessful set of recordings with RCA.

The group returned to the *Hayride* in the summer of 1951, then bounced back to the *Opry* at the start of 1952. Shortly thereafter, Kitty Wells emerged as country music's first female superstar with her 1952 recording of "It Wasn't God Who Made Honky-Tonk Angels." The song was composed by southern Louisianan J. D. Miller, an independent producer in Crowley, Louisiana, who recorded pioneer Cajun, hillbilly, and, later, blues on his Feature Records as early as 1947.[44] Miller wrote the song as an answer to Hank Thompson's recent hit, "The Wild Side of Life," which includes the line: "I didn't know God made honky-tonk angels." He originally enlisted

Alice "Al" Montgomery to record the tune for Feature.[45] Miller's song used the same tune as Thompson's hit, which, in turn, had borrowed its notes from the sacred song that Roy Acuff brought to the *Opry* in 1936, "The Great Speckled Bird." Furthermore, the related Carter Family's 1929 song, "I'm Thinking Tonight of My Blue Eyes" preceded Acuff's tune and the melody has deep roots in Anglo song tradition.[46] "It Wasn't God" began a series of hit recordings by Wells, who eventually took a figurative throne as "Queen of Country Music." After they left Shreveport and followed Hank to the *Opry*, Wells's career overshadowed that of her husband's duo, though Johnnie and Jack continued to release successful recordings as a duet until their career was cut short by Anglin's death in a 1963 car accident.[47]

Wells's subsequent hits demonstrate the same clarity, intensity, and sincerity that made her treatment of Miller's tune a tremendous success. At a live *Hayride* guest performance, a visit occurring after Wells had left for the *Opry*, Wells performs the 1955 hit "Making Believe."[48] The lyrics typify her most successful material—a heartbroken lament over a lost love, about whom the singer can now only fantasize. Supported by a smooth fiddle and mellow background counterpart by the steel guitar, Wells pushes her voice steadily through each of the straightforward lines and simple melodic contours. It is a vocal style that conjures the somber traditional style of Anglo mountain ballad singers while at the same time it communicates a world-weariness that perhaps comes from having experienced both the Great Depression and World War II. Whatever its source, the determined resignation in Wells's style rang true with her audience just as it expelled stereotypes about the honky-tonk limitations of the female voice (fig. 5.5).

In different ways, both Williams and Wells brought to the *Hayride* stage music that marked Shreveport's position as a regional intersection of northern and southern Louisiana cultures. Williams bridged north and south Louisiana with his Anglo pop variant of a Cajun tune in "Jambalaya." Likewise, Miller's appropriation of an alternately romantic/religious Anglo waltz is yet another way in which southern Louisiana Cajun culture made a showing in mainstream culture via *Hayride* stars. Their successes broke ground for later *Hayride* performers who straddled north and south Louisiana traditions even more directly, as Louisiana natives at once fluent across two distinct traditions. Jimmy C. Newman stands out among the handful of highly respected Cajun musicians on the *Hayride*, whose performances lay the groundwork for the Cajun genre's gradual more mainstream acceptance.

First appearing on the *Hayride* in June 1954, Newman brought a breadth of influences and experience, and nurtured an ability to connect musically to both Cajun and conventional country audiences. Born in 1927 on the prairies of Big Mamou, Newman first began performing with a Bunkie, Louisiana band that played country and some Cajun tunes.[49] With this band, led by fiddler and "Jambalaya" inspiration Chuck Guillory, Newman made his first recordings in 1946 on Modern Records, singing mostly Cajun songs in his native French patois. Old phonograph records by the Carter Family and Jimmie Rodgers and broadcasts of the *Grand Ole Opry*

Fig. 5.5 Kitty Wells with Johnnie [Wright] and Jack [Anglin] at the
KWKH studios. Louisiana Hayride Archives—J. Kent.

influenced Newman from childhood just as much as the Cajun music
played by local musicians, and he was comfortable with both.

By the late 1940s and early 1950s Newman started experimenting with
a mainstream country sound and won a songwriting contract from Acuff-
Rose, as well as a deal with Dot Records (he moved to MGM in 1958). Newman's first major hit, "Cry, Cry, Darling," reached the top five on the country chart in 1954 and led to an invitation to join the *Hayride*. For the most
part, he continued pursuing a broadly aimed aesthetic during his two-year
Hayride stint. As a result, most of Newman's mid-1950s repertoire was mainstream country with the exception of "Diggy Liggy Lo," a Cajun melody
given English lyrics. His more straight country hits during the *Hayride*
years included "Daydreamin'" and "Blue Darlin'," in 1955 and "Seasons of
My Heart" the following year.

According to the by-then-typical pattern, Newman's career gained momentum in Shreveport until he left to join the *Opry* in 1956. He kept his
strong ties to Louisiana close by. Newman gradually began to experiment
with blending Cajun and country styles (songs like "Alligator Man" in
1961) and even recorded an acoustic album of Cajun music, all the while
excelling in mainstream country.[50] During the late 1970s, Newman organized a band called Cajun Country, including his son Gary Newman, fiddler
Rufus Thibodeaux, and accordion player Bessyl Duhon, which continued

performing over the next two decades at the *Grand Ole Opry*. With the exception of his biggest country hits, Newman's band ever since performs "about 99 percent Cajun."[51] Cajun music now enjoys status as a significant subgenre within mainstream country, but the initial working out of that relationship found an early formal arena at the *Louisiana Hayride*.

Hank Williams and Kitty Wells signify an auspicious beginning for the *Hayride* both as portents of the show's significance to postwar country music and as reminders of the region's rich heritage as a point of cultural intersection. Against the historical background of Shreveport's Red River, upon which commerce and culture flowed roughly between north and south, the appearance of prominent Cajun musicians on Shreveport's *Hayride* is fitting. Likewise, the land route of goods and people over the Texas Trail runs in symbolic parallel to the flow between east and west captured in the country subgenre known as honky-tonk. Williams and Wells both traveled west from Alabama and Tennessee, respectively, to Shreveport, where they adapted and defined the sound for the decade.

"Honky-tonk" as a phrase predated them, first appearing on a 1937 country record, "Honky-Tonk Blues," by east Texas native Al Dexter.[52] Honky-tonk style originated even earlier, particularly in the oil-boom towns of east Texas, north Louisiana, and Oklahoma, and already reached a national audience via recordings by Ernest Tubb, among others. As a musical style, honky-tonk defines itself by a moderate two-step dance tempo and a small ensemble with a loud lead instrument, often electrified guitar or steel guitar, capable of cutting through the din of small, raucous clubs typical of the area. Early honky-tonk is also characterized by lyrics about prodigious drinking and licentious women. Honky-tonk reached its stylistic peak in the postwar decade, exemplified by Williams and Wells, whose sense of form and manner of delivery continue to inform country aesthetics to this day.

Most of the successful honky-tonk performers who followed Williams and Wells at KWKH did not attain their eventual stature as popular culture icons, but nevertheless made lasting contributions to the genre. In Shreveport, they found an audience warmly receptive to honky-tonk, and at the *Hayride*, an opportunity to refine a distinctive voice within the honky-tonk tradition. Among these performers was Woodrow Wilson "Red" Sovine, who stepped directly into the place opened by Hank Williams when he left the *Hayride* in June 1949. In the wandering fashion then still typical of professional country radio entertainers, Sovine had been at KWKH before, in the spring of 1948. He originally left for WFSA in Montgomery to take the radio job Williams vacated to come to Shreveport. Thus, Sovine's return to Shreveport was his second time filling a void left by Williams. Once there, Sovine took up Williams's post as the "Ol' Syrup Sopper," the host of a KWKH morning radio show sponsored by locally manufactured Johnny Fair Syrup.

Sovine and his band, the Echo Valley Boys, drew an enthusiastic following among KWKH listeners. In fact, Sovine sold so much Johnny Fair syrup and became so identified with his sponsor that he changed his band

Fig. 5.6 Red Sovine and announcer Ray Bartlett
grapple over a bottle of Johnny Fair Syrup in a KWKH
publicity shot. Louisiana Hayride Archives—J. Kent.

name to Red Sovine and His Syrup Soppers[53] (fig. 5.6). Sovine's onstage
charisma comes across in a live *Hayride* performance of "I Hope You Don't
Care," where a few slow lines of free-metered introduction break into the
jaunty, swing-tempo tune. The song's lyrics follow the protagonist as he
moves in on the wife of a two-timing Johnny, eventually convincing her to
go "on a moonlight ride" where he will "squeeze you tight and hold you
near."[54] Ultimately the speaker seems to lose his nerve in the last line, "if
we part here." Despite its suggestion of double adultery, the performance
maintains a lighthearted feel both in Sovine's sung parts and in a straightforward steel solo break. The song represents the basis of Sovine's success
as a performer: it is a solid honky-tonk dance number, instrumentally speak-
ing; lyrically, the song suggests sin more graphically than many songs and,
at the same time, keeps a safe distance from that tainted world.

   Sovine eventually won a spot on the *Grand Ole Opry*. He became well
known for his mastery of the country music genre of sentimental recitation
songs, notably 1965's "Giddy-Up Go" and "Phantom 309" and—remarkably,
over a decade later—"Teddy Bear."[55] Although he never experienced the

chart success of some contemporaries, Sovine enjoyed a long career that garnered accolades for his convincing ability both to render tear-jerking sentiment and to tread convincingly into the honky-tonk style. As demonstrated in the live *Hayride* recording, Sovine communicates a broad appeal as a good-hearted, old-fashioned country singer and a solid interpreter of an important style with deep regional connections.

Sovine's friend and eventual label mate Webb Pierce epitomized the era's honky-tonk sound with his own rough-edged vocals accompanied by a lithesome steel guitar. For years, Pierce honed his skills over radio stations in his native north Louisiana home area of Monroe and in Shreveport, where early on he made a living working in the local Sears, Roebuck men's department. Pierce sought a spot with the *Hayride* cast more than once, but producer Horace Logan rejected him every time. According to Tillman Franks, who was Pierce's manager at the time, he arranged for *Hayride* staff guitarist Buddy Attaway to call in sick so that Pierce could take his place, giving him a chance to prove himself on stage.[56] Now with a foot in the door, Pierce made a solo *Hayride* debut in 1950. Two years later, he scored his first big hit, "Wondering," a tune written in 1935 by Louisianan Joe Werner, which became the biggest-selling country song of 1952. Franks recalled planting his own young guitar students in the audience to stimulate applause for "Wondering," thus, successfully jockeying an encore for his client.[57]

Pierce followed his first hit a few months later with "That Heart Belongs to Me." The string of subsequent recordings made Webb Pierce the eminent country performer of the 1950s and one of the most prolific singers in country music chart history.[58] Pierce's influence over honky-tonk happened not only because of his myriad chart success with this and other honky-tonk-styled hits but also because of his talent for hiring highly capable musicians for his band. While on the *Hayride*, Pierce's band included two future stars, pianist Floyd Cramer and vocalist Faron Young. Both Jimmy Day and Bud Isaacs played steel guitar for Pierce, along with Pierce's regular steel player Basil "Sonny" Burnette. Isaacs later drew acclaim for his extraordinary role in bringing the instrument to new prominence on the 1954 Pierce hit "Slowly."[59]

Pierce's style comes across well in a live *Hayride* recording of "I Don't Care," which became a hit for Pierce after he had left his regular *Hayride* gig for Nashville. Pierce's nasal caw—an almost literal honking—delivers lyrics that address a woman the singer is courting, promising no questions asked about her checkered past. Pierce's voice combines to great effect with the steel guitar, which, with the exception of a fiddle break, remains at the instrumental foreground throughout and maintains an ongoing dialogue with the singer. It is no coincidence that Pierce found a receptive audience in Shreveport, central to the region known as the Ark-La-Tex, which was once populated by the smoke-filled, state highway joints evoked by Pierce's recording.

From the perspective of postwar country music, it is somewhat confounding that Pierce is relatively unknown today compared with some of his less successful contemporaries, given that his career included fifty-five top ten singles, thirteen of which reached number one. Most of his consignment to the periphery of music history can be explained by his vocal delivery. His flat, nearly wooden tenor warble struck a chord with contemporary fans, but did not stand the aesthetic test of time, particularly as the silky Nashville sound and all its attendant sensibilities emerged in the 1960s. Even in spare, return-to-roots country—as in so many revival trends—certain sounds from the past simply are not welcome by modern ears. Pierce's voice is one such unwelcome guest. Inside the country music industry, both Pierce's sound and garish personal image rubbed against the increasingly sophisticated and urbane aura of the genre in the latter twentieth century. Pierce was not elected to the Country Music Hall of Fame until 2001, ten years after his death. But Pierce was a country music superstar relative to his era and a peerless honky-tonk stylist in his day. From the perspective of *Hayride* history, Pierce represents not only another star in a long procession launched to fame there but also a native to the region whose musical sensibilities created one of the era's definitive country sounds.

Another performer with connections to Webb Pierce was Faron Young, who joined Pierce's group as a guitarist and vocalist while a 19-year-old student at Shreveport's Centenary College. During his 1951–52 *Hayride* tenure, Young emerged as a solo performer in his own right. The Shreveport native capitalized on his youth and good looks, and on his versatility as a performer who could record everything from bubblegum to schmaltz to borderline raucous.[60] Before long, Young acquired a Capitol Records contract and moved to Nashville to join the *Opry*. In addition to his regionally appropriate stylistic scope, Young's particular appeal to teenage girls and his six-month catapult to stardom signaled imminent changes in country music—changes that would move all of U.S. society toward a youth culture characterized by passing fads and overnight sensations. In short, Young's success, beginning with his first major hit record "Goin' Steady" in October 1952, tapped into many of the same cultural impulses that engendered rock-and-roll.[61]

The tune "Live Fast, Love Hard, Die Young," captured in a live performance on the *Hayride* stage, rests squarely in the tradition of country music at the same time it flirts with the youth culture that stirred all around during the postwar era.[62] Young clearly was well versed in the music of Hank Williams and, specifically in the case of this tune, Lefty Frizzell's "If You've Got the Money I've Got the Time." Honky-tonk guideposts mark the song, with lyrics eschewing commitment and a steel guitar solo fading into fiddle. But there is something striking beyond the lilting laid-back country beat with a prominent bass on the live recording. The tune captures an incipient rock-and-roll spark in lyrics like "I got a hot rod car and a cowboy suit," which, in hindsight, seem to straddle two worlds. The title sentiment itself suggests a tinge of detached nihilism absent in many of the most heart-wrenching honky-tonk laments. Young's delivery attests to a regional honky-tonk apprenticeship even as it hints at the attitude that became one of the immutable qualities of rock-and-roll performance.

Hayride audiences and producers were as ready to receive an up-and-coming firebrand like Young as they were to embrace the most traditional of country music performers. For musicians themselves, a chance for exposure on the *Hayride* grew increasingly invaluable, for the show transmitted each week not only over the 50,000-watt Shreveport station but over the Universal network and on the *Louisiana Hayride* network of twenty-seven stations in four states after February 1950.[63] In addition, a second simultaneous 50,000-watt broadcast aired the *Hayride* when KTHS in Little Rock increased its power in late 1952. Beginning in 1953, the barn dance was also heard every third Saturday for a half-hour on the CBS national network of more than 200 stations. The *Hayride* gained the allure of a spot where aspiring young performers of early country music could gain a foothold.[64] This was true not only of relative neophytes like Young but also of seasoned troubadours like guitarist-singer Billy Walker, who recognized the *Hayride* as a vehicle for his aspirations toward national fame.

Although Walker was only 23 when he joined the *Hayride* in 1952, he already brought nearly a decade of performing experience that began on radio station KICA in Clovis, New Mexico. At 15, Walker won a KICA amateur musician contest and was awarded a weekly fifteen-minute radio program every Saturday. By that time, his family had moved to Whiteface, Texas, so the high school guitarist/singer hitchhiked 80 miles each way every Saturday to make his unpaid gig.[65] Walker spent the next several years performing in a variety of settings: as a solo guitarist and singer on station KRBC in Abilene one summer; as a singer and front man for Jake Miller and the Mustangs, a Western swing band in Lubbock, Texas; as a guitarist in a band at a "high class honky-tonk" in Santa Rosa, New Mexico; then as front man for Columbia recording artist Jimmy Lawson, touring the Southwest and the Midwest for a year; as a member of a cowboy group called the Sons of the Prairie in San Angelo, Texas; and finally, as a solo performer on station KWTX's *Ranch Time Show* in Waco. While there, he joined another western swing group called the Lone Star Playboys.[66]

Walker's biography is a reminder of the hardscrabble rural life that shaped so many of the era's legendary country performers, a life so remote from the promise of wealth that lured most of them to Nashville. Like so many rural Americans born during the Depression, Walker's childhood was difficult, marked by the death of his mother when he was 4. With eight children, his father lost his farm over a $15 payment, and Walker, along with two brothers, went to live at a Methodist-run home for orphans in Waco until his father could get back on his feet. When he was 11 years old, his father moved the family to Portales, New Mexico, to manage a small dairy farm; he had remarried a woman who had four children of her own and, together, they had one more child. Soon, the family moved to Clovis, where Walker's father managed the ice cream department of a larger dairy, and then to Whiteface.

Walker's guiding inspiration for a musical career was the Gene Autry movie *Public Cowboy No. 1*, which he saw in 1942 when he was 13 years old. After picking 329 pounds of cotton one day, Walker received 25 cents from his father to see the movie. He still has paraphernalia from the movie on his office wall today. He soon earned $6.00 for a cheap guitar, plus 25 cents for an instruction book, by plucking turkeys for two weeks that autumn for his uncle in Clovis, at 8 to 10 cents a turkey. Outside of a brief period of work for the JC Penney shoe department when he was 17, Walker supported himself through his music for the rest of his life.

In 1949 he auditioned for the radio barn dance known as the *Big D Jamboree*, taking the train from Waco to Dallas every weekend to perform as "The Traveling Texan, the Masked Singer of Folk Songs." Meanwhile, country singer Hank Thompson invited Walker to be the opening act for a five-day-a-week radio show. Thompson also helped Walker secure a record contract with Capitol. His first recording session for Capitol Records was in July that same year, but Walker's songs won little chart success.[67] Walker left Hank Thompson in 1951 to host a radio show on KWFT in Wichita Falls, sponsored by the alcohol-heavy pharmaceutical Hadacol. In Wichita Falls, Walker was on the air four times per day, on a sixteen-station regional network; this was his first exposure to a large audience. He switched to Columbia Records in 1951 and charted his first top ten record, "Anything Your Heart Desires," the next year.

Walker had become a regional star when, according to Horace Logan, Webb Pierce recommended that he join the *Hayride*.[68] Walker's arrangement with Hadacol was ending due to the company's legal and financial problems, so Walker came to Shreveport in July 1952. In an interview, Walker reflected on the significance of the *Hayride* to his career.

> The *Louisiana Hayride* was [big] in those days. There was only three national programs that meant anything to an artist as far as building a career was concerned. One was the *Louisiana Hayride*. . . . And in those days, people don't realize, but the *Louisiana Hayride* was a very popular show. Our Saturday night performance had two 50,000-watt radio stations hooked together, KWKH and KTHS in Little Rock, and they broadcast that simultaneously and, buddy, we got out to a great deal of [territory]. We was giving the *Grand Ole Opry* a fit for the money.[69]

On the strength of the show's tremendous territory, Walker continued to build success. In 1954, while on the *Hayride*, he recorded another hit for Columbia, "Thank You for Calling." For Walker, it was not the immediate allure of Nashville but of television that took him away from Shreveport. Of the era's handful of attempts to bring the barn dance format to the new visual medium, the *Ozark Jubilee* in Springfield, Missouri, hosted by country singer and comedian Red Foley enjoyed the most longevity. Walker left Shreveport in 1955 to join the *Jubilee*, and finally made it to the *Grand Ole Opry* in 1960. He shortly thereafter recorded "Funny How Time Slips Away," a song by a young struggling songwriter named Willie Nelson.

Thanks to the KWKH stepping stone, Walker remained in the *Opry* cast for over thirty years, continuing to make records that were successful in the United States and abroad.[70]

Williams, Wells, Newman, Sovine, Pierce, Young, and Walker form only a representative handful of the artists who set the tone of success for the relatively young *Louisiana Hayride*. They also sufficiently demonstrate the pattern upon which the station built its reputation, of drawing solid talent, giving it recognition and audience, and bidding it adieu. And though the *Hayride* always played farm team to Nashville's more senior major league, its position as stepping stone to country music stardom never gave *Hayride* producers much pause. Quite the contrary, by coining the epigram "Cradle of the Stars," the *Hayride* embraced this role for all its lucrative potential. The procession of new talented voices to Shreveport remained steady for more than a decade. Every time a popular performer left for Nashville, a relative newcomer stepped into the spotlight. The momentum did eventually slow down because the *Hayride* did not keep pace with the changing expectations of professional country musicians during the post–World War II decade.

Around the time the *Hayride* started, country music underwent a transition toward an increasingly competitive big business. As much as KWKH stood at the foreground of musical trends, the station lacked vision in regard to the transformation of the industry. In some ways, the *Hayride* never broke free from assumptions about professional country music life of the 1930s and 1940s when performers got by on a grueling schedule of daily sponsored spots and local live performances, supplemented at times by sales of photos, song folios, and sometimes recordings. In the changing atmosphere of country music as big business, these forums no longer adequately made ends meet. Yet the *Hayride* never took a deliberate or long-sighted approach to ensuring its viability. In some ways, KWKH still iterated the seat-of-the-pants quality of radio as it was for the Sheltons during the 1930s or even Tillman Franks after the war, just when those realities were becoming obsolete. An ingenuous, intuitive quality gave the show much of its energy and spontaneity at the same time it assured its gradual decline.

Shreveport lacked nearly all the attendant music industry trappings that drew musicians to Nashville—large studios, music licensing houses, record companies—and Shreveport never developed the means to stop the constant migration of its stars to Tennessee. The musical infrastructure there promised a chance for success and security that no previous generation of country musicians could have anticipated. Guitarist and Nashville recording executive Jerry Kennedy, who grew up in Shreveport and began his career on the *Hayride*, reflected on the absence of interest and capital necessary to create a competitive recording industry in his home city:

> I wonder if the *Hayride* wouldn't have been a lot bigger and meant so much more if there had been a great recording studio in that city. Because when people would come up here—they had to come to Nashville to record—they would do a guest shot on the *Opry*. If they went

over real well, the people in the *Opry* zapped them up. And I just won-
der if they hadn't have had to come here to do the records if they
[might have stayed at the *Hayride*].[71]

Shreveport's status as a springboard settled early on and a pattern repeated itself time after time: Performers cut their teeth at the *Hayride* in
order to advance as proven talent to the country music mecca.

Besides studios and record companies, other supporting industry never
materialized in Shreveport. For example, the *Hayride* neglected to establish a successful central organization for booking the performances by
which their musicians made a living. A handful of individuals, driven most
often by a love of the music, sometimes by a desire for extra income, took
it upon themselves to fill the void and acted as informal agents. Among
these were local bandleader Pappy Covington; Kyle Bailes, who pursued
booking after he quit playing bass for his brothers; *Hayride* producer and
emcee Horace Logan; and, most active of all, musician and manager Tillman Franks. But their isolated toils could not achieve what a centralized
booking office could.[72]

In 1951 music businessman Jim Bulleit came to Shreveport from Nashville with the intention of creating a formal booking agency at KWKH along
the lines of what the WSM Artists Services Bureau did in Nashville for *Opry*
acts. Bulleit had much experience in radio and recording, having started
his own label in 1946, which he called in allusion to his own name Bullet
Records. For reasons that remain unclear, Bulleit abandoned the effort
within a year and returned to Nashville to rejoin his family. During his stay
in Shreveport, he helped to hire several *Hayride* performers including Jim
Reeves, Slim Whitman, and the Wilburn Brothers.[73] A few others repeated
Bulleit's failed attempt to centralize performance schedules for artists.

In 1954, in another instance, Horace Logan arranged a meeting between
a promoter named "Colonel" Tom Parker and station manager Henry Clay
about the establishment of a WSM-style artists service bureau. Parker's career had evolved already from carney man to concert booker, promoter,
and artist manager, most notably of superstar Eddy Arnold. Along the way,
in 1948, he finagled an honorary colonel's commission from Jimmie Davis
during the singing governor's first term in Louisiana office.[74] Clay already
felt he had made a concession in paying Parker's expenses to come to the
meeting; when Parker announced the bureau would require $12,000 from
KWKH up front (twice the yearly salary of a radio announcer at the time),
Clay scotched the plan.[75] Within a few years, Parker would become famous
as Elvis Presley's flamboyant personal manager.[76] Of course, once Elvis became a national phenomenon, it was apparent in hindsight not only that
the $12,000 would have been easily recovered but also that KWKH had
missed the brass ring of unprecedented profits.

The third push for KWKH to form a centralized booking agency for its
artists succeeded, but it was too late. In 1957, at the same time Horace
Logan left the *Hayride* for California, Henry Clay formed Cajun Publishing
as a subsidiary of KWKH. Clay named Tillman Franks as the artists serv-

ice manager. Under this arrangement, Cajun Publishing received a percentage of a performer's income from bookings, songwriting, and recording during the period of the contract.[77] By this time, Franks had developed a well-established system of connections, especially within the region of Louisiana, Texas, and Arkansas, and to the west in Texas and New Mexico. But the *Hayride* had passed its peak, and the ever-lax yet affable management had become unwilling to fund efforts to revive the floundering show.

In many ways, the same qualities that hindered the *Hayride*'s viability beyond the late 1950s enhanced the show in its heyday. These dual-sided qualities spring from the *Hayride*'s status as a neophyte. By the time the *Hayride* began, the *Opry* was over two decades old and had enjoyed the national spotlight on NBC for almost half that long. Because of its age and prestige, the *Opry* inadvertently assumed the role of gatekeeper for country music form, imposing relatively strict limits on the music that won a place on its stage. In its established position of preeminence, the *Opry* functioned as a watchdog, a burden that never weighed on the more junior *Hayride*. The *Opry* management concerned itself over instrumentation and song content that might compromise the down-home atmosphere. For instance, Kitty Wells's breakthrough hit, "It Wasn't God Who Made Honky-Tonk Angels," was initially banned from the *Opry* and NBC because its candor about marital infidelity was deemed racy.[78] In hindsight, it was precisely that quality that elevated conjugal candidness to a hallowed trope of honky-tonk lyricism, spawning countless songs of cheating and heartbreak.

In contrast, the *Hayride*'s greenhorns necessitated an openness to untried musical styles, an attitude that fostered some of its greatest performers. Station owners at the local Shreveport *Times* newspaper cared nothing about dictating the show's content so long as it proved profitable. This accentuated the laissez-faire attitude already brought by the relative youth of the *Hayride* as an institution and of its staff. The threads that weaved the free spirit and eclecticism of the *Hayride* were those of its youth and its region. If these threads eventually unraveled, they held together many contributing factors to create a show of extraordinary vitality and edge for nearly a decade.

In the liberal atmosphere of the *Hayride*, artists enjoyed free reign to experiment with different styles on stage. They were, in fact, urged to do so. Logan recalled the attitude he tried to communicate to the artists who came to Shreveport:

> You had to have enough intelligence to take those natural attributes that you have, watch audience reaction to them, and create an individuality. . . . Every artist who has been nationally prominent for any extended length of time—if you had the ability to mimic, you could imitate them. If you don't have a style that's strong enough to be imitated, you don't have a style.[79]

Logan pushed them to excel by scheduling in room for encores. If a performer inspired enough applause, then he or she might encore once, twice, or more on later segments. This established a built-in motivation for performers to dazzle the audience, even to stretch their limits. Hank Williams's farewell *Hayride* performance in 1949 set the record for such encores when he performed "Lovesick Blues" seven times in a row, and quit then only because time had run out.[80] Not until Elvis Presley in 1954 did another *Hayride* performer so raise the bar on audience exhilaration.

Although *Hayride* musicians were limited to only one or two songs in a row, as a rule they fashioned their time in the spotlight as they saw fit. They called the tune and were at liberty to promote a recent release. Performers often tested out different styles to see what incited the most response from the auditorium. As Frank Page reflected:

> Webb Pierce would stand on his toes and the glands on the side of his neck would pop out when he hit a high note. Well, the audience loved that. He was trying hard, you know. And then he'd move his guitar from side to side and they liked that, so he'd do more of it. And Elvis the same way. Elvis wiggled his legs a little bit and they responded and so he wiggled them more. He snarled and mumbled and they liked that, so he did that more. So they learned as they experimented, and as we did.[81]

In this way, the *Hayride* acted as a kind of artist's hothouse, which nurtured the stage personae of its performers into full bloom before they were transplanted to Nashville.

The interest of *Hayride* managers extended to specifics little beyond concerns with licensing fees. KWKH engineer Bob Sullivan recalled that song lists mainly functioned in helping the station negotiate the demands of BMI and the more expensive ASCAP as economically as possible:

> We'd have the singers turn in a list of the songs they were going to do . . . and if two or three of them had an ASCAP song they would put them within a 15-minute segment because they could pay ASCAP in 15-minute increments. Instead of just getting a blanket license . . . we want them all done within a 15-minute period so we can just pay them for 15 minutes, you know, and then move on.[82]

In encouraging performers to craft whatever musical idiosyncrasies they had into unique styles, Horace Logan intuitively guided many of them into the level of success that comes only to the immediately recognized artist. Thus, Slim Whitman employed violinists from the local symphony in recording the title song from a 1920s operetta years before the "Nashville sound" used similar strings support. Drums never troubled *Hayride* managers in the way they confounded *Opry* directors, who long resisted them.[83] Entrepreneurial by necessity, the *Hayride* concentrated on innovation and freshness, and left most judgments about artist style or material up to its audience.

Fig. 5.7 Slim Whitman and his band (including Tillman Franks on bass) on the *Hayride*. Louisiana Hayride Archives—J. Kent.

Because of its open attitude, a number of performers with styles that did not precisely fit the parameters of country music found an enthusiastic reception in Shreveport. Ottis Dewey "Slim" Whitman stands out as one of the legendary *Hayride* performers whose corpus diverged from mainstream country tradition. With styles ranging from waltzing cowboy ballads to yodeling light opera pop, Whitman forms his own subgenre of country music[84] (fig. 5.7). Before coming to the *Hayride*, Whitman had recorded several songs for RCA beginning in 1949 with such country music luminaries as mandolin player Kenneth C. "Jethro" Burns and guitarist Henry D. "Homer" Haynes (who together also formed the best-known country music parody group, known simply as Homer and Jethro), steel guitar player Jerry Byrd, and guitarist Chet Atkins. But with the exception of the minor hit that became Whitman's theme song, "I'm Casting My Lasso to the Sky," none of the other RCA recordings received much notice.[85]

He made his debut on the *Hayride* in April 1950, leaving the Light Crust Doughboys, a Western swing group from Fort Worth, Texas then doing a show on the Mutual Network. Whitman's artistic vision seems to have been clear early on. During the next year, Whitman released his first record on the Los Angeles-based Imperial label, "Love Song of the Waterfall." He made the record with members of the *Hayride* staff band in the KWKH studios, Hoot Rains on steel guitar, Curley Herndon on lead guitar, Curley Harris on bass, and Sonny Harville on piano. During his years in Shreveport, because of a moral aversion to nightclubs, Whitman worked as a city mail carrier to supplement his income from a daily radio show and the regular Saturday night gig. Since the post office does not allow time off for its employees to make recordings, Whitman cut the record at the radio station after hours and sent the tape to Lew Chudd at Imperial, who pressed it into vinyl and released it to his small group of distributors. It reached the top ten for one week.

In 1952 the same group gathered at the KWKH studio to record "Indian Love Call," which sold a million copies and earned Whitman national acclaim.[86] The song, composed in part by Oscar Hammerstein for Rudolf Friml's 1924 operetta *Rose Marie*, gained new life via Whitman's yodeling treatment. The version won immediate approval from Shreveport audiences, and upon release of the album, from record buyers around the nation and beyond.[87] Whitman's idea to record the song met with the same flexibility that generally guided *Hayride* programming. As Logan recalled his interchange with Whitman years later:

> He walked into my office one day and told me he wanted to record "Indian Love Call," which is . . . a light operetta-type thing. And I said "Why not?" He said, "Well, it ain't hillbilly." I said, "It will be when you get through with it." I said, "You make an arrangement that's so dog-gone hard that nobody else can do it like that unless they have a voice just like yours, and I don't know of anyone else with a voice just like yours."[88]

Whitman's subsequent hits included a western ballad, "Bandera Waltz," and "Rose Marie," the title song from the operetta, both of which received Whitman's characteristic soaring falsetto treatment.

Whitman achieved as much success on popular charts as on country charts, and developed an enormous following in Great Britain.[89] In a live 1958 recording of a broadcast commemorating the *Hayride*'s tenth anniversary, the "Smiling Starduster," as Frank Page introduced him, returned to the Municipal Auditorium and performed "Careless Hands."[90] By this time, Whitman's U.S. career had peaked, but he continued to draw enthusiasm from European crowds. In the tune, Whitman's tenor floats in its famous way above a lilting accompaniment, an ongoing clippity-clop that evokes the spaghetti-Western. A high violin strain punctuates each vocal phrase and emphasizes the heartbreak of the faithful lover who only gets rejection in return. Whitman's style is not his only distinctive trait among *Hayride* alumni. Unlike many, he avoided the trail from Shreveport to Nashville; upon achieving international acclaim, he made his native state of Florida the home base of his later career.[91]

Whitman was not the only successful *Hayride* performer who did not graduate to stardom via the *Grand Ole Opry*, nor was he the only one whose style stretched the boundaries of country music. When Johnny Horton auditioned for the *Hayride* late in 1952, he was already an experienced performer in clubs along the West Coast and on the *Hometown Jamboree* (formerly the *Dinner Bell Roundup*) at Los Angeles television station KSLA-TV. He had recorded for small West Coast labels like Cormac and Abbott, the latter owned by his manager Fabor Robison, but these never brought much commercial success. Born in 1925, Horton grew up in the east Texas town of Tyler, an avid sportsman especially fond of basketball and fishing. He won basketball scholarships to Baylor University and then to Seattle University, but never completed his degree, leaving college to work as a fisherman in Alaska and Los Angeles. It was in 1950 at the Anaheim Harmony Park Corral in California that Horton won an amateur musician contest, which led to a job with radio station KXLA in Pasadena.[92]

On the *Hayride*, Horton remained a popular performer for years, with a full-throated, bellowing vocal style couched in a rhythmic, guitar-driving sound that prefigured the sensibilities of soon-to-emerge rock-and-roll. In 1955 Horton retained Tillman Franks as his personal manager, having severed ties with Fabor Robison in 1953. Robison's dubious business practices weave in and out of the early careers of several mid-1950s *Hayride* artists, including Jim Reeves, the Browns (a sibling duo, Jim Ed and Maxine, later a trio with the addition of Bonnie), Mitchell Torok, and Floyd Cramer, along with Horace Logan. Like Colonel Parker, Robison wed a hustler's persona to an ever-watchful eye for a dollar. Colin Escott sums up Robison's legacy as an early talent scout and independent producer: "He would discover, manage [*sic*] and record an astonishingly rich variety of artists, but lose every one and have them all hate him."[93] In turn, Horton, Reeves, and the Browns split from Robison with ill feelings over Robison's underhanded dealings.

In 1956 Horton and his new manager Franks penned the song "Honky-Tonk Man," included on a release of live *Hayride* recordings in addition to studio takes.[94] Performed with the stripped-down sound that characterizes much early rockabilly, the song celebrates the free-wheeling lifestyle of the honky-tonk rambler without fiddle or steel. Instead, a moderate boogie-woogie beat and simple lead guitar carry Horton's straight ahead vocals, unadorned except for the characteristic opening growl and an occasional stuttered vowel ("lay my moh-o-ney down"). The Columbia release of the tune gave Horton his first chart success, but he had yet to record the song that would launch him into the national spotlight.

That song came in 1959, when Horton recorded "The Battle of New Orleans." It was an adaptation of a fiddle tune from the British Isles, "The Eighth of January," with lyrics that recounted General Andrew Jackson's rout of British forces in the *ex post pax* Battle of New Orleans. It had been written and recorded the previous year by Jimmie Driftwood, a schoolteacher from Arkansas.[95] Franks first heard Driftwood's version on the radio late one night and did not particularly like it; he later dreamed that Horton recorded it to great acclaim and followed through on his premonition.

Like Whitman, Johnny Horton sidestepped Nashville. Instead, he appeared on national pop forums, most notably *The Ed Sullivan Show* and *American Bandstand*. He followed the "Battle of New Orleans" with recordings of a similarly hardy nationalist spirit: "North to Alaska" (written for a John Wayne movie of the same title), "Sink the Bismarck," "Johnny Reb," and "The Battle of Bull Run." Although billed as "King of the Saga Songs," Horton was equally adroit at love songs like "All for the Love of a Girl," honky-tonk heartbreak tunes like "Everytime I'm Kissing You," and novelty numbers like the archetypal hunting song, "Ole Slewfoot."[96] *Louisiana Hayride* audiences in Shreveport embraced the breadth and diversity of his style for years before Horton enjoyed the national spotlight.

Johnny Horton's last appearance on the *Hayride* was on 29 June 1959, designated "Johnny Horton Day" by Shreveport's mayor; by then, he was no longer a regular *Hayride* performer, as the *Hayride* had quit its weekly Saturday night schedule. In the meantime, Horton continued to pursue his songwriting, performing, and recording, as well as his love of angling (Horton's other epithet was "The Singing Fisherman," which he earned in California). He lived in Bossier City, across the Red River from Shreveport, with his wife, Billie Jean, who was Hank Williams's widow, and their two children. At the peak of his career, on 5 November 1960, Johnny Horton was killed in a car crash returning to Shreveport after a show at the Skyline Club in Austin, Texas. Horton was driving, with bassist/manager Tillman Franks and guitarist Tommy Tomlinson his sleeping passengers. An eerie coincidence of his death has been noted more than once: Not only was Johnny married to Hank Williams's widow but also Williams's last gig was at Austin's Skyline Club.[97]

Had Horton lived longer, his unique style might have influenced the direction of commercial country music during the 1960s with his blend of gutsy, high energy, and hard-strum rhythm, so far afield of the Nashville "country pop" or "countrypolitan" sound simultaneously emerging. Perhaps he might have carved a space for the initial rockabilly spark to stay aglow within the parameters of a country sound. As it stands, his early work remains a foreshadow of rock-and-roll. With a recorded corpus that makes Horton difficult to categorize neatly, he remains one of country music's most distinctive voices.

Known for a style antithetical to Horton's, Jim Reeves first joined the staff of KWKH as a golden-throated announcer in December 1952. Nicknamed "Gentleman Jim" for his soft-spoken politeness and smooth-toned voice, Reeves met Horton's old manager Fabor Robison in Shreveport and recorded for Robison's Abbott label. His release of "Mexican Joe," written by fellow east Texan Mitchell Torok (later a *Hayride* regular himself) reached the top of the country chart in April 1953. According to Logan, Reeves's shot on the *Hayride* began when Hank Williams was too drunk to sing one night, although that version of the story has not been fully established.[98] Reeves impressed the audience and he began to sing regularly. Over weeks of radio performance, he developed a breathy singing style particularly suited to microphones, moving close in and crooning lightly in his velvet baritone.[99] Following "Mexican Joe," Reeves soon scored another hit with a cover of the song "Bimbo," recorded with less success by singer Rod Morris a few months prior.

By 1955 Reeves moved to Nashville, signed with RCA Victor, and joined the *Opry*. Like Johnny Horton before him, Reeves became disenchanted with Robison's shyster business dealings and abruptly ended his relationship with his former manager, producer, and publisher.[100] In contrast to Horton, Reeves's smooth vocals fit the evolving Nashville country-pop aesthetic, though early RCA recordings still reflect the honky-tonk influence of his east Texas home. A live recording of the song "Red Eyed and Rowdy," written by Reeves while still with Robison and performed during a *Hayride* tour into Texas, bears out the early rural influences from which Reeves eventually distanced himself.[101] The tune jauntily celebrates the happy drunk and, while Reeves pulls it off effectively, it seems clear that honky-tonk was not his ultimate destiny. Words like "hunky dory" seem odd in the context of a honky-tonk song and lines like "free and easy like a big pig when he's greasy" are hard to reconcile with the pop-oriented "Gentleman" Jim that was his most famous persona. By the late 1950s and early 1960s, through tunes like "Am I Losing You" and "He'll Have to Go," Reeves had acquired a "touch of velvet" voice that fit well into the "Nashville sound" of overdubbed arrangements, swelling strings, and background vocal choruses dripping wet with reverb.[102] Like Slim Whitman, Reeves commanded attention from audiences abroad, especially in Europe, Scandinavia, and South Africa, where he filmed a movie *Kimberly Jim*. And Reeves's recordings remained popular even after his career was cut short by a private plane crash on 31 July 1964.

A handful of other headliners from the mid-1950s and after suggest that the *Hayride* continued to draw talented performers from throughout the region, and that the show's aptitude for identifying fresh voices and its willingness to embrace a breadth of styles endured. For example, a few years after Reeves, the Browns, made up of siblings Jim Ed and Maxine, joined the *Hayride* in 1954. They are notable alongside Reeves not only for their series of entanglements with Fabor Robison but also for the pop sensibilities they brought to an act otherwise squarely centered in traditional country music. A brother and sister duet from Arkansas, the pair had recently signed a contract with Robison's new Fabor Records label on the strength of their novelty song "Looking Back to See." The tune was already popular with audiences of the *Barnyard Frolic* in Little Rock. A third Brown sibling, Bonnie, joined the act in 1955, and the trio soon experienced success with Fabor recordings "Draggin' Main Street," "Here Today and Gone Tomorrow," and a remake of "Looking Back to See" recorded in the KWKH studios with Jim Reeves on guitar and Floyd Cramer on piano.[103]

Near the end of 1955, the Browns left Shreveport to join the *Ozark Jubilee*, and switched to the RCA label the following year. They became adept at the country-pop sound of Nashville, recording a huge crossover success in 1959, "Three Bells," followed soon by "Scarlet Ribbons" and "The Old Lamplighter." They joined the *Grand Ole Opry* in 1963, but their appeal as a trio waned. Jim Ed Brown remained on the *Opry* and made a series of successful solo recordings between the late 1960s and mid-1970s. Maxine and Bonnie returned to Arkansas in semi-retirement, except for a brief success in 1968 of Maxine's solo, "Sugar Cane Country."[104]

George Jones joined the *Hayride* in 1955 after approaching Horace Logan in Conroe, Texas, for an audition at a *Hayride* package show, one of the touring shows the *Hayride* performed on the handful of weekends the Municipal was not available. Jones's ambition to be a singer began by at least the age of 12, when he sang with his guitar on the streets of Beaumont, Texas. He had experience as a radio performer and announcer in small stations around that area of south Texas. In 1954 Jones recorded two songs, "No Money in This Deal" and "You're in My Heart," for the Starday label in Beaumont. After hearing his audition, Logan let Jones open the Conroe show and offered the singer a regular spot with the *Hayride* cast that night.[105] Jones stayed with the *Hayride* for less than a year, during which he returned to Beaumont to record his first hit, "Why, Baby, Why," on Starday Records. A live *Hayride* recording of the tune still bears traces of the early influences of Roy Acuff, coming to terms with the dual inspirations that would eventually hold sway: the styles of both Hank Williams and Lefty Frizzell. Jones received an invitation to the *Opry* in 1956, signed with Mercury Records, and began his legendary career. His mastery of melisma and his expansive range from soaring bray to fruit-cellar bass epitomize modern honky-tonk vocals, while his lifelong public trail of conspicuously empty bottles and pathetically broken marriages embodies an accompanying live-hard ethos.[106]

Like Jones, Johnny Cash first pursued music by way of a career in radio. Following his discharge in 1954 from the Army, where he often entertained his fellow soldiers in the barracks playing guitar and singing songs, Cash returned from Germany to Memphis. There, he enrolled in radio announcer's school in hopes of becoming a country music disc jockey. In June of 1955, Cash and a few friends went to Sam Phillips's Sun Records studio, where they convinced Phillips to record two songs. The first was "Hey Porter," a train song with a driving rhythm; afterwards, Phillips sent Cash home to write lines with sharper pop hooks. The next day, Cash recorded "Cry, Cry, Cry." The record was an instant hit. Later that year, Cash joined the *Louisiana Hayride* where he remained until July 1956, when he joined the *Grand Ole Opry*. Cash developed a remarkable ability to communicate with audiences across genres, gifted with the artistry both to turn his own experiences into vivid portraits-in-song and to bring vision to the material of others. Both talents come through clearly on two live *Hayride* performances with Cash's rockabilly trio of the era and a stripped-down sound that remained characteristic. "Five Feet High and Rising" commemorates a devastating flood that displaced his family in Arkansas when Cash was a child, while "Rock Island Line" recasts the folk railroad tune famously recorded by Huddie Ledbetter as well as the Weavers (fig. 5.8).

Fig. 5.8 Johnny Horton and Johnny Cash backstage at the *Hayride*.
Louisiana Hayride Archives—J. Kent.

While less renowned than Cash or Jones, David Houston had a much
longer and much more varied association with the *Hayride*. He first appeared on the *Hayride* in 1951 when he was 12 years old. While he is best
known for his squarely Nashville-centered Epic releases of the 1960s and
1970s, the Shreveport-area native performed off and on the *Louisiana
Hayride* throughout the 1950s, drawing from a stylistic palette that attests
to the eclecticism of both show and singer. His performance career took
a temporary hiatus in order to pursue his degree at Faron Young's alma
mater, Shreveport's Centenary College, before he dropped out to work for
a time in his family's construction business. For a period following Presley's appearance, Houston performed rockabilly songs like "Sugar Sweet"
and "Teenage Frankie and Johnny." He traveled to California with *Hayride*
producer Horace Logan in 1957 and, along with fellow *Hayride* members
and later rockabilly icons Bob Luman and James Burton, filmed a bit of
rockabilly memorabilia *Carnival Rock*.[107]

In a live *Hayride* performance, Houston announces the tune "One & Only"
from the movie that "seems to be doing real well for me right now." Houston rhythmically spits out rapid-fire lyrics like "Come on baby let's have
some fun" between choruses that vary repetitions of the line "Mmmm Boy,
(Whooooo) sure could kiss." The monotone execution is surprising from a
singer later celebrated for the melodic range he brought to country ballad
singing. This along with the backup from an equally rhythm-focused guitar, bass, and drums bring a nascent punk quality to the performance. That

this performance was a featured part of a live *Hayride* broadcast incontrovertibly confirms the absence of stylistic strictness that had characterized the show since Williams first performed his version of the Tin Pan Alley song "Lovesick Blues." It also represents a turning point in country music, part of a broad cultural upheaval in the form of rock-and-roll that threatened the ways of thinking about music established in the 1920s by Peer's black-and-white paradigm of race and hillbilly.

Houston, himself, did not continue to pursue rock-and-roll. In 1963, he affiliated himself with manager Tillman Franks, who took Houston to Tyler, Texas, in order to record the song "Mountain of Love." Franks took the studio tapes to Epic Records in Nashville and landed a recording contract for his client. The song reached number two on the country charts that year and was followed by other successful records throughout the 1960s, including "Livin' in a House Full of Love," and the 1967 Grammy-winning song "Almost Persuaded." He joined the *Opry* in 1972, and his success continued throughout the mid-1970s, highlighted by duets with Tammy Wynette and Barbara Mandrell. Although his popularity waned after 1976, Houston was one of Nashville's most popular singers for a period, with fifteen consecutive top ten records between 1966 and 1971. Houston on the *Hayride* stage in the late 1950s, however, takes on symbolic importance. In one way, the performance embodies the spirit of the *Hayride*. Only in this kind of open atmosphere could performers as varied as Kitty Wells, Faron Young, Slim Whitman, and Johnny Cash hone their distinctive styles. At the same time, Houston's performance represents a late 1950s identity crisis in country music incited by all the posture and abandon of the rockabilly moment. Houston here also signals the slowing of the *Hayride*'s near-decade-long momentum.

What happened on the stage in Shreveport's Municipal Auditorium during the mid-1950s was the country music equivalent of what happened in Shreveport's streets during the 1850s. Then, the town was a commercial center for goods traveling in four directions, over land and water. As a matter of course, these goods brought with them the culture of the people who bought and sold them. At the *Louisiana Hayride*, Shreveport became a country music center for sounds traveling north from Cajun country with Jimmy C. Newman, Doug Kershaw, and others; south from Arkansas with the Browns and Johnny Cash; east with Mitchell Torok, Billy Walker, and George Jones; west with Red Sovine and Slim Whitman, Hank Williams and Kitty Wells. The convergence of creativity inspired and nurtured talented musicians from within the region, like Jim Reeves, Webb Pierce, Faron Young, and David Houston. But where culture had followed commerce a century before, commerce did not follow country music culture in Shreveport. Thus began the siphoning of talent to Nashville and the gradual decline of the show.

Were this story told from the perspective of Nashville, it might focus on the centripetal force of concentrated music industry capital to slowly but forcefully draw talent from regional peripheries toward the center. Were it told from the perspective of Shreveport history, it might be the story of how multiple streams of country music flowed together for a time, until the channels shifted and the riverbed dried up. But from the perspective of U.S. culture during the post–World War II decade, the story takes on even more far-reaching significance. As it turns out, Shreveport's *Hayride* in the mid-1950s stood on the fault line of a cultural paradigm shift—perhaps the key musical paradigm shift of American popular culture. And this tremor began quietly, on an October night in 1954.

6

Beyond Country Music

Shreveport was a great place to cut your teeth on music because
there was so much going on.
　　　　　　　—Jerry Kennedy, musician and producer

On 16 October 1954 the *Louisiana Hayride* scheduled a guest appearance of 19-year-old Elvis Presley, calling himself "The Hillbilly Cat."
From that moment, in the fertile ground of a KWKH radio show, a new
sapling was successfully planted, one that conspicuously exposed its country roots. On this autumn night during the dawn of nuclear anxiety, no one
could foresee the megaton explosion of popular music aimed at teenagers.
The mostly white audience at Shreveport's Municipal Auditorium saw an
unsung "cat" with herky-jerky legs sing a few quirky covers, including a
high-octane version of Bill Monroe's bluegrass standard "Blue Moon of
Kentucky" and a driving rendition of Arthur Crudup's rhythm-and-blues
tune "That's All Right, Mama." He introduced his trio as the Blue Moon
Boys, referring to the Monroe song or to the Rodgers and Hart tune "Blue
Moon" they had played around with some, or to both.[1] To anyone there
that night, it was just another Saturday evening at the *Hayride*.

The *Hayride* had a six-year history of taking chances on unproven artists
with unique styles. It was a young show with a young staff, and its entrepreneurial producers always sought artists they thought might captivate
and expand the audience, increasing both revenue and the program's stature
as a prominent forum for country music entertainers. Thus, KWKH hoped
to find in Presley another example of that which it consistently sought— a
new artist with the distinct sound and the charisma to boost profit. What
they got was a pivotal performer destined for a life and musical career that
mixed triumph and tragedy in proportions extraordinary enough to inspire countless writers to reflect on his place and meaning in U.S. popular
culture. They got a performer whose image and recordings between the
years 1954 and 1958 represent a transformation of musical aesthetics on
the *Hayride*, in country music at large, and within the whole society.

Presley's story on the *Hayride* reflects the snowballing of changes following World War II on both a national level and a local level in Shreveport. For U.S. culture as a whole, these changes culminated in the most dramatic social markers of the mid-to-late 1950s: the emergence of youth culture, the breakdown of legal race-based segregation, the transformation of media industries, and the rise of rock-and-roll. In ways both tangible and emblematic, Presley connects these same social forces to a generation of Shreveport musicians who, like him, grew up steeped in black and white music that came to them on phonograph records, radio, and through live performance. The stories of four famous sidemen who musically matured in Shreveport during the *Hayride* era form a critical counterpart to those of the *Hayride's* headliners from Hank Williams to Elvis Presley. These sidemen make it apparent that the dynamic musical atmosphere in postwar Shreveport fed on a rich local culture with at least a century-long history. Two of these players, D. J. Fontana and James Burton, share a direct connection to Presley, since they spent long portions of their careers in Presley's band. The other two, Joe Osborn and Jerry Kennedy, eventually brought the instincts they developed in postwar northwest Louisiana to the newly dominant arena of recording studios. Through these musicians, the unique energy of their native region reached places even beyond the powerful reach of the KWKH radio signal.

Yet a mid-1950s Shreveport—like anywhere in the United States, especially the South—must be understood against the social back story of the postwar era. If it is true that Shreveport and other southern cities were hotbeds of mutual sharing between black and white musicians, it must be understood that these exchanges often crossed tempestuous rivers. These rivers broke their banks in the postwar United States. For African-Americans, the 1950s was a decade when the gross social inequality and economic disparity that had defined their citizenship in the legacy of slavery looked to be a waking steppenwolf at the doors of the Supreme Court. Obversely, for many institutions of Euro-American power, the civil rights movement that emerged during the 1950s and threatened radical shifts of power constituted little more than a barbarian at the gate.

Throughout the postwar decade, the entire nation experienced the most radical social upheaval since the Civil War and the subsequent passing of the Thirteenth Amendment. Working-class blacks and whites migrated from the South to the North, and from the rural South to its urban centers. Suburbia began its crawl across the nation, slowly becoming the landscape of a new middle class. Pre-planned Levittown-styled communities appeared around cities, populated almost exclusively by young whites with a government-subsidized college degree, a newly expanded pocketbook, and a newly utopian image of an American social order.[2] Beneath the image, discontent rumbled softly as the bankruptcy of older frameworks for how gender and race dictated relationships between people became increasingly apparent. Women, many of whom had sensed new possibilities in pursuing college or gainful employment in industrial jobs vacated by drafted soldiers, experienced deep conflicts when, after the war, they were expected to resume domesticity. African-Americans who had served in the military returned to their homes with a heightened sense of dissatisfaction and unwillingness to tolerate continuing racial inequalities.

Earlier in the same year Presley first performed on the *Hayride*, the Supreme Court challenged the established social order, particularly in the South, in its decision in the case of *Brown v. Board of Education*. The process began more than a decade before, through a series of cases that gradually overturned the 1896 *Plessy v. Ferguson* decision that legitimized racial segregation. In this case, which addressed Jim Crow seating on south Louisiana railroad cars, the Court legalized segregation by establishing the theoretical criterion of "separate but equal" facilities for blacks in the South. In reality, however, separate facilities were rarely close to equal. In the case of Shreveport in 1910, for example, 62 percent of the total 58,200 residents of its Caddo Parish were African-American, but only 6.5 percent of the total value of Caddo Parish school property was dedicated to facilities for black students.[3]

In 1938, *Gaines v. Canada,* the Court ruled against Missouri, which maintained a law school for whites but not for blacks; rather, Missouri paid tuition for blacks to attend law school in a different state. The Court ordered Missouri to either build a separate facility for black law students or admit black students to the white school. In June 1950 two cases involving African-Americans, George W. McLaurin in Oklahoma and Heman Sweatt in Texas, called into question the idea that separate could also be equal, based on intangible benefits such as intellectual exchange with other students, tradition, and prestige offered by the graduate programs at the University of Oklahoma and the University of Texas. The watershed, however, was May 1954 *Brown v. Board of Education,* which unequivocally affirmed that the racial segregation of educational facilities rendered them necessarily unequal.[4] In May 1955 the Court issued a dictum that school desegregation should proceed "with all deliberate speed."

It was not incidental that the phenomenon of rock-and-roll emerged during a period when the legal strictures of segregation in the South were breaking down. Presley's early recordings and performances, particularly those during his subsequent year-and-a-half stint with the *Hayride*, assume paramount significance within the context of *Brown v. Board of Education*. The watershed court decision became a gestalt for the erosion of a racially determined social order. Likewise, popular music has a foreshadowing moment in Presley's *Hayride* debut, when the tensions underlying the long and tangled history of musical exchange between southern blacks and whites began coming to a head. As a southern white musician, Presley did more than appropriate or mimic African-American music. He fused the southern musical aesthetics in which he had been immersed since childhood—country, rhythm-and-blues, pop, gospel—into a hybrid musical identity that was equally indebted to them all. On the *Hayride*, Elvis Presley performed country songs like "Just Because" by the Shelton Brothers (recorded by them as the Lone Star Cowboys in 1933) and "I'll Never Let You Go (Little Darlin')," a 1941 song by Jimmy Wakely. He also performed rhythm-and-blues songs like "Mystery Train" by Junior Parker, and "Good Rockin' Tonight" by Wynonnie Harris. Presley performed "I Don't Care If the Sun Don't Shine," originally written for the Disney animated feature *Cinderella* by Mack David, and the Rodgers and Hart "Blue Moon."[5]

Moreover, Elvis Presley's music and his presentation stood as an overt expression of the social and cultural implications that *Brown v. Board of Education* portended. In sound, in repertoire, and in posture, Elvis Presley of the mid-to-late 1950s represented nothing short of a desegregation of musical aesthetics. This signaled a degree of desegregation of the music business itself, as companies marketed him and rock-and-roll artists like Little Richard, Fats Domino, Carl Perkins, and Jerry Lee Lewis to teenagers across racial lines. But the implications extended far deeper than a new market category somewhere between white country and black rhythm-and-blues. Presley's presentation inadvertently set off an earthquake. Although he was not the first musician to manifest the rock-and-roll impulse, he touched a cultural nerve as no one had before him.

Two years before Presley appeared on the *Hayride*, a moderately successful Western swing bandleader and country music disc jockey from New Jersey named Bill Haley recorded the song now considered the first white rock-and-roll record. In 1952, still known as Bill Haley and the Saddlemen, his band recorded a 1949 rhythm-and-blues hit by Jimmy Preston and his Prestonians, "Rock the Joint." The flip side of this record was "Icy Heart," based on the Hank Williams song of the year before, "Cold, Cold Heart." The following year, 1953, Haley changed the name of his band to Bill Haley and Haley's Comets, and became famous for both his recording of "Shake, Rattle and Roll," written by Charles Calhoun and originally recorded by rhythm-and-blues singer Big Joe Turner, and of "(We're Gonna) Rock around the Clock." The latter song won prominence in the 1955 movie *Blackboard Jungle* and sold more than twenty-five million copies.[6] "Rock around the Clock" became famous for setting the tempo and mood for rock-and-roll music to come, despite its origins (like Williams's "Lovesick Blues") in Tin Pan Alley.[7]

To a level that alarmed some onlookers, Haley excited audiences just as pop crooners like Frank Sinatra before him. However, his music ignited neither the hysteria of fans nor the obloquy of critics that Presley sparked, both of which were unprecedented in degree. By the time Presley left the *Hayride*, headlines read "Beware Elvis Presley" in newspapers across the country and warnings appeared in *America* magazine in June 1956; his effigy was burned in Nashville; the East Berlin newspaper *Neues Deutschland* called him a "Cold War Weapon" against communism and a NATO conspiracy to infiltrate East German society.[8] Presley's sexuality and the frenzied reaction it evoked among teenage girls only exacerbated the disquiet he inspired in many adults. In the context of postwar America, that disquiet seems to have less to do with sexuality, per se, and more to do with the tempestuous social changes occurring at the same time. More specifically, in the context of white southern resistance to African-American demands for full civil rights, Presley's stage persona and his music conveyed a rebellion of manners through an intuitive blend of black and white styles. This was the quintessence of rockabilly—its definitive musical integration—and, for this, it caused a stir.

As a potent manifestation of the broader rock-and-roll phenomenon, rockabilly was the music of the emerging youth culture, which strove to create new means of expression—in dress, attitude, patois, and sound-track—that would distinguish teenagers from the world of adults. For white teenagers, this involved the open embrace of aesthetics identified with African-American culture, which entered wider cultural circulation after the war. Beginning in the late 1940s, radio and recordings offered broader access to the music of African-American performers. At the same time, white teenagers of the post–World War II era had money to spend on entertainment as had no generation before them. Much of this money went to purchasing records. A whole new market of young record-buyers snatched up releases by white rockabillies and by black rhythm-and-blues artists. Among whites, young musicians first tapped into the rich resources of rhythm-and-blues records in the late 1940s, but that interest spread during the early 1950s to white teenagers in general.[9]

This process fit into the same postwar cultural phenomenon that Norman Mailer pondered in his essay on the late 1950s stereotyped figure, "the hipster." In "The White Negro: Superficial Reflections on the Hipster," originally published in 1957, Mailer characterizes the hipster as a racially hybridized individual, born when "the bohemian and the juvenile delinquent came face-to-face with the Negro."[10] In Mailer's view, the hipster faced the new challenges of the postwar world head-on, when the larger society suffered from "a collective failure of nerve."[11] Elvis Presley's *Louisiana Hayride* debut occurred three years before Mailer published his portrayal of a phenomenon he observed largely in New York's Greenwich Village. Taken out of its East Coast context, Mailer's prose could easily have described the early performances of Presley—suggesting hedonism, youth culture, and African-American culture—in the context of a white country music radio barn dance in Shreveport.

The manifestation of this hybrid aesthetic that took place among southern white youth took on the name "rockabilly," coined around the mid-1950s for the obvious mixing of elements from country or hillbilly music with, as country music historian Bill Malone puts it, "rocking" black music.[12] In June 1956 the term appeared in the lyrics to Gene Vincent's first release, "Be-Bop-A-Lula," and, later that month, in print as a description of a new release by Ruckus Tyler in a *Billboard* review column, "Reviews of New C&W Records."[13] Rockabilly music existed before then, however, the product of musically fecund environments like Shreveport, where white country musicians could incorporate the energy from African-American rhythm-and-blues into country music. It was then a musical impulse without a name. During Presley's *Hayride* tenure, contemporary Shreveport newspaper writers wrestled to find adequate descriptors of Presley's "unusual singing style" or "wriggling style of song delivery" or the "unique musical arrangements" of his band. Shreveport *Times* writer Pericles Alexander described him in March 1956 as the "21-year-old guitarist-singer who straddles the fence as a purveyor of both country and western songs and the type of ballads you expect to emanate from the larnyx [*sic*] of Perry Como, Sinatra, or Der Bingle."[14]

Even as Shreveport journalists groped for words to describe it, rockabilly's most striking characteristics—including backbeat meter, slap bass, prominent electric guitar, instrumental solo breaks, and spontaneous whoops and hollers—had direct precedents within country music tradition. For one, attention to and influence from contemporary black music extended to the genre's commercial beginnings in the 1920s and long before. But the musical energy and onstage intensity that distinguished rockabilly had forerunners as well, even on the *Hayride*. One of the best examples is the family act known as the Maddox Brothers and Rose, whose long career included *Hayride* cast membership for parts of 1953 and 1954 (fig. 6.1). During these periods the group worked out of Shreveport, with a daily KWKH radio show sponsored by a Chicago company selling baby chicks.[15] Before coming to Shreveport, the Maddox family, originally from Alabama, had hitchhiked and jumped boxcars to California, where they spent several years working as migrant fruit pickers. They began performing music and won such local acclaim that they soon pursued entertainment full time, creating a high-energy, colorful stage act. In elaborate sequined costumes, they delighted crowds with spontaneous antics, comedy bits, and brassy singing by sister Rose.

Their sound foreshadowed rockabilly in the melodic guitar work by Roy Nichols and the slapped-bass technique of Fred Maddox.[16] Music writer Nick Tosches, citing in particular their late 1940s version of Jimmie Rodgers's "Blue Yodel No. 8" titled "New Muleskinner Blues," comments that the group "recorded stuff that not only rocked, but also contained many of the vocal fireworks—yelps, screams, howls—that became watermarks of rockabilly."[17] Elvis Presley admired their showmanship and their flashy costumes. As Rose Maddox recalled in an interview with country music historian John Rumble:

> We was backstage there [at the *Hayride*], and the boys had their jackets to these pink costumes hanging in a room . . . and we went back there and Elvis . . . had one of the boy's jackets on, looking in the mirror, just so proud. You know, he said, "One of these days, I'm going to have me a suit like this." And Mama came back there and seen him with that on and she made him pull it off. She didn't want nobody else wearing their clothes.[18]

In both their sound and their flamboyance, the Maddox Brothers and Rose presaged many of the future qualities that distinguished rockabilly.

The Maddox Brothers and Rose continued a distinctly rowdy tradition long part of country music at the same time they anticipated the mid-1950s musical transformation. The tradition that engendered Jimmie Davis's ribald, sometimes downright dirty songs of the early 1930s found its mid-

Fig. 6.1 An old photo of Rose Maddox and her brothers on the *Hayride*. Noel Memorial Library Archives, LSU in Shreveport.

1940s and early 1950s manifestation in the style known as honky-tonk. Rockabilly, as a hallmark of the postwar atmosphere of accelerated cultural interchange, exploded and exploited this raucous tradition in country music, just as it drew from the characteristic bawdiness of rhythm-and-blues. Rockabilly epitomized in music the same breakdown of aesthetic borders across racial boundaries that Mailer portrayed in his late-1950s hipster.

In a dramatic way, Presley's debut on Shreveport's *Hayride* stands as a pivot point where the natural extension of a long tradition made a sudden abrupt shift toward a new musical paradigm. Like several other southern cities—Memphis, New Orleans, Atlanta, Dallas, Houston, St. Louis, Kansas City—Shreveport had a tradition of white and black musicians listening to and borrowing from one another. During the late 1940s and early 1950s, this dialogue became national. Cultural exchange across racial lines accelerated and intensified, spurred on by records and radio, in a way that permanently altered conceptions of popular music in the United States. Shreveport presents this process in microcosm at the same time the live music and records broadcast over station KWKH helped to push it forward.

Records sales to a growing, enthusiastic, and youthful audience during the postwar era led to the success of a number of independent labels that had up until then barely kept afloat. The result was upheaval in the record industry as a whole, which only a few years before had been dominated by a handful of big companies.[19] A glut of small postwar independent labels, like Chess, Modern, Specialty, Imperial, and Sittin' In With Records, captured an unprecedented wealth of blues and rhythm-and-blues by African-American musicians. Besides being a boon to black audiences, young white musicians now more than ever took these records home and studied them, unconstrained by the ubiquitous borders—social, political, and especially in the South, legal.

Many of these small labels depended on a less formalized, less centralized model of product distribution than the bigger companies. Radio stations like KWKH played an important role in getting these records into the hands of young consumers. For instance, during the early 1950s Shreveport's KWKH began broadcasting *Stan's Record Review*, sponsored by local music store entrepreneur Stan Lewis and hosted by Frank "Gatemouth" Page.[20] Lewis had opened his record shop in 1948 on Shreveport's downtown Texas Street and, from the beginning, built a symbiotic relationship between his business and KWKH. Lewis purchased time for a radio show that sold records on KWKH and eventually expanded to KTHS in Little Rock, Arkansas. As he recalled:

Frank Page did the show on KWKH. We had a program on which we sold records by mail. So I would program and tell him what to play—I'd make a list every night. And we would have, like, six records for $3.49—the same way that they do today on TV with the big artists you see on TV . . . I started with fifteen minutes, and then I went to thirty and then to an hour.[21]

Lewis's mail-order records and radio shows became an important avenue for young white musicians across the region to absorb African-American music, as well as experiment with new styles and new sounds.

The same could be said of the rhythm-and-blues disc jockey shows that began airing after the war all over the South. Beginning in the late 1940s, *Hayride* announcer Ray Bartlett, calling himself "Groovie Boy," spun the newly introduced single-song 45-rpm records in nightly KWKH disc jockey shows called *In the Groove* or *Groovie's Boogie*.[22] Like many southern stations of the postwar decade, KWKH juxtaposed its rhythm-and-blues with a variety of other music, particularly country music on the still-popular Saturday night barn dance shows. A generation of future professional musicians from Shreveport, like guitarist James Burton and musician-producer Jerry Kennedy, developed their musical ears by tuning into both the *Louisiana Hayride* and Bartlett's rhythm-and-blues disc shows. This juxtaposition of the *Louisiana Hayride* and *Groovie's Boogie* on KWKH speaks volumes about the postwar rise of rock-and-roll. And the iconic moment of Presley's debut comes out of this intensified mingling of white and black music on the airwaves.

A few overlapping, sometimes competing stories account for Presley's first appearance on the *Hayride*. Sam Phillips at Sun Records in Memphis had recorded the covers of Monroe and Crudup during the week after Independence Day in 1954.[23] Both cuts showed promise, generating a positive response from Memphis radio audiences right away. Phillips looked around for ways to promote his label's young artist. On 18 July Phillips called Bob Neal, a prominent local disc jockey who hosted an early morning country radio show called the *High Noon Round-up* on Memphis station WMPS. Neal also did booking and promotions in the area.[24] Neal had put together a show that featured *Louisiana Hayride* headliners Slim Whitman, who was riding the success of "Indian Love Call," "Rose Marie," and "Secret Love," and Billy Walker, whose recording of "Thank You for Calling" had just entered the top ten on country charts. As Walker recalled it, Neal approached them before their scheduled show at the Overton Band Shell in Memphis on 30 July:

> Bob Neal came to me and Slim and said, "I've got this kid here. Would you mind if I put him on for a couple of songs?" And I said, . . . "Well if he's good enough for you, I guess he's good enough for us." And so I watched this kid. . . . He knocked the crowd out. We got back the next week and I was in Horace Logan's office talking about Elvis Presley. I got the kid's phone number. And I was talking to Horace about him and Slim walked in about that time and Slim said, "Yeah, but he's got some kind of funny name." And I said, "Yeah, his name is Elvis Presley." So I gave Horace his phone number and Horace called him up and gave him an audition shot to be down on the *Hayride*.[25]

Logan's own recollection likewise includes the connection with Whitman and Walker.

According to Tillman Franks, Thomas Clinton "T. Tommy" Cutrer, singer and country music disc jockey on Shreveport's station KCIJ at the time, played a Presley record on his show. The sound caught Franks's attention and, as he recalled, "I called him up and I said, 'T., boy, that record by that black boy that you're playing is unreal.' He said, 'Tillman, he's not black, he's a white boy and Sam Phillips has got him. He got [*sic*] a funny name.'"[26] At that time, Franks both managed and played bass for a *Hayride* duet known as Jimmy and Johnny (Jimmy Lee Fautheree and "Country" Johnny Mathis). Jimmy and Johnny wanted to play a lucrative gig in Carlsbad, New Mexico, on an upcoming Saturday night, but Horace Logan hesitated to free them of their *Hayride* commitment. As Franks continued:

> I said, "Well, I'll get the boy with the funny name." He said, "You can't get him." I said, "Well I'll call him up." And I didn't have a phone and I called him from [bandleader/booking agent] Pappy Covington's office. Told Sam who I was and I said I'm in Pappy Covington's office. He called Pappy. Pappy handed me the phone. . . . That's the way he come [*sic*].[27]

In the meantime, Sam Phillips had arranged with *Grand Ole Opry* manager Jim Denny for Presley to appear as a guest in early October. Presley and his fellow band members, guitarist Scotty Moore and bassist Bill Black, performed the two songs to a lukewarm reception from the audience and left Nashville feeling defeated. On the bright side, they would play a guest spot on the *Louisiana Hayride* in only a couple of weeks. Regardless of the precise circumstances leading to the *Hayride* invitation, Presley's trio performed with enough success that they entered into a one-year KWKH contract three weeks later. Still a minor, Presley signed along with his parents on 6 November 1954. Before long, the show's producers began placing Presley's group at the end of *Hayride* performances to avoid upstaging other performers. Bob Neal, who had become Presley's manager in early 1955, negotiated the bandleader's second one-year contract with the *Hayride* in September 1955 (to become effective the coming November). By that time, Presley's salary raised from the union scale of $18 per appearance to $200 per appearance, with a side agreement that stipulated a penalty of $400 per show for missed performances beyond the allotted five[28] (fig. 6.2).

In March 1956 Presley adopted Colonel Tom Parker as his new exclusive manager. Parker bought out the second year of his client's contract for $10,000 the next month, with the stipulation that Presley return to perform a charity concert at Shreveport's Youth Building (later renamed the Hirsch Coliseum) before the year's end. Presley's final Shreveport performance took place on 15 December 1956, and the proceeds of the concert aided the local YMCA.[29] The ride cymbals crashing and tom-toms pounding in time with Presley's farewell burlesque on KWKH made the performance a watermark for Shreveport's *Louisiana Hayride* in the story of rock-and-roll. According to Logan, female fans after the show mangled his Mercury automobile climbing onto it to get into the high windows of the coliseum's back stage area. Inside the coliseum, Logan admonished the teenagers leaving en masse for a glimpse of their hero to keep their seats for upcoming acts, famously assuring them: "Elvis has left the building"[30] (fig. 6.3).

Ironically, Presley's ascendance to fame on the *Louisiana Hayride* also marks the beginning of the show's gradual decline. According to some Hayriders, the Saturday-night crowds at Shreveport's Municipal Auditorium began to look and act differently after Presley. For one thing, more teenagers attended, particularly girls who screamed and rushed the stage, often even before the music began. Jimmy C. Newman cites the resulting audience shrinkage as a reason he sought a position at the *Opry*: "When he [Presley] came there, the older audience, a lot of them didn't come back to the *Hayride* because it was such a change, you know, to a young audience. But once he left, the younger audience left and the older ones didn't come back much."[31] Pianist Sonny Harville, who performed for years in Slim Whitman's band and in the *Hayride* staff band, remembers Presley's impact as less immediate. He felt that the show suffered more from attempts by the *Hayride* management to replace Presley with young singers of similar appeal: "Elvis is a phenomenon and that was all right. . . . The country people could take him, but when they got . . . too many Elvis imitators, the country folks just quit coming."[32]

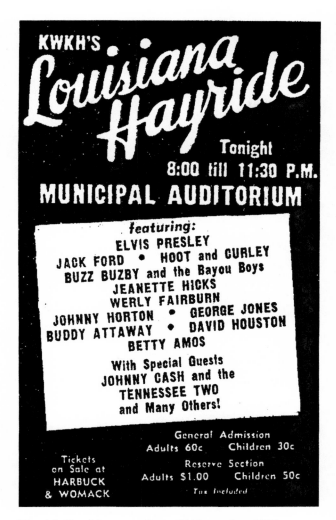

Fig. 6.2 *Hayride* poster from 31 December 1955.
Louisiana Hayride Archives—J. Kent.

In this way, Presley represents a cultural phenomenon that shook the country music industry to its core and resonated far outside the region of Shreveport. Even at the *Opry* where Presley never again performed, ticket sales decreased by almost 44 percent during the period 1953–1960.[33] Country music as an industry eventually responded to the threat of rock-and-roll by adding mellow-toned choruses and swelling strings, and de-emphasizing the fiddle and steel guitar in a cross-over country-pop style intended to have broader appeal—the "Nashville Sound." The *Hayride* tried to do as it always had and find the next shining talent. After Presley, other rockabillies appeared on the *Hayride* stage, but never filled his blue suede shoes.

Fig. 6.3 Elvis Presley, D. J. Fontana, and Bill Black on *Hayride* stage in March 1956. Louisiana Hayride Archives—J. Kent.

Rockabilly luminary and native Louisianan Jerry Lee Lewis actually auditioned for the show, but was turned down. As Sonny Harville recounted with some bemusement:

> Before Jerry Lee Lewis was known, he came in to the *Hayride* and went to Horace Logan who was boss of the *Hayride* at that time and asked Horace for a job playing the piano. . . . Horace sent him to me, 'cause I was playing piano at that time on the *Hayride*, to listen to him and I told Horace that he wouldn't work out. He's too show but no music, you know. Couldn't play well enough to be on the staff band.[34]

The Lewis anecdote attests that the *Hayride*'s timely instincts about musical flair were not always infallible. At the same time, it points to the dilemma rockabilly brought to the *Hayride*, as well as to white southern roots musicians in general. How would a white country musician, or a white country barn dance for that matter, carry on in a world where older ways of understanding music—black and white, race and hillbilly—were proving less and less adequate? Either during or after Presley's tenure, George Jones, Johnny Cash, and Johnny Horton upheld the popular momentum of the *Hayride* just as the *Hayride* searched for direction. Each of these performers reckoned the impact of rockabilly in different ways around this period. Yet, as noteworthy as they were in sustaining the show's standing, the *Hayride* never again regained the edge it had in late 1940s and early 1950s country music.

Other prominent rockabilly performers appeared during the late 1950s and specifically appealed to the newer teenage audience, including Tommy Sands and, most notably, Bob Luman. While Luman later won notoriety between 1965 and his untimely death in 1978 as a country-pop singer on the *Grand Ole Opry*, his early musical style from recordings between 1955 and 1957 reflected his immersion in the rockabilly sounds of the day and the singular impact of Elvis Presley on white southern teenagers of his generation. After seeing Presley perform at a *Louisiana Hayride* package show in his hometown of Kilgore, Texas, as Luman put it, "That's the last time I tried to sing like Webb Pierce or Lefty Frizzell."[35] Shortly thereafter, Luman won a talent show in Tyler, Texas (judged by Johnny Horton, Johnny Cash, and Carl Perkins), and subsequently joined the *Hayride* in 1956, filling a vacancy left by Cash. He appealed to a teenage audience with his rakish charisma and gutsy energy. On the strength of his *Hayride* success, Luman also appeared, along with singer David Houston and guitarist James Burton, in the teen flick *Carnival Rock*. Following the film, he gained a regular spot on the *Los Angeles Town Hall Party*, the same show that had earlier in the decade featured Johnny Horton.

But the biggest and farthest reaching story in the *Hayride*'s shaping of popular music after the mid-1950s lies not in its stars. For at the same time its status as "Cradle of the Stars" vis-à-vis Nashville slowly slipped away, the *Hayride* nurtured a group of influential sidemen, players who typify the postwar generation of young southern white musicians with one foot in country and the other in rhythm-and-blues. Among this generation, Dominic "D.J." Fontana, James Burton, Joe Osborn, and Jerry Kennedy were all born in and around Shreveport during the era when the Lone Star Cowboys traveled between KWKH and other well-positioned southern radio stations. Members of the same generation as Presley (born between 1931 and 1940) they share his immersion in diverse musical influences.[36] These musicians grew up during the age when radio enriched their lives with a daily dose of music from their own cultural milieu as well as distant sounds they might never have heard otherwise. All four musically matured during the time when the *Louisiana Hayride* carved out a permanent place in the annals of pop music. Each one of these players left Shreveport to achieve high levels of success in the music business. Common threads bind together the stories of their developing musicianship, including KWKH and the *Hayride*, Presley, Luman, and Ricky Nelson, and the power of records, radio, and live musical performance from the mid-1940s through the early 1950s.

Radio echoes throughout their early memories. Jerry Glen Kennedy, a guitarist, record executive, and producer born in Shreveport in 1940, soaked up live country music from the family radio as a child. As he recalled:

My first memories are of country music and a guy named Harmie Smith on KWKH. He had a daily radio show at . . . 4:15 in the afternoon. And I was 4 or 5 years old and I remember that I would have my mom call me because I couldn't miss that. I wanted to be in the house listening to that whenever it came on.[37]

Bassist Joe Osborn, born in 1937, also recalled the singularity of radio during his childhood, since his family did not own many phonograph records. When he began playing guitar around age 12 after his uncle showed him a few chords, live country radio took on new significance. Eminent guitar picker Chet Atkins in particular caught his ear and, as Osborn recalled, he would "listen to the radio and wait until Chet came on and play along."[38] On Saturday nights, he tuned into the radio barn dances, especially the *Opry* and the *Louisiana Hayride* where, in the early 1950s, he especially remembers hearing guest appearances of Texas honky-tonker Lefty Frizzell. The airwaves likewise brought Chet Atkins to another developing Shreveport musical legend, James Burton. Born in 1939, he picked up the guitar at age 13, and quickly absorbed not only the licks of Atkins but also the sense of timing and musical phrasing of early 1950s country singers like Williams, Frizzell, and Carl Smith. Explaining the influence of country music on his budding guitar style, Burton once said: "Also, I really admired the way people like Hank Williams and Lefty Frizzell sang, and I got into their style of singing and overall feeling. I thought that this was how a lead instrument should treat a line—like a lyric—and that was always my approach to playing a solo."[39]

During the same period in his early development, Burton tuned in to the afternoon and late-night rhythm-and-blues shows on KWKH and other stations where he heard the likes of Lightnin' Hopkins, Muddy Waters, and Howlin' Wolf. Enthused by all the sounds, black and white, that poured through the radio speaker, Burton bought records and listened intently, learning new licks and incorporating them into his own playing. Kennedy too discovered early on the sounds of rhythm-and-blues artists like Muddy Waters, Fats Domino, and the Platters via radio shows like the one "Daddy-O Hot Rod" broadcast over the Shreveport station KOKA, as well as Groovie Boy's show on KWKH. As Kennedy grew up, his musical palette continued to expand and by the late 1940s and early 1950s, his ear bent to pop artists like Jo Stafford, Patti Page, and Joni James, as well as close-harmony quartets like the Four Aces and the Ink Spots. All of this music shaped his developing sensibilities from early in his childhood in the same way that blues, string bands, parlor songs, and hymn-singing shaped Jimmie Davis's style from a half-century before. They formed the foundation of his later success in the music business.

Drummer D. J. Fontana also recalls phonograph discs of his youth. Born in 1931, the oldest of the four Shreveport sidemen particularly remembers the Stan Kenton, Woody Herman, and other big band jazz records of his cousin A. J. Lewis. Lewis, an avid collector and later Shreveport music store owner, also owned a distinguishing asset in the local community, a complete set of drums that he encouraged the aspiring musician to use. Fontana gained much of his early technical skill from his band director at the local Ford Park High School. But even more critical to his developing proficiency were the opportunities for live performance abundant in Shreveport during the postwar era. By the time he reached his teens, Fontana worked in local nightclubs like the Carousel, usually with trios who specialized in Dixieland and standards like "How High the Moon" and "Stardust."[40]

The live musical contexts that cultivated Fontana's talent included both informal jam sessions and paid gigs, most often in a nightclub area across the Red River from Shreveport known as the "Bossier strip." Like Fannin Street had been earlier in the century, the Bossier strip was a thriving music scene in mid-century. As Fontana remembered, "Shreveport had a lot of clubs. Bossier, that strip there was just one club after another, you know. They must have had fifteen clubs, it was like a small Vegas is what it was."[41] A musician like Fontana could find plenty of work in Shreveport during the late 1940s and early 1950s. The key to success in this environment was flexibility across a wide range of musical genres. Fontana described the blossoming of the music scene and the demands of playing local clubs:

Back then they had an influx of musicians. . . . They just start showing up from everywhere, mostly out of the South. They were out of Mississippi, Alabama, and south Louisiana. And some great players come out of there, whether it be country, whether it be blues, pop. You know, back then—you worked a club, you had to play a mixture. You just couldn't play country or rock or whatever.[42]

Eventually, this local music club scene beckoned all four future sidemen and played a formative role in the directions their talents would take them. While still in high school, for instance, Burton fine-tuned his instincts in these area clubs—for which he needed a special underage permit—building a reputation around town as a guitarist of unique ability. Likewise, Joe Osborn played in local clubs, mostly around the Bossier strip, beginning at age 14 or 15. There, he first gained experience with the commingling of country and rhythm-and-blues music that would prove essential to his later success. Like Fontana, Osborn recalled the liveliness of the club scene and the music that resonated together there:

At that time [the Bossier strip] was really booming. It was like just alive, you know, wall-to-wall clubs and music. You can still see some of those old places boarded up and see what it was, or what it must have been. It all [country and rock and roll music] sort of gelled. . . . You could go ahead and do your old country standards but maybe with more drums, you know.[43]

Shreveport's 1950s music scene emerged from the same dynamic post-war southern musical atmosphere that wrought rockabilly. But while the area's clubs mingled music styles in a way akin to the era's radio, the clubs accomplished what radio never could. These nightclubs became sites for face-to-face interaction between black and white musicians themselves. In Shreveport clubs and along the Bossier strip, the racial constraints of the segregated South loosened among musicians much as they had on Fannin Street when Leadbelly played its brothels. As Fontana recalled his experience:

> If we had a jam session, you'd call everybody you knew. And they'd show up . . . black, white, . . . they didn't care. If you played, come on, bring your horn, bring your drums, whatever. We'll all have a good time. Sometimes we'd play all night. Different songs, you know. Guys would sing, everybody'd just work together, have a good time and go home. We used to do that about once or twice a month.[44]

This open attitude among musicians extended to paid gigs as well. Fontana further reflected upon his experiences during the postwar era:

> Amongst musicians we had no problems. We could play and have a good time. I think it was just the people, the people who wanted to be segregated. But we didn't care. If the guy could play his horn or play saxophone or whatever, well, hey man, come on and play something tonight. We'll be at such-and-such a place. They'd show up and nobody would bother them. We'd go to a black club maybe and play and they wouldn't bother us cause we were with that band.[45]

Fontana's experiences suggest that the status as a musician sometimes eased the turbulent waters that separated whites and blacks during the era.

Jerry Kennedy also absorbed music from African-American contemporaries, not only as a fellow musician but as a member of the audience. As a teenager, Kennedy attended shows of rhythm-and-blues artists who traveled to the area, particularly at a local black nightspot on Shreveport's Texas Street known as Club 66. As Kennedy described it, the African-American club allowed whites to attend these shows, but circumscribed their participation:

> I remember that they had a little cage, a glassed-in place where white people could go in. Sort of like the opposite of the way it was during segregation down there with theaters and stuff like that. It was a place set aside. . . . I saw Jimmy Reed there. That's where I saw Bobby Blue Bland. If I'm not mistaken, I probably saw Chuck Berry, Bo Diddley, for sure. But anyway, there was only room for like twelve people to get into this little space.[46]

Even more than Presley's *Hayride* association, the live musical experiences of Fontana and Kennedy point to a long-standing, yet constrained, tradition of cross-racial interaction in the South just as they form a live context for the postwar acceleration of musical exchange that transformed U.S. culture.

Along with the Shreveport club scene, station KWKH and its *Louisiana Hayride* form a meaningful thread in the experiences of these four sidemen. Osborn's *Hayride* connection was the most peripheral of the four, extending past his Saturday nights by the radio to occasional attendance at a live *Hayride* show in the Municipal Auditorium. Osborn recalls one particularly memorable night when he attended the *Hayride* with a friend who knew Presley, as well as Fontana, then a member of the staff band. As Osborn described:

> I met Scotty back in the dressing room, and he showed me the lick he played on "That's All Right, Mama." See, these guys were new too, you know what I mean? Elvis had had his first hit, but he wasn't the star yet. They were accessible. You could go in and meet them and sit and talk with them. "How'd you do your lick?" you know.[47]

For Osborn, the backstage interchange counts as a singular moment of inspiration with one of rockabilly's guitar icons. For the others, the *Hayride* formed a regular laboratory for their training. Fontana, Burton, and Kennedy each served apprenticeships as members of the *Hayride* staff band. In different ways, these experiences pointed the way for their eventual professional accomplishments.

Fontana's *Hayride* association determined the direction of his musical career in a decisive way. Following a stint in the Army, Fontana returned to Shreveport where he helped out in his parents' grocery store, acquired his own set of drums, played in clubs around town, and joined the *Hayride* house band. As staff drummer for several years during the early 1950s, Fontana backed many of the artists who were regulars or guests on Saturday nights. True to the *Hayride*'s typical stylistic berth, it made drums available for any group who wished to use them. At first, in Fontana's words, "most of the artists didn't want me to play behind them anyway." Throughout the early 1950s, drums steadily gained acceptance as a standard part of a country band, and this transformation played out on the *Hayride*. As Fontana tells it, "Gradually one or two of them said, 'Yeah you wanna play—just [play] real quiet.' And pretty soon it got to where I had to work behind everybody. They got used to the idea."[48] The audience grew accustomed to the addition just as the players did.

On Saturday nights at the *Hayride*, Fontana learned the secret of playing drums in country music, which was to use quiet, subtle brush strokes. This introduction to country drumming put Fontana behind the likes of Jim Reeves (with whom he toured), Mitchell Torok, Johnny Horton, Webb Pierce, Faron Young, Lefty Frizzell, and Slim Whitman. The experience served him well in years to come, as an in-demand Nashville studio musician with an instinctive understanding of when to keep his instrument in a subdued, supporting role and when to assert his presence. Fontana later recorded with Tommy James, Patti Page, Porter Wagoner, Dolly Parton, Webb Pierce, Floyd Cramer, Nat Stuckey, Red Sovine, and many others. However, even more than a portent of his future Nashville success, Fontana's role as staff drummer was a harbinger of the transformations to come on the *Hayride*, as well as within country music as a whole. By allowing an instrument fundamental to rock-and-roll, the same instrument decisively absent from the *Opry* stage, the *Hayride* set in place a key variable in unleashing the pent-up energy of rockabilly. In more concrete terms, the *Hayride's* openness to drums led to a fortuitous meeting between Fontana and Presley (fig. 6.4).

According to the drummer's recollections, Tillman Franks and Pappy Covington, both of whom had booking offices on the KWKH floor of Shreveport's Commercial National Bank building, called Fontana into their office one morning to listen to Presley's first single, "That's All Right, Mama," which had also been playing on local radio stations. They asked Fontana if he would like to play with the group when they came to town. In Fontana's words, "I said, 'Well, they don't need me.' They had such a unique sound. I said, 'I'll just make them sound bad,' you know."[49] Not long after, Scotty Moore approached Fontana about their trio's interest in adding drums and suggested they try working up a couple of tunes. The four musicians gathered in one of the dressing rooms at the Municipal Auditorium to experiment. Fontana described his approach early on:

> The secret was not to get in the way. Let them do what they do well. I just played a brush, real quiet and easy, . . . later on I played more, but early on the sound they had with that slapped bass was so unique. I didn't want to clutter that up. Maybe that's why I got the job. Simplicity, you know.[50]

Fontana began playing regularly with the band on the *Hayride*, as well as on tours booked through east Texas and southern Arkansas. In spring of 1955, Fontana officially joined Presley's band, an association that lasted until 1969.

Ultimately, the restraint required by most *Hayride* bandleaders was not what the Blue Moon trio was looking for. Perhaps this fact encouraged Fontana to accept Presley's invitation since, as David Sanjek points out, country music has generally neglected its instrumental virtuosos like Fontana, with the notable exception of bluegrass.[51] For his part, Fontana offered the key element that pushed the Blue Moon trio to a new level of energy. Fellow drummer Levon Helm (of the group known as The Band) once described Fontana's contribution to Presley's band, recalling a performance he witnessed in Arkansas during the mid-1950s where Fontana was "building up to the solos, riding the solos in and riding them out again. He had incredible technique and fast hands . . . he played like a big-band

Fig. 6.4 A youthful D. J. Fontana at the drums.
Noel Memorial Library Archives, LSU in
Shreveport.

drummer—full throttle. Now Elvis had a real foundation, some architecture, and he made the most of it. D.J. set Elvis *free*."[52]

Throughout their long association, on approximately 460 RCA recordings with Elvis, Fontana employs the full range of his drum technique, even those subtle brush strokes from his barn dance days, which he brought to the tender ballads that entered Presley's post-Sun repertoire. Fontana also created definitive rock-and-roll licks to certain tunes, like his emphatic conversation with Moore's guitar in "Heartbreak Hotel" or the machine-gun punctuation that fills empty spaces in "Hound Dog." Still today, Fontana maintains a steady income from Presley-related events all over the world—from Argentina to Tunisia, and throughout Europe. As a drummer, the flexibility Fontana demonstrates, not only with Presley but as a Nashville studio musician and producer, began during his formative years in Shreveport, soaking in the variety of musical styles that converged in the region. His attitude toward his music is not philosophical, but rather the pragmatism of a musician whose acumen seems to flow naturally from the depth of his experiences. "I never did adapt to a change," Fontana commented, "I just played what I learned when I was a kid and it all fit. It all fit, so why change?"[53]

Guitarist James Burton shares with Fontana both a critical *Hayride* apprenticeship and an intimate connection with Presley, though this came much later for him. At age 14, Burton became the *Hayride* staff guitarist. There he played behind George Jones, Jimmy and Johnny, Billy Walker,

Johnny Horton, and others, continually honing his craft. The first recording Burton ever made came a year later, when he was 15. In the KWKH studio, he played behind a young singer named Dale Hawkins whose "Suzie Q," based on a blues tune by Howlin' Wolf, became his first and biggest hit record. The song is now anthologized as one of the seminal rockabilly recordings of the mid-1950s.[54] Stan Lewis, the local record store owner who was just beginning to dabble in record-making, oversaw the session with KWKH engineer Bob Sullivan at the board.[55] Like other recordings made at the KWKH studio, this one used only three or four RCA ribbon microphones and an aging Collins broadcast board, with no equalizer, no echo—in the words of Sullivan, "just bare bones."[56] Burton devised the distinctive lick later imitated on covers of the song, most famously by the California pop-rock trio Creedence Clearwater Revival. The recording marked him as a guitarist whose style inspired imitation and sealed his association with rockabilly so that when he joined Presley's band in 1969, remaining until the singer's death in 1977, he became what music writer Rich Kienzle referred to as the "sole remaining rockbilly touchstone in Elvis' music."[57]

Between his years on the *Hayride* and his association with Presley, Burton gradually innovated a flatpick/fingerpick style (holding a pick between thumb and forefinger and a fingerpick on his middle finger). The resulting sound, an understated voice that included a staccato, percussive effect he dubbed "chicken pickin," made him one of his generation's most influential and emulated guitarists.[58] As a self-taught player, the evolution of Burton's distinct voice was not so much a deliberate, conscious melding of the influences of country and rhythm-and-blues that he absorbed throughout his childhood, but their innate by-product. As he commented, "It's just the way I started doing it. . . . I didn't notice anything peculiar until I went into a music store one day and some guy said, 'Man, you're doing it all wrong.'"[59]

Burton's career took shape after Bob Luman joined the *Hayride* in 1956 and Burton began playing regularly with him both on Saturday nights and in area tours. When Luman left Shreveport for California in 1957, he took Burton with him, along with bassist James Kirkland and drummer Butch White. The 1958 movie *Carnival Rock* includes lively footage of their rockabilly numbers "All Night Long," "This Is the Night," and an instrumental, "The Creep."[60] Several of the group's recordings, including Luman's version of "Red Hot," remain part of the standard rockabilly corpus.

The following year, Burton and Kirkland joined Ricky Nelson of *The Adventures of Ozzie and Harriet* television show and also an aspiring singer. In the earliest sessions with Nelson, Burton plays the rhythm guitar while another musician, country guitarist Joe Maphis, plays lead. Beginning with Nelson's song "Believe What You Say," Burton played lead. He thus gained wide notoriety among fellow musicians and producers for his sound, and a visual boost via the band's regular *Ozzie and Harriet Show* performances when the camera often focused on the unusual work of Burton's hands. Burton left Nelson's band in 1964, bored with the exclusivity of a contract that left him working for only one month or so out of the year. He began applying his signature technique in studios, on both guitar and dobro, and in 1965, played lead guitar with The Shindogs, house band for the short-lived rock-and-roll television show *Shindig*. Burton's studio work continued, running the gamut from country to pop to rock. During the late 1960s, he recorded with Buffalo Springfield and Judy Collins, as well as Merle Haggard and Buck Owens, where his distinctive guitar helped to define the "Bakersfield sound" of the mid-1960s.[61] By the time he replaced Scotty Moore in Presley's band, Burton often sounds more like a second soloist than a supporting instrument, as he weaves a wah-wah-inflected polyphony against the singer's line, adding new energy to tunes like "Hound Dog," which by that point Presley had been singing for more than a decade.

Following Presley's death, Burton played with John Denver for seven years, and continued to pursue studio recording with Gram Parsons, Joni Mitchell, Emmylou Harris, and others during the 1970s. On his versatility in both country and rock-and-roll, dobro and steel guitar player Steve Fishell once wrote of Burton that he "has refined his country and rock and roll chops with equal mastery: He is equally poised curling a tasty signature flourish around a ballad's chorus line or plunging pell-mell into a double-time country cooker."[62] Since 1984 Burton has toured with an aging but still vital Jerry Lee Lewis, adding his distinct sound to Lewis's mixture of gospel, rockabilly, and country, the same mix in which Burton was schooled during his days in 1950s Shreveport. He returned to his home city during the mid-1990s with his wife, also a Shreveport native, to open a downtown club, James Burton's Rock-and-Roll Cafe, drawing locals along with the patrons of the recently developed casino boats on the Red River.

Joe Osborn shares with Burton a well-worn trail between Shreveport and California, where he likewise crossed paths with Luman and Nelson, and a career built on flexibility in the studio. Between the early 1960s and the late 1980s, Osborn's bass was the lynchpin for hundreds of hits, from rockabilly to pop to soul to country. His own story might be said to include an indirect *Hayride* apprenticeship. Osborn's career reflects the way Shreveport's position as a regional crossroads fostered a unique kind of musical fluency that echoed across a breadth of popular music for decades after the *Hayride*'s final broadcast. Osborn was married and selling hardware at the local Sears Roebuck when his close friend Dale Hawkins had his hit with "Suzie Q." At the time, Osborn regularly played around town. Hawkins's brother Jerry managed his band while Dale was touring to promote his song. The group lived above a Bossier strip joint called the Skyway Club, where they played regular gigs when Osborn joined the band in the latter 1950s. Their repertoire mirrored the same eclectic mix that KWKH blasted over its airwaves. As Osborn described it,

> We were doing that old south Louisiana R&B, I mean whatever was a hit, we just copied whatever was a hit. Jerry Lee had some things, whatever those were—"Whole Lotta Shakin'" and "Great Balls of Fire"— and some of those things like Chuck Willis. And Fats Domino had a few hits by then. So just that kind of stuff. We had a couple of horns. That's where I met [guitarist] Roy Buchanan.[63]

Jerry Hawkins acquired his own record deal in Los Angeles, so Osborn and Buchanan traveled with him to California (fig. 6.5) Unfortunately, the plans derailed and, as Osborn recalls, "Roy and I were left alone starving to death. Couldn't get our clothes out of the cleaners. Had hair down to there before long hair was supposed to be in."[64] In stepped Bob Luman, whose acquaintance they had made during Luman's membership on the *Hayride*. As it turned out, the association decisively altered Osborn's career. Osborn knew that Luman, by then a *Town Hall Party* cast member, was coming through town on his way to Las Vegas to open the Showboat Hotel along with other *Town Hall* stars. When Osborn caught wind that Luman needed a band, he and Buchanan resolved to "go sit on his doorstep and wait on Bob.'"[65] Luman rehearsed with Osborn and Buchanan and agreed to hire them. In Osborn's account, "He got our clothes out of the cleaners, took us to Las Vegas, got us a hair cut, and so that's how we wound up there. Stayed about a year. And during that time he did his hit record in Nashville. And that's when I started playing the bass."[66]

Until the Las Vegas job with Luman, Osborn played guitar. But two guitars were one too many for the Showboat gig. Since, by his own estimation, Buchanan was a better guitar player, Osborn picked up the electric bass. It was a fortunate turn of events for the musician now considered one of the innovators of the instrument. His guitar background led him to use a pick, a practice uncommon for a bass player at the time. As Osborn recalls,

> I plugged in and turned a lot of treble on the amp, just clicking and clacking and it's great, you know. [Other bass players said,] "You can't do that. You're supposed to feel the bass, you're not supposed to hear it." Well I didn't have a choice. I didn't know anything about playing the bass. It's the only way I knew how to do it. It turned out to be a good thing.[67]

In decades of band and studio work that would follow, Osborn fashioned a fresh melodic type of bass line, a flat-pick style that increased the instrument's prominence, and a characteristic "slide" technique. A pioneer in the relatively young profession of the studio musician, Osborn used the new tools of electric bass and multi-track recording technology to alter notions about the role of the bass in a band.

The Las Vegas job with Luman ended with the bandleader's draft notice in 1960. Osborn and Buchanan played for a while in Chicago, toured out of New Jersey with Dale Hawkins, and finally returned to Shreveport to rejoin Jerry Hawkins at the local Stork Club. Upon the recommendation of Burton, who happened into the club one night and first heard Osborn play bass instead of guitar, Osborn soon returned to California to join Rick Nelson's band. There, at the cusp of a period of musical flowering in Los Angeles studios, Osborn caught the attention of local producers and musicians with the near-human roundness of his sound on Nelson's biggest hit, "Traveling Man." The bassist began a decade-long association with two other session musicians—drummer Hal Blaine and pianist Larry Knechtel—

Fig. 6.5 Jerry Hawkins and his band. Louisiana Hayride Collection, Noel Memorial Library Archives, LSU in Shreveport.

that comprised the rhythm section on innumerable recordings of the 1960s and early 1970s. Lou Adler and Bones Howe are among the notable producers who depended upon the trio. Meanwhile, Osborn opened the Los Angeles nightclub called Whiskey A-Go-Go with musician Johnny Rivers and pursued continuous studio work—as many as twenty sessions per week—until 1974 when he grew tired of the hectic big city pace. As Osborn told the story:

> I had to get out of town. I thought we were going to move to the Ozarks and quit. A friend of mine said, "You don't want to do that. You need to do what you're doing but in a different place." Nashville was the obvious place. I might have gone to New York but that would have been worse than L.A. So Nashville. And that whole thing mushroomed again, you know.[68]

Osborn remained active in Nashville studios until 1989, when he retired and returned to Keithville, Louisiana, just outside of Shreveport.

Among the many pop and country acts over the years whose bass lines were laid by Osborn, most often anonymously, were the Mamas and the Papas, the Fifth Dimension, the Carpenters, Neil Diamond, Simon and Garfunkel, Helen Reddy, Barbra Streisand, Kenny Rogers, America, Mickey

Gilley, and Hank Williams Jr.[69] This partial list testifies to the flexibility and professionalism of Osborn as a studio bass player. His pioneering sound is epitomized in the Fifth Dimension's cut of "Aquarius/Let the Sun Shine," where drum, horn, and even vocals seem tethered to the direction of Osborn's undulating deep groove. The variety of musical contexts in which Osborn thrived reflect his past.

In a way, his experiences in the studio extend the musical dexterity demanded of him in local nightclubs around Shreveport. Osborn viewed his talent as a cumulative process of learning that began on the Bossier strip: "If you're just in a band doing whatever's a hit, you know, you learn the record. And you learn to play what's on the record. So that's got to influence your style somewhat, you know, because you're playing that lick." As he moved to the studio, he maintained the same ears-wide-open attitude: "You're always learning. Especially doing recordings with people that have an idea about what they want to hear, and they lead you into playing things you never played. So okay that's another lesson. And you take all that knowledge with you to the next one, you know."[70] Osborn's upbringing in Shreveport established the foundation for a stylistic breadth that would keep him in demand for nearly three decades. As he said, "I think this has always been a magical place for music. And it could happen again."[71]

Jerry Kennedy's relationship to the *Hayride* goes deep, from his earliest memories beside the family radio to the Municipal Auditorium's wooden seats on Saturday nights to its stage. More closely than the other sidemen, his pathway to studio success mirrored the direct Shreveport to Nashville trail patterned after Hank Williams's initial trajectory. In Nashville, he made a name not only as a musician but as a producer as well. His early experiences all seem to point there. From his childhood, going to the *Louisiana Hayride* every Saturday night was a weekly ritual. Kennedy arrived there at 5:00 p.m. in order to get a front-row seat for the 8:00 p.m. show. In the audience, he became acquainted with Roger Sovine, the son of Red Sovine and now a BMI executive, and befriended the children of Johnnie Wright and Kitty Wells.

Kennedy learned to play guitar from Tillman Franks, and he gained some performing experience playing over the weekly station KCIJ Saturday-morning broadcasts of the *Tillman Franks Guitar Club*. By age 10, Kennedy won first place in the local Bob Wills Talent Contest, then went on to compete in Dallas for second place. Subsequently, RCA signed the young guitarist-singer to a recording contract. At his first session in Dallas he recorded the Johnnie Masters song, "16 Chickens and a Tambourine," also covered by Roy Acuff. Kennedy's version made it to the Top Five on the charts. The following year, he traveled to Nashville, where he recorded under the direction of Steve Sholes in a session backed by Chet Atkins.

By his early teens, he and Roy Dey, a friend who, like Kennedy, eventually became a Nashville record executive, continued to attend the *Hayride* on Saturday nights, now intent on getting a close look at the guitar technique of a player whose recording they tried to "pick apart" already. According to Kennedy, "We'd go up to the *Hayride* . . . and try to listen to this

guitar player, but we couldn't hear his guitar because the girls were scream-
ing so loud because this weird guy was dancing."[72] Of course, the gyrating
lead singer was Presley, but it was Moore's rockabilly blend of country and
rhythm-and-blues that lured Kennedy.

Kennedy's childhood prodigy and his regular *Hayride* attendance gradually evolved into performances, as Franks booked him to play behind artists
like Webb Pierce, the Carlisles, Faron Young, and Slim Whitman whenever
they performed close to Shreveport. As a sophomore or junior in high
school, Kennedy traveled south to Alexandria, Louisiana, where he filled
in for Johnny Horton's guitarist, Tommy Tomlinson. He handled the gig
well. Kennedy joined the *Hayride* staff band the next year as electric guitar
player, where he remained for a year and a half (fig. 6.6). By his senior year
of high school, Kennedy started traveling on long road tours with *Louisiana Hayride* package shows as far away as Arizona and Colorado, booked
by Franks. After returning from a tour of Canada in 1959, Kennedy lost his
taste for road life and quit the stage. He took a job in a warehouse for the
Morris Dickson Drugstore Company, in the meantime marrying *Hayride*
singer Linda Brannon.

In 1961 Kennedy met Shelby Singleton, artists and repertoire ("A & R")
man for the Southeast for Mercury Records. Singleton hired Kennedy to
assist in record production and the two cut albums together in Dallas and
New Orleans. Kennedy moved to Nashville and worked as a session musician and, by 1969, a recording executive for Mercury Records. He left his
position as vice-president over Mercury's country music recordings in 1984,
opening his own JK Productions company. He demonstrated his capability early on as the producer for Roger Miller's Grammy-winning signature
song, "King of the Road," as well as other Miller albums and singles. That
Kennedy produced the spare, intimate country-folk of Miller attests to the
acoustic sensibilities and country roots of the Shreveport native. On the
other hand, two decades of producing the barbershop-tight country vocals
of the Statler Brothers often demonstrated his studio acumen more dramatically. A good example is their 1964 hit "Flowers on the Wall," whose
alternating walking banjo and driving tom-tom accompanies quirky lyrics
and a lurching metrical arrangement. The staying power of the delightful
pop oddity earned it inclusion in the soundtrack to the 1994 counter-
culture breakthrough film *Pulp Fiction*.

Kennedy earned many other credits over the decades after he left Shreveport. As a studio musician, he carved a distinct musical voice on both guitar and dobro during the 1960s, playing on Roy Orbison's seminal tune
"Oh, Pretty Woman," Jeannie C. Riley's novelty hit "Harper Valley PTA"
and Bob Dylan's album *Nashville Skyline*. Kennedy's later work as producer includes recordings of Jerry Lee Lewis, Tom T. Hall, Patti Page, and
Reba McEntire, to whom he signed her first recording contract. In all, he
has had one of the most diverse and long-lasting careers in the Nashville
music industry.[73] Kennedy's coming of age in post–World War II Shreveport, amid the influences of live clubs, records, and, most powerfully, radio
station KWKH schooled him for his later pursuits, and he carried these

Fig. 6.6 Linda Brannon and Jerry Kennedy on the
Hayride stage. Louisiana Hayride Archives—J. Kent.

formative experiences throughout his professional life in Nashville. As Kennedy mused,

> Shreveport was a great place to cut your teeth on music because there
> was so much going on. I wonder if I had been from Tyler, [Texas], I'm
> not sure that it would have worked. Just being there and hanging
> around KWKH and going to the *Hayride* and living there, all those
> things probably set up everything like a domino effect—everything
> that's gone on up until right now.[74]

Against the backdrop of musicians from the Shreveport region like Lead-belly and Jimmie Davis, along with musicians drawn to the region like Hank Williams and Elvis Presley, the four sidemen illustrate a postwar phenomenon in Shreveport with deep national implications. The cultural milieu that shaped them in youth included the eclecticism of KWKH radio, the plethora and availability of small independent record labels, and the dynamic local music scene. These four players emerged during a period when the accidental momentum and momentous accidents of history—

the social, cultural, and geographical forces that shaped the region—set off an earthquake that shook any notion of a simple black and white paradigm of popular music to its foundation. As the *Hayride* faded away, these musicians, no longer subject to the galvanized categories of recorded music, entered the music business during an era when the studio supplanted the stage as a litmus test for industry success. Drawing from cross-racial instincts developed in Shreveport, they recorded scores of songs that would influence the direction of rock-and-roll, country, and rhythm-and-blues for decades to come.

Conclusion

The *Louisiana Hayride* stakes a claim in the annals of country music and rock-and-roll in postwar U.S. history by the simple fact that it brought to the national spotlight both Hank Williams and Elvis Presley. But the *Hayride* assumes even deeper meaning when these two musical icons are placed upon a historical trajectory extending both backward and forward in time. Going backward, the story begins in the mid-nineteenth century, when Shreveport stood at the commercial center for a four-state area including parts of Texas, Louisiana, Arkansas, and Oklahoma, along a geographic and cultural border between the South and the West. Going forward, the story ends not with the *Hayride*'s final broadcast but with the multiple directions taken in the musical careers of four influential side-men whose instincts formed in post–World War II Shreveport.

Commerce plays an essential role in this story of music, for wherever commerce arises there follows culture. Shreveport's position as a nineteenth-century crossroads for business along its Red River, as well as along the Texas Trail, gave way a century later to its position as a meeting ground for vital strains of postwar country music. Along the way, the characteristic nature of radio broadcasting as a mass medium enabled the rise of a radio station of distinct sway in Shreveport, first in airing the indignations of the cantankerous iconoclast who founded it and, later, in spreading music. As host to the famous KWKH radio barn dance, Shreveport's Municipal Auditorium became a site where the history of commerce and media intersected, creating a powerful manifestation of a larger socio-cultural paradigm shift in the postwar United States (fig. C.1).

Race, too, flows from the troubled depths of Shreveport's history as another critical undercurrent in the story of a forum for mid-century white country music. The nineteenth-century plantation culture kept more than half of northwest Louisiana's population shackled to King Cotton in service to a white plutocracy. A system of racial segregation arose around the turn of the century in slavery's shadow, given its legal sanction in 1896 with

Fig. C.1 Shreveport's Municipal Auditorium in 1956. Louisiana Hayride Archives—J. Kent.

Plessy v. Ferguson. The racially determined social order upended in legal terms in May 1954, the same year that Presley debuted on the *Hayride*. The history of legal constraints and harsh social injustices that characterized U.S. race relations plays out most dramatically in places like Shreveport, where blacks and whites have been present in nearly equal numbers since the mid-1800s. By the same token, amid this troubled history, the close proximity of two racial groups makes cultural exchanges between them inevitable.

In the context of country music, Presley dramatically manifested a fluency across elements of black and white southern musics that has deep roots in the religious singing of the South's evangelical denominations, and in the music of Leadbelly, the Allen Brothers, Bob Wills, the Maddox Brothers and Rose, and others. In the context of broader post–World War II U.S. culture, Presley on the *Hayride* underscores the radical (and sometimes overlooked) country foundation of rock-and-roll and presents a local manifestation of a national phenomenon—the rise of rock-and-roll and its attendant youth culture.

In concrete terms, Shreveport gains a central position in this story of country music and its place in larger southern musical culture largely because of its radio station, the 50,000-watt KWKH, and the influence it wielded. From the 1920s, when its idiosyncratic owner, "Hello World" Henderson, broadcast Jimmie Davis, KWKH played a significant role in the commercial history of country music (not to mention in the future of Louisiana politics). KWKH continued to broadcast live country performers—the Shelton Brothers, the Rice Brothers, the Blackwood Quartet, to name a few—during the 1930s and 1940s. Several years after World War II, KWKH began airing the *Louisiana Hayride*.

The *Hayride* might have remained just another live radio broadcast of provincial importance were it not for the fortuitous coincidence of several factors. The appearance of Hank Williams on the show three months after it started and the singer/songwriter's sudden rise to stardom established the *Louisiana Hayride* as a potential launching pad for commercial success. The show reached a large audience, which continually broadened during the early 1950s, as it was simultaneously aired over a sister station in Little Rock (KTHS, also 50,000 watts), as well as several regional networks and the CBS national network. Young and talented musicians flocked there, and many of them went on to become the most distinct and influential voices of country music during the postwar period and after. As Hank Williams Jr., a successful country music performer in his own right, narrates in the documentary about the *Hayride*, *Cradle of the Stars*, "If the *Grand Ole Opry* was the Promised Land for country musicians on their way up, then the *Louisiana Hayride* was heaven's gate."

Meanwhile, station KWKH began to broadcast afternoon and late-night disc jockey shows of rhythm-and-blues records by African-American performers. These programs attracted a generation of young listeners, many of whom were drawn equally to the *Hayride*'s country music broadcasts as to the rhythm-and-blues discs spun by Ray "Groovie Boy" Bartlett and Frank "Gatemouth" Page, both also *Hayride* announcers. KWKH and its listeners presented a microcosm of what was happening all over the South, as the musical and cultural exchange between black and white musicians accelerated along with the rest of society during the postwar decade.[1] It was then that rhythm-and-blues and country players alchemized musical genres into something more than music. Unlike any other time in history, musicians made culture.

The dominant figure in the 1950s rise of youth culture was Elvis Presley, who, like Hank Williams before him, gained his first widespread national exposure on the *Louisiana Hayride*. On the *Hayride*, Elvis Presley performed a wide array of songs, including country tunes, rhythm-and-blues songs, and pop songs. For his eclectic repertoire and distinctive musical style, Presley found a receptive audience in Shreveport's Municipal Auditorium and on tour with *Hayride* package shows. Presley's music made sense in Shreveport, which had long been a crossroads for a variety of musical styles and cultural impulses. Shreveport inadvertently grew a culture of close and constant contact between its white and black citizens, whose musical traditions have influenced one another so deeply that their boundaries frequently lose distinction and overlap at surprising turns.

Presley's performances associated with his year-and-a-half on the *Hayride* and his recordings on Sam Phillips's Sun Records label in Memphis epitomize the strain of rock-and-roll music known as "rockabilly." The rockabilly of Presley, Carl Perkins, Jerry Lee Lewis, and others, along with the rock-and-roll sounds of Bill Haley, Chuck Berry, and Little Richard, eroded the record industry's notions of racially segregated musical categories, established in the 1920s by "race" and "hillbilly" recording pioneer Ralph Peer. Rock-and-roll and its country cousin equally undermined the industry's understanding of "popular music" as songs by Haley, Berry, Presley, and Fats Domino topped the popular charts in the mid-1950s. Elvis Presley, the Everly Brothers, Jerry Lee Lewis, Johnny Horton—all white performers originally within the context of country music—recorded songs between 1956 and 1960 that simultaneously scaled the country and western, rhythm-and-blues, and popular music charts.[2] Racial desegregation that would take painful decades to progress significantly was occurring with relative speed in the music dubbed rock-and-roll.

The critical significance of the *Louisiana Hayride* to U.S. culture refuses to cooperate with the paradigm Ralph Peer unwittingly established for conceiving southern roots music along segregated lines of race. Presley alone makes it impossible to confine the *Hayride*'s influence to its whiteness just as the historical circumstances that made the show possible cannot be understood apart from Shreveport's mixed racial situation. The region's milieu makes it clear that tumultuous dynamics of race and culture existed under the Anglo veneer of mid-century country music.

The history of these dynamics in Shreveport included religious camp meetings, community picnics, medicine shows, and shows in theaters, tents, and on board steamboats; informal settings like Shreveport's Fannin Street "sin district," back porches, and storefronts; colorblind forums like hymnbooks, and, eventually, mass media. In many ways, blacks and whites in the South unconsciously assimilated one another's culture, even as white culture's racist and paternalistic view of African-Americans policed these interactions. On the other hand, the white musicians described on these pages—from Jimmie Davis, Jimmie Rodgers, through Hank Williams and Elvis Presley, to Jerry Kennedy, D. J. Fontana, and Joe Osborn—listened to and learned from black musicians, just as black musicians did from whites, out of an impulse toward musical dialogue. So said, none of these musicians deliberately strove to dissolve racial barriers in their explorations of different aspects of a continuous southern cultural landscape. It just came with the territory.

The *Louisiana Hayride* points to other rich possibilities for popular music scholarship that looks outside the established music industry centers (Nashville, New York, and Los Angeles). It suggests the limitations for tacitly adopting Ralph Peer's segregated commercial categories for southern roots music as fully viable parameters for understanding the music in its wholeness. It suggests how a region like northwest Louisiana breathes life into the clay lungs of a shared history: in it, the rise of radio, the expansion of country music, and the tectonic shifts of U.S. culture during the postwar era all point to hope for our future both in light of, and in spite of, our past.

Notes

Preface

1. Russell, *Blacks, Whites, and Blues*, 10.

Introduction

1. This is a creative retelling of Horace Logan's account included in his memoir *Elvis, Hank, and Me*, 7.

2. By 1927 this show aired two or three times per month. See Malone, *Country Music, U.S.A.*, 33–34; and Ewen, *All the Years*, 306.

3. WSB in Atlanta first began broadcasting hillbilly music prominently as early as 1922, though it did not use the barn dance format. Examples of shows that emulated the early prototypes include: the *Wheeling Jamboree* on WWVA in Wheeling, West Virginia, beginning in 1933; the *Boone County Jamboree* in 1938 on Cincinnati's WLW (who renamed it the *Midwestern Hayride* in 1945); the *Renfro Valley Barn Dance* in 1939 on WHAS in Louisville, Kentucky; the *Tennessee Barn Dance* in Knoxville on WNOX in 1942; the *Old Dominion Barn Dance* in Richmond, Virginia, on station WRVA in 1946; the *Ozark Jubilee* over KWTO in Springfield, Missouri, in 1947; the *Big D Jamboree* on Dallas station KRLD, also in 1947; the *Town and Country Jamboree* on KMAL in Washington, D.C., 1947; and the *Town Hall Party*, a television broadcast over station KTTV begun in 1950, Compton, California. This list is taken from Tucker, "Louisiana Saturday Night," 393–94. A list of radio barn dances also appears in Gentry, *A History and Encyclopedia*, 168–75.

4. Roger M. Williams, "Hank Williams," in *Stars*, ed. Malone and McCulloh, 238. Writing from the centrality of Nashville, R. Williams refers to the show as the "farm club," the "minors," or (abandoning the parallel to baseball) one of the "way stations on the country music line" in his biography *Sing a Sad Song*, 73, 198, 1.

5. Malone, *Country Music, U.S.A.*, 207.

6. Hank Williams Jr., foreword to *Elvis, Hank, and Me*, by Horace Logan, vii–viii.

7. Nachman, *Raised on Radio*, 158.

8. Sleepy Brown, interview by Rachel Stone.

9. Monte Mountjoy (Texas Playboys drummer), liner notes to Bob Wills, *The Tiffany Transcriptions*, vol. 6, *Sally Goodin*; also see Carr and Munde, *Prairie Nights to Neon Lights*, 62; and Townsend, *San Antonio Rose*, 103, 289.

10. Franks and Murrell Stansell, interview by Rachel Stone. Escott identifies the upstaging gymnast as Ray Atkins, who performed with Johnnie and Jack; Franks asserts that it was Bartlett.

11. Ray Bartlett interview. All interviews are by the author, unless otherwise indicated.

12. Frank Page interview. According to announcer Page, the *Hayride* toured four or five times per year, selling out most shows.

13. "Louisiana Hayride," 32–33; in Tucker, "Louisiana Saturday Night," 425.

14. Davis recorded with the Sheltons and Chappelear during his last recording session for Victor Records in Chicago, 4–5 August 1933, before he moved to Decca. Tony Russell describes session details in notes to *Governor Jimmie Davis: Nobody's Darlin' But Mine*. This is the first box of a two-box set of Davis's entire opus.

15. For more discussion of these performers recruited by Upson and the Baileses, see Tucker, "Louisiana Saturday Night," 408–11. A picture of Curley Kinsey and the Tennessee Ridge Runners shortly after their arrival at KWKH appears in the Shreveport *Times*, 11 January 1948. Announcement for the beginning of daily broadcasts by Johnnie and Jack and the Tennessee Mountain Boys, at 5:45 a.m., 1:30 p.m., and 10:30 p.m. Monday through Friday appears in the Shreveport *Times*, 8 February 1948; both articles in the scrapbook compiled by Gentry, *The Louisiana Hayride*, vol. 1, *1948–55*, 3, 5. In the early 1960s, Johnnie Wright changed the spelling of his first name to "Johnny." I will use the original spelling, as he was still using it during the period discussed.

16. Malone, *Country Music, U.S.A.*, 207. A brief entry listing some other stars appears in Kingsbury, ed., *The Encyclopedia of Country Music*, 304–5. Also of interest is an essay from the late 1950s written by Horace Logan and printed as part of a *Louisiana Hayride* publicity layout in Gentry, *The Louisiana Hayride*, vol. 2, *1956–60*, 362–63.

17. Tucker, "Louisiana Saturday Night," 396–97.

18. Hall, "A Historical Study," 183. See also Summers, ed., *A Thirty-Year History*, 208.

19. Johnny Cash, introduction to *Elvis, Hank, and Me*, by Logan, xii.

20. Hall, "A Historical Study," 183.

21. Bartlett's program also went by the name *Groovie's Boogie*. Bartlett was the same *Hayride* announcer who turned back flips during "Lovesick Blues." In discussing the instrumental "Juke," released by Chess Records in 1952, Muddy Waters reflected on a tour his band made in that year to Monroe and Shreveport, Louisiana, set up by a "disc jockey, called him the Groovy Boy [*sic*]". See Palmer, *Deep Blues*, 211.

22. See KWKH program logs in Shreveport *Times*, 4 August 1948, 4 April 1950, and 23 June 1951; in Gentry, *The Louisiana Hayride*, vol. 1, 23, 78, 101. A photo caption of KWKH announcers in the Shreveport *Times*, 15 January 1950, describes Bartlett's program as "the most popular locally produced program heard in Shreveport"; in Gentry, *The Louisiana Hayride*, vol. 1, 75. Disc jockey programs of all types expanded and a glance at KWKH radio logs underscores the eclecticism of the era. For example, Bartlett's show during one period immediately followed a live hillbilly show

by Harmie Smith. Performer Johnnie Bailes also hosted a hillbilly program, and Frank Page hosted both a pop program and a rhythm-and-blues show in addition to his *Hayride* announcing.

23. Rufus Thomas on station WDIA in Memphis is among the most famous of African-American disc jockeys of the era; he began in 1951 doing an hour-long Saturday program and, by 1954, he was doing four hours late night every day. See Rob Bowman, liner notes to Rufus Thomas, *Can't Get Away from This Dog*. A number of stations started between 1948 and 1952 that were solely aimed at an African-American audience; many of these were white-owned, but there were exceptions, like WERD in Atlanta. See Barnouw, *The Golden Web*, 289–90.

24. Lhamon, *Deliberate Speed*. Malone writes of the dynamic in *Southern Music/American Music*, among other places. Mailer's famous essay "The White Negro" is discussed in chapter 6.

1. The Character of a Region

1. Mary Taylor, Steamboat Livingston, to Maria H. Marshall, letter dated 11 March 1837. Taylor was traveling through Shreveport from the eastern United States.

2. The Shreve Town Company members were Col. J. B. Pickett, Gen. T. T. Williamson, Angus McNeil, Sturges Sprague, Bushrod Jenkins, W. S. Bennett, Col. J. H. Cane, and Capt. Shreve. Sources conflict as to the exact date in May. Hardin, "An Outline," 788, lists 27 May, while McCall, *Conquering the Rivers*, 217, states 24 May. The transfer initially occurred to McNeil, then to the larger company, which may explain the discrepancy of dates. According to Henrici, *Shreveport: The Beginnings*, 43, formal incorporation of the town did not occur until 20 March 1839.

3. Estimates of the length of the logjam range from 160 to 214 miles, as figured by the government engineer sent to survey Shreve's work. McCall, *Conquering the Rivers*, 198 and 224.

4. Humphreys, "The 'Great Raft' of the Red River," in *North Louisiana*, vol. 1, ed. Gilley, 76–77.

5. Among the tribes were "the Natchitoches, the Nacogdoches, the Adai, the Yatasee [*sic*], and the Kichai, whose names are still perpetuated in the region, and some eight or nine others of which no trace remains." See Hardin, "An Outline," 762.

6. See Flores, "A Very Different Story," 2–17; and Tyson, *The Red River in Southwestern History*, 70–75.

7. Flores, "A Very Different Story," 17. Also Flores, ed., *Jefferson and Southwestern Exploration*.

8. Malone, *Country Music, U.S.A.*, 3.

9. Hunter, *Steamboats on the Western Rivers*, 52.

10. Hardin, "An Outline," 846.

11. McCall, *Conquering the Rivers*, 191–92.

12. Woodruff, "Removal of the Red River Raft," 641.

13. McCall, *Conquering the Rivers*, 230; Lowery, "The Red," in *The Rivers and Bayous of Louisiana*, ed. Davis, 56, suggests the date was 7 March 1838.

14. Carruth, *Caddo 1000*, 9. Also discussed in McCall, *Conquering the Rivers*, 215 ff.; and Henrici, *Shreveport: The Beginnings*, 25.

15. U.S. Congress, House, *The Caddo Indian Treaty*, 27th Cong., 2nd sess., 1842, H. Rep. 1035, p. 118; also in Henrici, *Shreveport: The Beginnings*, 23.

16. Gute and Jeter, *Historical Profile*, 34.

17. McCall, *Conquering the Rivers*, 224.

18. Hardin, "An Outline," 831.

19. See Thomson and Meador, *Shreveport: A Photographic Remembrance: 1873–1949*, 10. Also see Gute and Jeter, *Historical Profile*, 4.

20. A table appears in Burton, *On the Black Side of Shreveport*, 157, showing the Caddo population in 1850 to include 3,639 whites, 5,208 slaves, and 42 free blacks; figures for the same groups a decade later were 4,733, 7,338, and 69. The figures are confirmed in other sources, including Thomson and Meador, *Shreveport: A Photographic Remembrance: 1873–1949*, 9. Statewide statistics are found in Smith and Horton, eds., *Historical Statistics of Black America*, 1818, 1820–21; and Calhoun and Frois, eds., *Louisiana Almanac*.

21. Leonard, unfinished memoirs; also reprinted in Gute and Jeter, *Historical Profile*, 35.

22. Ibid., 192–241. This source reprints the 1850 Census for Shreveport. The population according to the 1850 census numbered 1,040 and included 256 residential dwellings.

23. Donovan, *River Boats of America*, 85.

24. Leonard, unfinished memoirs, 28. Leonard uses the phrase "floating population" on p. 41.

25. John Edington to his sister, Mrs. Johnson, letter dated May 1838. Punctuation in original. Edington refers to The Catfish, the town's only hotel at the time. Later in the letter, the author predicts: "This is bound to be a great place say in 2 or 3 years as there is such a fine Back Cotton Country, and they ship it all at this Port." Edington remained in Shreveport and prospered.

26. Leonard, unfinished memoirs, 16–17. Leonard's long and varied life included stints as a Confederate soldier, a state senator, a U.S. district attorney, a private attorney, a banker, and a planter. In addition he was founder and publisher of the Shreveport *Times* newspaper. He began writing his autobiography in 1917 but died before it was completed. Leonard includes an account of an attempt by a group of Texans to overtake Shreveport by force: "Sometime in 1839 a company of Texans fully armed (about 100) and equipped (for war) marched into Shreveport and occupied the Court House Square." The local citizenry rallied together, exchanged "some parley," and escorted their invaders back to Texas; these events occurred a decade before Leonard arrived in Shreveport. See ibid., 27–28.

27. McCorkle, ed., *1849 Texas Journal of Samuel Wear McCorkle*, 39–40.

28. Henrici, *Shreveport: The Beginnings*, 61–62. See also Leonard, unfinished memoirs, 31–33, for a colorful description of John Sewall's death.

29. Lowery, "The Red," 57. This new raft started 3 miles above the head of the former Great Raft.

30. Tyson, *The Red River in Southwestern History*, 100. Some private contractors during the 1840s attempted to keep the river clear. Their efforts ultimately failed, and, by 1845, the raft again blocked the channel. Due to public demand, the project was briefly reinstated in 1852 under the direction of Charles A. Fuller, but this effort, too, proved unsuccessful.

31. Hunter, *Steamboats on the Western Rivers*, 316.

32. Ibid., 52.

33. Ibid., 52, 317, 321, and 346.

34. Winters, "Secession and Civil War in North Louisiana," in *North Louisiana*, ed. Gilley, 193.

35. Taylor, *Louisiana Reconstructed, 1863–1877*, 380; also 372, 385.

36. Tyson, *The Red River in Southwestern History*, 101.

37. Shreveport *Times*, May 1873, 1.

38. Shreveport *Times*, 28 May 1872.

39. Shreveport *Times*, 19 November 1872 and 13 May 1873.

40. Letter from a Jefferson citizen, Shreveport *Times*, 21 February 1873; Tyson, *The Red River in Southwestern History*, 101; Lowery, "The Red," 57.

41. Today it is a quiet tourist town of quaint antique shops, horse and buggy rides, and bed and breakfast establishments. Shreveport *Times*, 9 December 1873, prints the date of completion. Lt. Woodruff had died one month earlier, possibly the result of a local outbreak of yellow fever in Shreveport around the same time.

42. Hardin, "An Outline," 854.

43. Shreveport *Times*, 27 February 1872 and 25 June 1872.

44. Hunter, *Steamboats on the Western Rivers*, 589. According to Hunter, when the Texas and Pacific Railroad completed its Red River to New Orleans connection, cotton receipts "dropped by two-thirds, while rail imports soared."

45. Thompson, "Transportation," in *Glimpses of Shreveport*, ed. McLaurin, 56–58, 60–61.

46. Hunter, *Steamboats on the Western Rivers*, 218.

47. Lane, *American Paddle Steamboats*, 38.

48. Stuck, *Annie McCune, Shreveport Madam*, 5. The quote comes from Stuck's interviews during the 1970s, asking senior citizens to recollect the early part of the century.

49. Leonard, unfinished memoirs, 39. Scholars from other disciplines occasionally ponder the region's competing cultural impulses. For example, see Owens, "Regionalism and Universality" in *The Texas Literary Tradition*, ed. Graham, Lee, and Pilkington, 69: "Where does the South end, the West begin? . . . [The boundary] lies somewhere along an irregular line where the myth and mystique of the South yield to the myth and mystique of the West, where a traveler passing through senses a change, where cultural historians, cultural geographers can find predominant the fields and customs of one or the other." Similarly, the theme emerges in Tarpley, "Cultural Clash in the Vocabulary of the Red River Valley." Indeed, still today, one finds a strange local allegiance among pro football fans to the Dallas Cowboys over the New Orleans Saints; and often on the same individual, attire that refers to the West (cowboy boots, hats) and to what one writer calls the "Cult of the Confederacy."

2. Shreveport Music before Modern Media

1. Price, "A History of Music in Northwestern Louisiana until 1900," 107. Price concentrates much of his study on the town of Natchitoches, approximately 100 miles south of Shreveport and the head of Red River navigation before 1836. See also Graham, *Showboats*, 23; and Lindsey, "The History of the Theatre in Shreveport, Louisiana to 1900," 6–7. The weekly *South-Western*, published in Shreveport from 1852 to 1872, regularly reported visits by the *Banjo*.

2. Cockrell, *Demons of Disorder*, 1–61, discusses the complex pre-history of blackface. Also see Nathan, *Dan Emmett and the Rise of Early Negro Minstrelsy*, 3–49.

3. Millard, *America on Record*, 85, 96–97. Tambo and Bones were the

names generally given the "endmen" and also referred to the instruments they played, a tambourine and the clacking, rhythm instrument known as the bones.

4. Toll, *Blacking Up*, 66–67. See especially chapter 3, 65–103, where Toll describes the images of African-Americans portrayed in minstrelsy. Another source on blackface minstrelsy is Lott, *Love and Theft*.

5. In January 1999 PBS aired a well-crafted presentation on these two seminal artists, "I'll Make Me a World." Also see Sanjek, *American Popular Music and Its Business*, vol. 2, *From 1790 to 1909*, 279–81, 285–90; Ewen, *All the Years*, 36–50, 118–19, 185–87; and Toll, *Blacking Up*, 218, 257–58. A discussion of the Broadway phase of Walker and Williams's careers appears in Riis, *Just Before Jazz*, especially 113–24.

6. Graham, *Showboats*, 24; in Price, "A History of Music in Northwestern Louisiana until 1900," 109.

7. Graham, *Showboats*, 24.

8. Donovan, *River Boats of America*, 94, 225.

9. See Wolfe and Lornell, *The Life and Legend of Leadbelly*, 16 and 28. A useful quick comparison is found in the two separate entries in Hitchcock and Sadie, eds., *The New Grove Dictionary of American Music*, vol. 4, 260–61. At times, "musicianer" can distinguish an individual able to sing and play an instrument, and "songster" describes one noted for improvising words. See Ramsey, *Been Here and Gone*, 40.

10. Wheeler, *Steamboatin' Days*, 8–9. Wheeler's informants lived mostly on the southern bank of the Ohio River, although many songs "tell a story of boats known on the Mississippi and the Tennessee as well," x. A contemporary mention of the steamboat song "I'm Gwine to Alabamy" appears in the 1867 study by Allen, Ware, and Garrison, *Slave Songs of the United States*, 89.

11. W. C. Handy often receives composer credit for the tune, but its history appears longer. See Meade, Spottswood, and Meade, *Country Music Sources*, 380–81, for "Jack of Diamonds," a variant title for "Rye Whiskey." For "Careless Love," Meade, Spottswood, and Meade, 540–41, list twenty-three recordings by white country (and one Cajun) artists under seven different titles between 1921 and 1942, seven recordings by African-American artists, and nine appearances in print. Other pertinent discussions of the tune include Crawford, "Notes on Jazz Standards"; and Handy, *Father of the Blues*, 153–54. Among African-American artists, Bessie Smith, Joe Turner, Josh White recorded the tune, along with southern blues musicians Fred McDowell (in the late 1950s) and Sam Chatmon (in the 1970s), both for Alan Lomax. See Lomax, *The Land Where Blues Began*, 353–55, 381.

12. See Donovan, *River Boats of America*, 226–27; and Price, "A History of Music in Northwestern Louisiana until 1900," 179–80.

13. Malone, *Country Music, U.S.A*, 6. Newspapers and magazines still reported the occasional circuits of modern medicine shows as late as the 1980s. For example, see Cherry, "The Medicine Show," 50, 41. Doc Tommy Scott led the last traveling medicine show into the early 1990s, hawking the FDA-approved Doc Scott's Snake Oil Liniment and Herb-O-Lac. See Gibson, "Doc Tommy Scott's Last Real Medicine Show," 26–29; and "Snake Oil Still Rolling Up Sales for Scott's Old Time Medicine Show," 51.

14. Malone, *Country Music, U.S.A.*, 6; also Mickel, *Footlights on the Prairie*, 5.

15. The first newspaper citation of Shreveport theater appeared in the

Shreveport weekly, the *South-Western*, on 13 December 1854; see Lindsey, "The History of the Theatre in Shreveport, Louisiana to 1900," 4.

16. Blind Tom's appearance was reported 30 April 1880 in Shreveport's *Daily Standard*. On Tally's Opera House, see Lindsey, "The History of the Theatre in Shreveport, Louisiana to 1900," 49–98; also 9–13, for a discussion of other performers arriving via the steamboat *National*, notably tragedian John McCullogh and actor John T. Raymond. See Leonard, unfinished memoirs, 61–63, for an assessment of Mencken's talents.

17. Penn, "While the Band Discoursed," 8.

18. Ibid., 25–30; also, Stuck, *Annie McCune, Shreveport Madam*, 6. Other minstrel troupes who visited Shreveport were Primrose and West's Minstrels; the Barlow, Wilson, Primrose, and West troupe in 1880 and in 1884; Duprez and Benedict's Minstrels in 1880; Goodyear, Cook, and Dillon in 1889; Richards and Pringle's Famous Georgies and Rosco and Holland's Operatic Minstrels (which combined in 1878).

19. Schafer and Allen, *Brass Bands and New Orleans Jazz*, 8.

20. Tucker, "Louisiana Saturday Night," 33–40; Penn, "While the Band Discoursed," 40.

21. Leonard, unfinished memoirs, 41. Reprinted in Gute and Jeter, *Historical Profile*, 40.

22. In Wolfe and Lornell, *The Life and Legend of Leadbelly*, 18. The quote appeared in Lawrence Cohn's notes to an Elektra box set, Leadbelly, *Library of Congress Recordings*. There is some ambiguity regarding the year of Leadbelly's birth, but this is the date supported by Wolfe and Lornell.

23. Ibid. The authors include other explanations, including Leadbelly's suggestion during another monologue that sukey may be "derived from the field term for cow and was used to call a cow, too." Also, the term "sukey jump" may be an adaptation of an African word.

24. Lipscomb, *I Say Me for a Parable*, 207. In compiling and editing Lipscomb's memoirs, Glen Alyn tried to capture Lipscomb's Texas-African-American dialect in print; I include the quote unmodified from Alyn's text.

25. Stuck, *Annie McCune, Shreveport Madam*, 5. He quotes the 1868 ordinance.

26. Ibid., 11. St. Paul's Bottoms and Fannin Street (the area's main thoroughfare) interchangeably refer to Shreveport's red-light district.

27. Ibid., 3 and 88.

28. Ibid., 88. See also Burton, *On the Black Side of Shreveport*, 64.

29. Malone, *Country Music, U.S.A.*, 9.

30. Wolfe and Lornell, *The Life and Legend of Leadbelly*, 35; their quote comes from a four-LP set titled *Leadbelly's Last Sessions*. For Leadbelly's tutelage in barrelhouse style, see also Russell, "Illuminating the Leadbelly Legend," 12; and Killeen, "Irene, Goodnight," 3.

31. Wolfe and Lornell, *The Life and Legend of Leadbelly*, 35. Although most famous as a twelve-string guitarist and folk singer, Leadbelly was also proficient on the "windjammer" (small button accordion), harmonica, Jew's harp, mandolin, and organ.

32. Lipscomb, *I Say Me for a Parable*, 211.

33. Wolfe and Lornell, *The Life and Legend of Leadbelly*, 29.

34. Ibid., 36. The authors write, "He always remembered the street [Fannin], always spoke and sang about it as if it were one of his most vital formative experiences."

35. "Fannin Street" and the variants "Tom Hughes Town" and "I'm on

My Last Go-Round," can be heard on the three-disc set *The Definitive Lead-belly*. Tom Hughes became Caddo Parish sheriff in 1916, serving in that office for many years, through multiple re-elections; see O'Pry, *Chronicles of Shreveport*, 358; and *Shreveport Men and Women Builders*, 93.

36. Wolfe and Lornell, *The Life and Legend of Leadbelly*, 35. Other tunes document Leadbelly's early Shreveport experiences, including "Easy Mister Tom," an instrumental "twelve-string rag" also on the *Definitive Leadbelly* compilation.

37. Wolfe and Lornell, *The Life and Legend of Leadbelly*, 85–87; their sources for this section include a 1948 interview with Ledbetter, conducted by Kenneth Britzius. When Neff signed the pardon on 16 January 1925, Leadbelly had served more than six-and-a-half years of a seven- to thirty-year sentence.

38. Ibid., 219 and 229. For Riker's Island incident, see 212.

39. For reflections on Leadbelly's posthumous legacy, see ibid., 264–66; also Killeen, "Testimony: Fred Ramsey (1915–1995)," 9.

40. "'Leadbelly,' Who Won International Fame as Interpreter of Negro Folk Songs, Is Dead," *New York Times*, 7 December 1949, 36(C); "'Leadbelly,' Blues Singer, Dies in New York," Shreveport *Times*, 7 December 1949, n.p. Also see Wolfe and Lornell, *The Life and Legend of Leadbelly*, 257.

41. Donna O'Neal, "'Ever-lovin' Light' Shines on Monument to 'Leadbelly,'" *Shreveport Journal*, 11 June 1982.

42. Gormanous and Williams, "Lead Belly Memorialized," 1, 5.

43. Leadbelly recorded extensively for the Library of Congress between 1933 and 1941, largely due to the continued urging of Alan Lomax; more than sixty sides were made during a session with Lomax in 1940 alone, in addition to the field recordings already made in 1933, 1934, 1935, and another session with Lomax in 1937. His extensive recordings are on Folkways, RCA Victor, ARC, and others. Around fifty Leadbelly recordings are housed in the Barnicle-Cadle collection of East Tennessee State University (in Johnson City). See Wolfe and Lornell, *The Life and Legend of Leadbelly*, 222, 227, 246, 211. Much of this recorded repertoire is a strong testimony supporting the assertion that black–white border crossing was common in the South, in general, and in Shreveport, in particular. The songs discussed here are all found on *The Definitive Leadbelly*.

44. See Wolfe and Lornell, *The Life and Legend of Leadbelly*, 91–94. Williard Thomas is the brother of Jesse "Babyface" Thomas, a bluesman active in Shreveport until his death in 1995. John Lomax came to Shreveport in 1940 and recorded Woods, along with two other local musicians with "songster" roots: Joe Harris from Bunkie, Louisiana, on guitar and Kid West on mandolin. Their repertoire included "Baton Rouge Rag," "Nobodies Business," "Bully of the Town," "Kid West Blues," "East Texas Blues," and "Out East Blues." Noah Moore (Leadbelly's cousin) recorded "Oil City Blues" for the Library of Congress.

45. Ivey, "Border Crossing: A Different Way of Listening to American Music," liner notes to *From Where I Stand*, 10. Also see Ivey, "Recordings and the Audience for the Regional and Ethnic Musics of the United States," 13.

46. Wolfe, "Black String Bands," 15, 17. Wolfe characterizes the story as "a typical encounter between the new mass media and one of the most potent but least-known examples of traditional musical: the black string band." The session producer was C. F. Lyons.

47. Ivey, "Border Crossing," 11.

48. Rumble, "The Artists and the Songs," liner notes to *From Where I Stand*, 31–32.

49. Not the Tin Pan Alley tune of a similar title, recordings of the song are listed in Meade, Spottswood, and Meade, *Country Music Sources*, 558; "Keep My Skillet" appears in ibid., 502. "Corrine, Corrina," copyrighted by the Sheiks in 1931, enjoyed a similarly wide circulation between black and white musicians. See ibid., 557.

50. Rumble, "The Artists and the Songs," 32.

51. Russell, *Blacks, Whites, and Blues*, 81–82.

52. Lines are quoted from "Tom Cat and Pussy Blues," found on CD 3 of Jimmie Davis, *Governor Jimmie Davis: Nobody's Darlin' But Mine*. For his part, Rodgers recorded with the Louisville Jug Band, an African-American group, a couple of years before.

53. In an essay about the historical connection between country music and African-American culture, pop music critic Claudia Perry used the term "cultural cross-pollination" and summed up some of the well-known examples of black influence in country and in its musical stepchild, rockabilly. She includes Rodgers, Bob Wills, Bill Monroe, and Hank Williams as predecessors to "rockabilly cats like Elvis Presley and Carl Perkins." See "Digging Country's Roots," liner notes to *From Where I Stand*, 13. Charles Wolfe cites other examples of African-American and Euro-American musicians in sessions together in "Black String Bands," 17.

54. Meade, Spottswood, and Meade, *Country Music Sources*, 422–23. They list five white acts besides Cutrell who recorded the tune between 1926 and 1934 and two other black musicians in addition to Collins.

55. Rumble, liner notes to "The Artists and the Songs," 33.

56. A live recording of Cash is found on *The Original Louisiana Hayride Archives*.

57. It should be noted that other groups outside commercial and academic interests also emphasized the black–white distinction, sometimes in pursuit of social or political aims. For example, Amiri Baraka, writing as a black cultural nationalist under the name LeRoi Jones, argued for the notion of a pure African-American music aesthetic during a critical era in the civil rights movement. See *Blues People*.

58. Quoted in Cohen, "The Folk Music Interchange," 43.

59. Ibid., 43–44; also Lomax, *The Land Where Blues Began*, 450. Alan Lomax reprints the story of Big Bill Broonzy's life as told to him in 1940s in *The Land Where Blues Began*, 426–58; here Broonzy, who was born in 1893, recalls the first few tunes he learned to play when he was a youngster in Arkansas were "Shortnin' Bread," "Old Hen Cackle," "Uncle Bud," and "The Chicken Reel." He recalls that after he was in his twenties, he played mostly for whites at three-day dances and at "fish fries, picnics, and all kinds of big gatherings all down through Arkansas and Mississippi and some parts of Texas" (432).

60. Malone, *Southern Music/American Music*, 7.

61. "I'll Fly Away" was composed in 1931; "Precious Lord" was written in 1932. These and other hymns were popular during the Depression and subsequently became part of the standard repertoire, especially among Baptists and Methodists in the South, white and black. See Malone, *Country Music, U.S.A.*, 131.

62. The earliest of the text-only songbooks were printed in the South. See Sanjek, *American Popular Music*, vol. 2, 182; and Jackson, *Spiritual Folk-Songs of Early America*, 10–12, for lists of early titles. Later publica-

tions of these revival spirituals, which were used by both whites and blacks, included notation in shape-notes.

3. Hillbilly Music and the Phonograph

1. See Malone, "Country Music, the South, and Americanism," 56–57. For discussion of the era's tensions and reactions, see Levine, *The Unpredictable Past*, 196; also Cash, *The Mind of the South*, 340; the topic threads thematically throughout the work of George B. Tindall and other historians of southern culture.

2. Millard, *America on Record*, 41.

3. Gelatt, *The Fabulous Phonograph*, 44; 33–45 provides a good overview of the phonograph's development. Also see Millard, "The Inventors," chap. in *America on Record*, 17–36.

4. See Gelatt, *The Fabulous Phonograph*, 47.

5. Moore, *A Matter of Records*, 3–4, includes a description of sessions with AtLee from his accompanist (and later EMI record company executive) Fred Gaisburg.

6. Millard, *America on Record*, 32, 125; Gelatt, *The Fabulous Phonograph*, 88. Vulcanization is the treatment by which rubber is rendered usable for any of its various purposes.

7. Porterfield, *Jimmie Rodgers*, 84. The word "phonograph" came into usage in the United States as a catchall term for all the devices previously distinguished as "phonographs," "graphophones," and "gramophones." Johnson avoided any confusion in terminology by naming his product the "talking machine." See also Millard, *America on Record*, 135. I use the word "phonograph" in its broad sense throughout the rest of the book.

8. Gelatt, *The Fabulous Phonograph*, 131. Victor profits continued to expand: by 1902, they reached nearly $1,000,000; by 1905, total business exceeded $12,000,000.

9. Ibid., 143, 153; Porterfield, *Jimmie Rodgers*, 85; Millard, *America on Record*, 59–64.

10. Millard, *America on Record*, 131.

11. The details of Smith's recording are now familiar in any study involving early roots recordings. For example, it appears in country music sources like Porterfield, *Jimmie Rodgers*, 92; and Malone, *Southern Music/American Music*, 46–47, 59. Composer and pianist Perry Bradford played an essential role in convincing Okeh executives to record the Cincinnati-born singer's treatment of his tunes; see his memoir, *Born with the Blues*, for his own reflections. Bourgeois, *Blueswomen*, 119, includes the lyrics to "That Thing Called Love" and "You Can't Keep a Good Man Down."

12. Sanjek, *American Popular Music*, vol. 3, 31 and 65; Malone, *Southern Music/American Music*, 62. Origins of the term "race records" are also discussed in Murray, *Stomping the Blues*; and George, *The Death of Rhythm & Blues*, 9.

13. Grundy, "'We Always Tried to Be Good People,'" 1599–1600.

14. For more on the development of Peer's understanding of the financial gain to be won from registering new copyrights, see Porterfield, *Jimmie Rodgers*, 96–100. Much of my understanding about Peer's role in the industry is drawn from Porterfield. The enormous issue of musical ownership in the 1920s is treated extensively in Sanjek, *American Popular Music*, vol. 2.

15. Levine, *The Unpredictable Past*, 201; italics in original. For general reflections on nostalgia and its relatively recent emergence in historical stud-

ies, see Levine's chapter, "Progress and Nostalgia: The Self Image of the Nineteen Twenties." He writes with broad insight: "The central paradox of American history, then, has been a belief in progress coupled with a dread of change; an urge towards the inevitable future combined with a longing for the irretrievable past; a deeply ingrained belief in America's unfolding destiny and a haunting conviction that the nation was in a state of decline" (191).

16. Wolfe, "Uncle Dave Macon," in *Stars*, ed. Malone and McCulloh, 42. I am indebted to Wolfe's essay for much of the biographical information on Macon.

17. Ibid., 59.

18. Ibid., 51.

19. See Tindall, *The Emergence of the New South*, 208–18. Malone expounds upon the South's conflicted image in *Southern Music/American Music*, 55.

20. Angoff, *H. L. Mencken*, 126; in Tindall, *The Emergence of the New South*, 210. Mencken's most famous essay on the South, "The Sahara of the Bozart," was published in *Prejudices*, 136–39. Others echoed Mencken's sentiments including populist politician and lecturer William Henry Skaggs and Columbia professor Frank Tannenbaum.

21. Harkins, *Hillbilly*, offers an excellent analysis of the complex associations of the label as it relates not only to music, but to visual and literary culture as well.

22. Charles Hamm traces the general presence of nostalgia as a thread common throughout U.S. popular music, especially after the 1820s and 1830s in *Yesterdays*. Millard, *America on Record*, 88, suggests the German sentimental tradition as another source for popular nostalgia.

23. Millard, *America on Record*, 89. Bland's song journeyed far from its original context and meaning when soul muscle funkster Rufus Thomas recorded a version titled "Take Me Back to Old Virginny" during the 1960s; included on Thomas, *Can't Get Away from This Dog*.

24. Sharp, *English Folk Songs from the Southern Appalachians*, xxvi.

25. Shapiro, *Appalachia on Our Mind*, 252.

26. See Whisnant, *All That Is Native and Fine*, 115; Whisnant points out that Sharp's fixation on the Child ballads was "almost universal among ballad collectors at the time." Olive Dame Campbell's work prior to her association with Sharp (as his assistant) is notable in its inclusiveness of other material. See also Wilgus, *Anglo-American Folksong Scholarship since 1898*; Malone, *Country Music, U.S.A*, 27; and Wolfe, *A Good-Natured Riot*, 13–14. Sharp's research coincided with an era of general fascination with Appalachia as a symbol of American culture, as a source of authentic folkways (music, crafts, dancing), and as a focus for social activism and organized benevolence.

27. Malone, *Southern Music/American Music*, 37. Malone continues: "The world at large, while enriched by these borrowings, received a decidedly limited view of the cultures of black and white southerners, and the total richness and diversity of their music remained largely hidden from the majority of the American public."

28. Green, "Hillbilly Music," 206–7; also mentioned in Porterfield, *Jimmie Rodgers*, 92.

29. Porterfield, *Jimmie Rodgers*, 339, 197, in a footnote. Also see 90 and 94.

30. *Chattanooga Times*, 14 December 1929, 10; in Porterfield, *Jimmie Rodgers*, 339; see also 226–27.

31. Cohen, "Early Pioneers," 4.

32. Millard, *America on Record,* 166–67, suggests that some companies used cheap materials like "waxed paper, chemically covered paper, and metal." This was done only occasionally and by minor companies; Tony Russell, e-mail message to the author, 4 June 2004. Also see Sanjek, *American Popular Music,* vol. 3, 122.

33. Malone, *Country Music, U.S.A.,* 95.

34. Millard, *America on Record,* 170.

35. See Grundy, "'We Always Tried to Be Good People,'" 1600; and Green, "Hillbilly Music," which discusses in detail the evolution of the labels.

36. Lakoff, *Women, Fire, and Dangerous Things,* 65.

37. For the "Age of Segregation," see Tindall, *The Emergence of the New South.*

38. See "The White Man's Blues, 1922–40." Wolfe, 39, defines "white blues" as a subtype of early country music, a blending of city and country blues styles performed by white musicians in the South. It thrived between 1925 and 1940. An earlier description of the brothers appears in Nelson, "The Allen Brothers," 147–50. Their story also appears in Malone, *Country Music U.S.A.,* 104–5.

39. Wolfe, "The White Man's Blues, 1922–40," 38.

40. Ibid.

41. Russ Shor, "Red Hot Jazz—Sizzling! Roasting! Scorching!" VJM Jazz & Blues Mart, http://www.vjm.htm (accessed 8 June 2004).

42. Wolfe, "The White Man's Blues, 1922–40," 39; also see Nelson, "The Allen Brothers," 148. The song, as well as reference to the incident in the liner notes, can be found on the compilation *Roots N' Blues.*

43. Lakoff, *Women, Fire, and Dangerous Things,* 65.

44. Walter Haden, "Vernon Dalhart," in *Stars,* ed. Malone and McCulloh. Haden untangles the history of Dalhart recordings including scores of pseudonyms here and in the article "Vernon Dalhart," *John Edwards Memorial Foundation Quarterly.* A theme of Haden's writing is the contrast between the historic treatment accorded Dalhart with that given the Carter Family and Jimmie Rodgers.

45. Ralph S. Peer, letter to the editor, "Ralph Peer Sees No Hypo [*sic*] for Late Jimmy Rodgers; Dalhart Not a Hillbilly," *Variety* 200/9 (2 Nov. 1955): 52. The letter was a response to musicologist Jim Walsh, who defended Vernon Dalhart's authenticity; see "Musicologist Jim Walsh on Hillbilly Champs: Dalhart vs. Rodgers, et al.," *Variety* 200/3 (21 Sept. 1955): 51, 54.

46. For "John Denver," see Porterfield, *Jimmie Rodgers,* 385, who quoted then-Country Music Foundation director Bill Ivey; for "coolly commercial," see Porterfield, *Jimmie Rodgers,* 55. For "Northerners," see Ewen, *All the Years,* 306. Also see Haden, "Vernon Dalhart," in *Stars,* ed. Malone and McCulloh, 77.

47. Ivey, "The Bottom Line," 283.

48. *My Rough and Rowdy Ways.* Armstrong is not mentioned on the session notes because he was under contract with another company at the time. Wolfe, "Satchmo Country: Louis Armstrong and Country Music," paper delivered at the International Country Music Conference, Nashville, May 2003.

49. Jones and Chilton, *Louis,* 236. The album was recorded in New York on Avco Embassy in 1970, the year before Armstrong died. For Porterfield quote, see *Jimmie Rodgers,* 258. Also, Wolfe, "Satchmo Country."

50. Guy B. Johnson, "Negro Folk-Songs," 558, writes in 1934: "The phonograph record companies employed colored blues singers and specialized in the sale of 'race records' to Negroes. These records became as popular with white people as with Negroes." His assessment of the white audience for commercial recordings by black performers is difficult to document, due to the absence of sales statistics. But his assertion that whites bought "race music" is echoed by later writers. See Millard, *America on Record*, 77; and Barnouw, *A Tower in Babel*, vol. 1, 130; and Fornatale and Mills, *Radio in the Television Age*, 37–39, who connect the practice to the late 1940s and early 1950s.

51. Malone, *Southern Music/American Music*, 82.

52. E. R. Fenimore Johnson, *His Master's Voice Was Eldridge R. Johnson*, 112; also in Millard, *America on Record*, 138.

53. Porterfield, *Jimmie Rodgers*, 338. He refers to *Variety*, 8 and 29 November 1932, both p. 53; see also *Billboard*, 3 October 1931, 20; and Millard, *America on Record*, 167.

4. Hillbilly Music and KWKH Radio

1. See Willey and Rice, *Communication Agencies and Social Life*, 186–205.

2. Presley's deep appreciation for blues, rhythm-and-blues, and black gospel quartets, as well as Pentecostal religious singing, country, and white gospel is widely acknowledged. The gospel connection received attention in a fairly recent documentary aired on PBS: *He Touched Me: The Gospel Music of Elvis Presley*. Also see Millard, *America on Record*, 252; Escott and Hawkins, *Good Rockin' Tonight*, 84; and Guralnick, *Last Train to Memphis*, where the racially mixed social milieu of Presley's boyhood is discussed in the first chapter, especially 26–28.

3. O'Pry, *Chronicles of Shreveport*, 355, 375–76.

4. Poindexter, *Golden Throats and Silver Tongues*, 87. Part of Henderson's bitterness sprang from the fact that the commission initially established twenty-five stations for clear-channel broadcasts and assigned twenty-three of these to NBC network affiliates. See McChesney, *Telecommunications, Mass Media, and Democracy*, 20.

5. Hall, "A Historical Study," 92.

6. Nikola Tesla patented the technology in 1897 and Guglielmo Marconi demonstrated its usefulness soon after. Marconi legally held the patent until 1943, when it was overturned by the U.S. Supreme Court in a suit brought by the U.S. government; Tesla, who died that same year, never benefited from the ruling. Jim Glenn, Margaret Cheney, and Robert Uth, "Tesla: Life and Legacy," Public Broadcasting Service, http://www.pbs.org/tesla/ll/ll_whoradio.html (accessed 8 June 2004).

7. Quoted from a 1917 book by Towers, *Masters of Space*, cited in Herron, *Miracle of the Air Waves*, 86. See also Archer, *History of Radio to 1926*; and Harlow, *Old Wires and New Waves*.

8. Walker, *Rebels on the Air*, 29; Archer, *History of Radio*, 203.

9. Archer, *History of Radio*, 204.

10. Archer, *History of Radio*, 211–13; Herron, *Miracle of the Air Waves*, 115.

11. Information on problems in early radio may be found in Archer, *History of Radio*, 280 (imprecise technology), 356 and 370–71 (territorial disputes), and 312 (ASCAP).

12. White, *The American Radio*, 29; Hilliard, ed., *Radio Broadcasting*, 4.

13. Rosen, *The Modern Stentors,* 62–63.

14. Hilliard, ed., *Radio Broadcasting,* 6; also in Hall, "A Historical Study," 2; and Fowler and Crawford, *Border Radio,* 4.

15. See Paper, *Empire,* on the history of CBS.

16. Barnouw, *The Golden Web,* 16–17. Also see Brindze, *Not to Be Broadcast,* 111–14 and 196–214.

17. See Smulyan, *Selling Radio,* 117–22; and MacDonald, "The Great Escape—The Story of Radio Comedy," chap. in *Don't Touch That Dial,* 91–153.

18. Barnouw, *The Golden Web,* 17.

19. Ibid., 6; also see 98–99.

20. In Fornatale and Mills, *Radio in the Television Age,* xix and xxv.

21. Malone, *Southern Music/American Music,* 58.

22. Bob Sullivan interview.

23. Archer, *History of Radio,* 370.

24. See Cohen, "Early Pioneers," 8.

25. Porterfield, *Jimmie Rodgers,* 86.

26. On Dalhart's tours, see Haden, "Vernon Dalhart," 70. Over half a century later, when audio tape became a staple medium for recorded music, market leader Memorex made a similar claim about its recordable product, asking, "Is it live or is it Memorex?"

27. Dalhart's style would have been completely unsuitable for the carbon microphones used in radio during the 1930s. See Wolfe, "The Triumph of the Hills," 60.

28. As Porterfield, *Jimmie Rodgers,* 311, points out, Rodgers's success sealed "the directions rural programming would take in the decades to follow."

29. Included on the DVD *Times Ain't Like They Used To Be.*

30. Antony's call letters (along with KDKA) predate the legislation that assigned stations east of the Mississippi River to begin with "W" and west of the Mississippi to begin with "K." See Albarran and Pitts, *The Radio Broadcasting Industry,* 10.

31. On WAAG and WGAQ, see Hall, "A Historical Study," 18–21, 22–23, 27.

32. Ibid., 29; Patterson retained a one-fourth share in the station.

33. Stedman Gunning, interview by Hubert Humphreys, 5, 16–17.

34. Hall, "A Historical Study," 36, 45–46. Also see Pusateri, "Stormy Career," 398; and Tucker, "Louisiana Saturday Night," 75.

35. Pusateri, "Stormy Career," 389; also Hall, "A Historical Study," 38, 50.

36. Stedman Gunning interview; also see Pusateri, "Stormy Career," 392–93, 403.

37. Stedman Gunning, interview by Hubert Humphreys, 5. A further boost to KWKH's power was the fact that amplitude-modulated (AM) waves behave in accordance with the "ozone skip effect," which means that they "bounce or skip off the atmosphere surrounding the globe in much the same way as a rock skips across a smooth pond." See Fowler and Crawford, *Border Radio,* 7.

38. Stedman Gunning, interview by Hubert Humphreys, 6; on *Radio Digest* award, see Pusateri, "Stormy Career," 401.

39. Pusateri, *Enterprise in Radio,* 103. Pusateri reports that more than $350,000 had been collected by this time.

40. Hall, "A Historical Study," 57–60.

41. May, *Hello World Henderson,* 57. The excerpt appears in this premature 1930 biography written by a Henderson family friend and published

by a company of which Henderson was at one time a vice-president. It functions more as a contemporary apologia than a historical account. As such, it is a fascinating set piece from Henderson's heyday.

42. See Pusateri, "Stormy Career," 402; also, Pusateri, *Enterprise in Radio*, 103, 106; also see Salassi, "Hello, World," 17.

43. Stedman Gunning, interview by Hubert Humphreys.

44. See Pusateri, "Stormy Career," 398; Hall, "A Historical Study," 54.

45. Pusateri, *Enterprise in Radio*, 74.

46. *Shreveport Journal*, 21 October 1930; in Pusateri, "Stormy Career," 402. A brief description of Long's radio oratory of the early 1930s is found in Craig, *Fireside Politics*, 160; it could safely be said that he perfected this style during his KWKH hook-ups.

47. In Pusateri, *Enterprise in Radio*, 100, from a January 1930 Henderson transcript.

48. *Supplement to the Annual Report of the Federal Radio Commission*, 1928, 48–50, 116–17; in Pusateri, "Stormy Career," 394.

49. KWKH File, Radio Division Records, Department of Commerce, National Archives, Washington, D.C.; in Pusateri, "Stormy Career," 393.

50. Pusateri, "Stormy Career," 401; also see Pusateri, *Enterprise in Radio*, 101.

51. Russell, liner notes to *Governor Jimmie Davis: Nobody's Darlin' But Mine*, 4.

52. Pusateri, "Stormy Career," 395–96; Russell, *Governor Jimmie Davis: Nobody's Darlin' But Mine*, 4, cites 167,000 supporting documents.

53. Kahn, "International Relations," 49; also see Barnouw, *A Tower in Babel*, 169, 259; and two biographies, Carson, *The Roguish World of Doctor Brinkley* and, more recently, Lee, *The Bizarre Careers of John R. Brinkley*. Also Benjamin, "'By Their Fruits Ye Shall Know Them': Brinkley, Baker, and Shuler," chap. in *Freedom of the Air and the Public Interest*, 89–107.

54. Among the many who trekked to Kansas for the operation was Dr. J. J. Tobias, Chicago Law School chancellor, who reported to local newspapers the great success of the operation and bestowed upon Brinkley an honorary doctor of science degree. Other high-profile clients were Senator Wesley Staley of Colorado and Harry Chandler, owner of the *Los Angeles Times*. See Lee, *The Bizarre Careers of John R. Brinkley*, 35, 46, 54, 82, and Fowler and Crawford, *Border Radio*, 17, 19–20. In 1939 Brinkley lost a lawsuit against Dr. Morris Fishbein for defamation via a series of articles called "Modern Medical Charlatans" for the American Medical Association journal, *Hygeia*; the verdict sparked a string of lawsuits from former patients, totaling over $1,000,000 "for everything from carelessness to 'criminal negligence in permitting a patient to bleed to death on the operating table.'" Again see Lee, *The Bizarre Careers of John R. Brinkley*, 211–30; and Fowler and Crawford, *Border Radio*, 43–44.

55. Barnouw, *The Golden Web*, 11–14.

56. Kahn, "International Relations," 50. KFKB won a similar distinction from the Chicago-based *Radio Times* in 1929; see Fowler and Crawford, *Border Radio*, 22. Frank J. Kahn, ed., *Documents of American Broadcasting*, 140–44, reprints the decision of the Justice to deny Brinkley's license renewal because the case set the precedent for the FRC to consider a station's past programming when reviewing a renewal application.

57. Kahn, "International Relations," 48.

58. The exception to the U.S. wattage limit was the Cincinnati station WLW, which in the mid-1930s was allowed to operate as an experimental

"superstation" with 500,000 watts of power, calling itself "The Nation's Station." In 1939 WLW was ordered to return to 50,000 watts at the behest of a Senate bill. See Barnouw, *The Golden Web*, 119, 133.

59. Fowler and Crawford, *Border Radio*, 154.

60. Malone, *Country Music, U.S.A.*, 98.

61. Quote from Fowler and Crawford, *Border Radio*, 6.

62. Tucker, "Louisiana Saturday Night," 138–39. During the period of Davis's employment with Dodd College, he avoided using his last name on air to avoid any sense of impropriety. After 1928 he used his full name; Kevin Fontenot, e-mail, 4 June 2004.

63. Russell, liner notes *Governor Jimmie Davis: Nobody's Darlin' But Mine*; also see Tucker, "The Singing Governor," chap. in "Louisiana Saturday Night," 131–91. Much of the following biographical information on Davis comes from Tucker's dissertation.

64. See Tucker, "Louisiana Saturday Night," 75–77, on the performers listed here and 138–39 on the Davis–Enloe broadcasts; also Weill, *You Are My Sunshine*, 47.

65. Russell, song notes, *Governor Jimmie Davis: Nobody's Darlin' But Mine*, 6.

66. Tunes with colorful titles like "She's a Hum Dum Dinger from Dingersville," "She Left A-Runnin' Like a Sewing Machine," "Organ-Grinder Blues," and "Tom Cat and Pussy Blues" were discussed in chapter 3. Also see Tucker "Louisiana Saturday Night," 145–54. Davis's entire opus is found on the two-box set *Governor Jimmie Davis: Nobody's Darlin' But Mine* and *You Are My Sunshine*; tunes from the bawdy period are also heard on *Jimmie Davis: Rockin' Blues*.

67. On both *Rockin' Blues* and *Governor Jimmie Davis: Nobody's Darlin' But Mine*.

68. Historian Charles Roland reports that American troops overseas were astonished to hear French and Polynesian children singing the song. See Roland, *The Improbable Era*, 165. Sleepy Brown recalled that the February 1940 session occurred in Chicago. According to Tony Russell (e-mail, 4 June 2004), the Decca matrix numbers indicate a New York location, although these numbers are not infallible.

69. See Russell, liner notes to *Governor Jimmie Davis: You Are My Sunshine*.

70. Ibid.

71. Tucker, "Louisiana Saturday Night," 82. Also Hall, "A Historical Study," 100–101.

72. In Fowler and Crawford, *Border Radio*, 6. See also National Association of Broadcasters (NAB), *The ABC of Radio*. Formed in 1923, the NAB's original purpose was to win royalty concessions from ASCAP.

73. See Barnouw, *The Golden Web*, 170.

74. *On the Level* (house organ published by KWKH-KTBS), 1 January 1936; in Hall, "A Historical Study," 102.

75. Hall, "A Historical Study," 102.

76. Ibid., 106.

77. Malone, *Southern Music/American Music*, 73; Wolfe, *A Good-Natured Riot*, 258–59.

78. Tucker, "Louisiana Saturday Night," 83.

79. Biographical information about the Sheltons (a.k.a. the Lone Star Cowboys and the Sunshine Boys) is in Tucker, "Louisiana Saturday Night," 77–81; and Malone, *Country Music U.S.A.*, 169–70.

80. McCloud, *Definitive Country,* s.v. "The Shelton Brothers," by Ivan M. Tribe, 724. With Davis, the Sheltons were also one of the earliest country musicians to sign contracts with Decca, newly formed in 1934.

81. Hall, "A Historical Study," 180. Also see [KWKH house organ] *On the Level* 1/9 (September 1936): 3.

82. *On the Level* 1/12 (December 1936): 1; quoted in Hall, "A Historical Study," 122; also appears in Tucker, "Louisiana Saturday Night," 83–84.

83. Hall, "A Historical Study," 180; and *On the Level* 5/9 (September 1940): 3. Also mentioned in Malone, *Country Music, U.S.A.,* 207; and Tucker, "Louisiana Saturday Night," 398.

84. Ewen, *All the Years,* 311.

85. Malone, *Country Music, U.S.A.,* 193; a version of the story appears in Charles Hirshberg and Robert Sullivan, "The 100 Most Important People in the History of Country," *Life,* 1 September 1994, 24.

86. See Malone, *Country Music, U.S.A.,* 182–83; and Fornatale and Mills, *Radio in the Television Age,* 81.

87. Morley, *"This Is the American Forces Network,"* 61–62.

88. Barnouw, *The Golden Web,* 160. According to Morley, *"This Is the American Forces Network,"* 73, "GI Jill" was the American answer to Tokyo Rose and Axis Sally.

89. Barnouw, *The Golden Web,* 192–93.

90. Frank Page interview; also Anne Wright, "Jenny, She Pass!!! Chiaroscuro: Chief Announcer Frank Page," *Shreveport Times,* 12 December 1948; clipping in Gentry, *The Louisiana Hayride,* vol. 2, 41.

91. Tillman Franks interview.

92. Brown, "Life and Times of T. E. 'Sleepy' Brown," unpublished memoir, 3.

93. Sonny Harville interview.

94. Sonny Harville interview. I Corps is the Roman numeral shorthand for First Corps.

95. Ibid.

96. Sleepy Brown interview.

97. Barnouw, *The Golden Web,* 165.

98. Ibid., 214 and 234.

99. Fornatale and Mills, *Radio in the Television Age,* 13; Barnouw, *The Golden Web,* 217.

100. Barnouw, *The Golden Web,* 109, 163–64. Also see Rothenbuhler and McCourt, "Radio Redefines Itself."

101. Barnouw, *The Golden Web,* 110; also see Sanjek, *American Popular Music,* vol. 3, 192; Kinkle, *The Complete Encyclopedia of Popular Music and Jazz,* vol. 1, xxxvii.

102. On the AFM ban see White, *The American Radio,* 50–54; and Barnouw, *The Golden Web,* 218–19.

103. White, *The American Radio,* 40; Craig, *Fireside Politics,* 105–6; and Barnouw, *The Golden Web,* 221, 168–81.

104. Barnouw, *The Golden Web,* 242. The proximity of television and FM spectrum space is the reason some television stations can be heard on the lower end of the FM band today.

105. Barnouw, *The Golden Web,* 126–27.

106. Fornatale and Mills, *Radio in the Television Age,* 3. Also see Hilmes, *Radio Voices,* 271–72.

107. Fornatale and Mills, *Radio in the Television Age,* 6; Barnouw, *The Golden Web,* 244–45.

108. Barnouw, *The Golden Web*, 285.

109. Fornatale and Mills, *Radio in the Television Age*, 4–5; and Barnouw, *The Golden Web*, 285.

110. See Fornatale and Mills, *Radio in the Television Age*, 23–33.

111. See Tucker, "Louisiana Saturday Night," 397; also "TV Comes in the Side Door," 17, 42.

5. Country Music Crossroads

1. Fornatale and Mills, *Radio in the Television Age*, 5.

2. Malone, *Country Music, U.S.A.*, 199. On the overall impact of World War II on country music, also see Tucker, "Louisiana Saturday Night," 392–95.

3. Tillman Franks interview.

4. See Franks's memoir, *I Was There*, 28–29.

5. Ibid.

6. Homer Bailes interview. Dean Upson's long association with WSM began before he became its artist service manager, when he was member of the Vagabonds, the singing trio that in 1931 became the first professional group to perform on the *Opry*. See Wolfe, "The First Professionals: The Vagabonds," chap. in *A Good-Natured Riot*, 179–89.

7. Tillman Franks interview. The exact recording date is listed in Tribe, "The Bailes Brothers," 13, although Tribe's discography lists Kyle Bailes on bass.

8. Homer Bailes interview.

9. Ibid.

10. Ibid.

11. Logan, *Elvis, Hank, and Me*, 16–17; also see Tucker, "Louisiana Saturday Night," 399 ff.; and Hall, "A Historical Study," 113–14.

12. See Gentry, *The Louisiana Hayride*, vol. 2, 362–63, which includes an undated photocopy of the *Hayride* publicity layout.

13. See "Louisiana Saturday Night," 414–15; and Logan, *Elvis, Hank, and Me*, 19–20.

14. See Tucker, "Louisiana Saturday Night," 415–16; and Malone, *Country Music, U.S.A.*, 207, which excludes the role of the Bailes brothers.

15. In discussing the friendship between the Baileses and Acuff, Homer recalled that Acuff sent them $1,000 to help stay on their feet when they first arrived in Shreveport. For relevant newspaper announcements, see "'Roy Acuff Show' to be in Shreveport," Shreveport *Times*, 14 March 1948; and "Acuff and Grand Ole Opry Troupe to Broadcast from Auditorium," Shreveport *Times*, 17 March 1948; and "KWKH Inaugurates New Radio-Stage Show: 'Louisiana Hayride' to Be Aired Each Saturday Night from Municipal Auditorium," Shreveport *Times*, 28 March 1948, in Gentry, *The Louisiana Hayride*, vol. 1, 9–10, 13.

16. Logan, *Elvis, Hank, and Me*, 117; and Tucker, "Louisiana Saturday Night," 428.

17. Frank Page interview.

18. Ibid. Page was the chief announcer for most of the period he describes. When Logan left in 1957, Page took over as producer.

19. Ibid.

20. Escott, *Hank Williams*, 106.

21. Bob Sullivan interview.

22. Ibid.

23. Sonny Harville interview. Also see Logan, *Elvis, Hank, and Me*, 20–22.

24. Frank Page interview.

25. Logan, *Elvis, Hank, and Me*, 5.

26. Frank Page interview. AM radio's skip effect is discussed in chapter 4.

27. Ibid.

28. See Escott, *Hank Williams*, 106.

29. Escott, *Hank Williams*, 89–92; Malone, *Country Music, U.S.A.*, 241–42; Tucker, "Louisiana Saturday Night," 435–36. Escott notes that the Miller and Griffin recordings were in Williams's personal collection and directly influenced his own version.

30. Tosches, *Country*, 107–9. Mills, a Jewish immigrant from Russia, is best known as manager of Duke Ellington's Orchestra during the period when Ellington moved from the Kentucky Club to the Cotton Club, 1926–32.

31. The exchange between them is detailed in Escott, *Hank Williams*, 86–87.

32. Ibid., 93.

33. Escott discusses the timing of Williams's death in relation to the development of his mythos and legend in the introduction to *Hank Williams*, ix–xii. The idea also appears in the autobiography of the singer's son, Hank Williams Jr., *Living Proof*, 12.

34. Jimmy C. Newman interview.

35. On *The Original Louisiana Hayride Archives*, vol. 1.

36. Hank Jr.'s comments along these lines appear in this book's introduction and in the foreword to Logan, *Elvis, Hank, and Me*, viii. On Williams's significance in pop music, also see Malone, *Country Music, U.S.A.*, 239.

37. Escott, *Hank Williams*, 143. Also see Logan, *Elvis, Hank, and Me*, 65. Logan names some other famous covers of Williams's songs: "Hey, Good Lookin'" was recorded by Frankie Laine, Jo Stafford, Helen O' Connell, and Tennessee Ernie Ford; "I Can't Help It" was recorded by Guy Mitchell; "Honky-Tonkin'" was recorded by Polly Bergen and Teresa Brewer; "Half as Much" was recorded by Rosemary Clooney. In the decades since his death, other songs have been covered extensively, including "Your Cheating Heart," "Jambalaya," "I Saw the Light," "Kaw-Liga," and "I'm So Lonesome I Could Cry." See Morrison, *Go Cat Go!* 33; and Hamm, *Yesterdays*, 411–12.

38. One of Shreveport's most renowned musicians today, drummer Brian Blade, played on the album with Jones. Another currently successful native Shreveport musician is guitarist Kenny Wayne Shepherd.

39. See Tucker, "Louisiana Saturday Night," 439; and Malone, *Country Music, U.S.A.*, 207.

40. Kitty Wells and Johnnie Wright interview. See also "Tennessee Mountain Boys on New KWKH Program: Group Comes to Shreveport Directly from 'Grand Ole Opry,'" Shreveport *Times*, 8 February 1948; in Gentry, *The Louisiana Hayride*, vol. 1, 5. Kyle Bailes recalled offering to promote Johnnie and Jack in Shreveport; see Kyle Bailes, interview by Ronnie Pugh.

41. Tucker, "Louisiana Saturday Night," 409; Malone, *Country Music, U.S.A.*, 215–16. Recorded transcriptions of the group's daily KWKH show, dating from mid-1949 until mid-1950 are preserved on *Johnnie and Jack (the Tennessee Mountain Boys) with Kitty Wells*. The CD covers the range of

their repertoire from fiddle breakdowns to gospel, from narrative ballads to broken-heart love songs and offers a taste of radio comedy by Johnnie Wright's alter-ego, "Cousin Nimrod," and dobro player Ray "Duck" Atkins.

42. Kitty Wells and Johnnie Wright interview.

43. Kitsinger, liner notes to *Johnnie and Jack*. According to Kitsinger, the group left KWKH to promote "Poison Love."

44. Broven, *South to Louisiana*, 56.

45. Kingsbury, ed., *The Encyclopedia of Country Music*, s.v. "J. D. Miller," by Daniel Cooper, 346.

46. Oermann, "Honky-Tonk Angels," 220. Jimmie Davis joined the long list of performers who recorded the Carter family song when he released it in a Western swing arrangement on Decca in 1941. More recently, the late Townes Van Zandt recycled the tune in his "Heavenly Houseboat Blues." These recordings are on *Governor Jimmie Davis: You Are My Sunshine* and *Townes Van Zandt Anthology 1968–79*, respectively. Meade, Spottswood, and Meade, *Country Music Sources*, 193–95 and 604, lists other recordings of "I'm Thinking Tonight" and "Great Speckled Bird." Wolfe further discusses the song in *A Good-Natured Riot*, 256–57.

47. See Tucker, "Louisiana Saturday Night," 409–10; Malone, *Country Music, U.S.A*, 215–26, 223–24; Kitsinger, liner notes to *Johnnie and Jack*; Broven, *South to Louisiana*, 61; McCloud, *Definitive Country*, s.v. "Kitty Wells," by Ivan M. Tribe, 854–55; and the relevant chapter in Bufwack and Oermann, *Finding Her Voice*. Tucker dates the group's appearance in Shreveport as 1947 and the move to the *Opry* in late 1952, after Wells's hit. Other sources, including Shreveport newspapers, confirm the dates given here. The Bear Family catalog also includes a CD box-set titled *Kitty Wells: Queen of Country Music (1949–1958)*.

48. Available on *The Original Louisiana Hayride Archives*, vol. 1.

49. Jimmy C. Newman interview.

50. The acoustic album, now out of print, was the 1963 Decca release *Folk Songs of the Bayou Country* and featured prominent Cajun musicians Rufus Thibodeaux on fiddle and Shorty LeBlanc on accordion.

51. Jimmy C. Newman interview.

52. Al Dexter is most famous for his 1942 composition, "Pistol Packin' Mama," which also became a big hit on pop charts after it was recorded by Bing Crosby and the Andrews Sisters. Born in 1902 not far from Shreveport, Al Dexter played with bands in oil boom towns throughout the area. During the 1920s and early 1930s, he played in a band with mostly African-American musicians in Longview, Texas. On the etymology of the phrase "honky-tonk," see Tosches, *Country*, 24–25. Also McCloud, *Definitive Country*, s.v. "Al Dexter," by Janet Bird, 229.

53. See various advertisements in the Shreveport *Times* (for example, on 13 July 1951, when Sovine was billed as "The Country Boy"). By 14 November 1952, Sovine, now known as "the Ol' Syrup Sopper," is scheduled to play a dance; both in Gentry, *The Louisiana Hayride*, vol. 1, 101 and 142. Also see McCloud, *Definitive Country*, s.v. Red Sovine," by Ivan M. Tribe, 753–54.

54. On *The Original Louisiana Hayride Archives*, vol. 1.

55. "Phantom 309" received a memorable treatment in Tom Waits's recording of it as "Big Joe and Phantom 309" on *Nighthawks at the Diner*.

56. Tillman Franks interview. Also see Tucker, "Louisiana Saturday Night," 447; and Logan, *Elvis, Hank, and Me*, 100–103.

57. Tillman Franks interview.

58. See "'Hayride' Cast Boasts Three of Nation's Top Folk Stars," Shreveport *Times*, 11 June 1953; in Gentry, *The Louisiana Hayride*, vol. 1, 150. Also see McCloud, *Definitive Country*, "Webb Pierce," 636; Tosches, *Country*, 197–98; Tucker, "Louisiana Saturday Night," 447–50; Malone, *Country Music, U.S.A.*, 232–34.

59. See Kingsbury, ed., *The Encyclopedia of Country Music*, s.v. "Webb Pierce," by Ronnie Pugh, 415–17, and s.v. "Bud Isaacs," by Mark Humphrey, 255–56. Also see McCloud, *Definitive Country*, s.v. "Webb Pierce," 637; Malone, *Country Music, U.S.A.*, 233–34; and magazine articles by Costa, "The Country Guitar," and Haggard, "Bud Isaacs."

60. Tucker, "Louisiana Saturday Night," 453–54, discusses Young's stylistic breadth.

61. Kingsbury, ed., *The Encyclopedia of Country Music*, s.v. "Faron Young," by Daniel Cooper, 606–7.

62. On *The Original Louisiana Hayride Archives*, vol. 1.

63. Tucker, "Louisiana Saturday Night," 512–13, lists members of the *Louisiana Hayride* network, a constantly-in-flux group of stations scattered throughout the four-state region of Louisiana, Texas, Arkansas, and Oklahoma. After 1951, many of these member stations broadcast tapes of shows recorded the week before. Also see Logan, *Elvis, Hank, and Me*, 97.

64. A full roster of successful *Hayride* performers from this era would need to include Mac Wiseman, the Wilburn Brothers, T. Texas Tyler, Van Howard, Martha Lawson, Leon Payne, Hank Locklin, Tommy Trent, the Carlisles, Claude Baum, Goldie Hill, Tibby Edwards, Carolyn Bradshaw, Tony Douglas, James O'Gwynn, Jimmy and Johnny, Werly Fairburn, Betty Amos, Jack Ford, Jeannette Hicks, Ray Hendricks, Floyd Cramer, and others.

65. Billy Walker interview, which is the source of most of the information on Walker.

66. Walker mentioned that Willie Nelson used to come watch them perform at the station during their noon time program.

67. See Carr and Munde, *Prairie Nights to Neon Lights*, 145–46. Carr and Munde place Walker's early career into the unique music scene in the West Texas region.

68. Logan, *Elvis, Hank, and Me*, 106. Walker recalls that he got to know Webb Pierce and Faron Young during a recording session in Nashville.

69. Billy Walker interview.

70. Other sources for Walker include: Tucker, "Louisiana Saturday Night," 465; Malone, *Country Music, U.S.A.*, 303; Logan, *Elvis, Hank, and Me*, 148; and McCloud, *Definitive Country*, s.v. "Billy Walker," 840. Walker's longevity is attested to by *Billboard* magazine's naming him as one of the Top 20 most played artists for the years 1950–70.

71. Jerry Kennedy interview.

72. Tucker, "Louisiana Saturday Night," 423.

73. Tucker, "Louisiana Saturday Night," 507. No other sources discuss Bulleit's role on the *Hayride*. I depend here on Tucker's account, based on his 1982 telephone interview.

74. Guralnick, *Last Train to Memphis*, 167; also Kingsbury, ed., *The Encyclopedia of Country Music*, s.v. "Colonel Tom Parker," 403–4.

75. Logan, *Elvis, Hank, and Me*, 153–54; Tucker, "Louisiana Saturday Night," 490.

76. On Parker, see Guralnick, *Last Train to Memphis*, who discusses him throughout his biography of Presley's career until 1958; also Logan, *Elvis, Hank, and Me*, 149.

77. On the Cajun Publishing setup, see Tucker, "Louisiana Saturday Night," 510–11.

78. See Bufwack and Oermann, *Finding Her Voice*, 178–79.

79. Horace Logan, interview by unidentified researcher.

80. Logan, *Elvis, Hank, and Me*, 54.

81. Frank Page interview.

82. Bob Sullivan interview.

83. See discussion of Wills's 1945 guest *Opry* appearance in the introduction.

84. Bob Sullivan, who recorded Whitman's early Imperial hits in the KWKH studio after hours, commented on Whitman's singularity of style: "Nobody has sounded like him since. He was an Irish tenor singing Sigmund Romberg, you know, and it was . . . just one of those things that happened. And I know Hank Williams couldn't stand him . . . Hank used to say, 'He ain't no damn hillbilly.'"

85. Malone, *Country Music, U.S.A.*, 238–39; Tucker, "Louisiana Saturday Night," 445. Also see Gibble, *Mr. Songman*, 50, which describes how the RCA recordings came about because of a meeting between Whitman and Tom Parker. Bob Sullivan suggested that RCA never intended to promote Whitman; rather they signed him to a contract in order to keep him out of the way of their already established yodeler, Elton Britt.

86. Tucker, "Louisiana Saturday Night," 444–45; Logan, *Elvis, Hank, and Me*, 109–12; McCloud, *Definitive Country*, s.v. "Slim Whitman," 865. Sonny Harville interview.

87. Hammerstein's work as lyricist on Rudolf Friml's 1924 operetta predates his more famous musicals like *Showboat* and *Oklahoma*. See Furia, *The Poets of Tin Pan Alley*, 182. A film version starring Nelson Eddy and Jeanette MacDonald had appeared in 1936. Whitman's recording of the operetta's title song became a hit in England within a few years.

88. Horace Logan, interview by unidentified researcher.

89. Tucker, "Louisiana Saturday Night," 446; "Slim Whitman Recording Still Riding High," Shreveport *Times*, 19 October 1952; in Gentry, *The Louisiana Hayride*, vol. 1, 141.

90. *The Original Louisiana Hayride Archives*, vol. 1.

91. Whitman was a member of the *Opry* for a very brief time during the summer of 1955, traveling each weekend from Florida to Nashville to appear on the show; this proved too great a strain, however, and he soon left the *Opry* cast. See Gibble, *Mr. Songman*, 98.

92. McCloud, *Definitive Country*, s.v. "Johnny Horton," by Steve Morewood, 393.

93. See Escott's excellent liner notes to Jim Reeves, *Welcome to My World*.

94. On *The Original Louisiana Hayride Archives*, vol. 1.

95. Tucker, "Louisiana Saturday Night," 458. "The Battle of New Orleans" has since entered the repertoires of diverse musicians; among them is African-American blues guitarist (and fiddler) Gatemouth Brown, who was born in Vinton, Louisiana, in 1914, and performed the tune in the 1970s. See Tosches, *Country*, 179.

96. Malone, *Country Music, U.S.A.*, 284.

97. On Horton, see Tucker, "Louisiana Saturday Night," 455–60; also see

Escott, *Tattooed On Their Tongues*, 115 and, in general, Escott's essay about Billie Jean Horton; also see Logan, *Elvis, Hank, and Me*, 189–206. Franks considered singer Claude King to be Horton's stylistic successor.

98. Evidently, this was the way Reeves himself told the story; Colin Escott contradicts this version, suggesting that Williams was most likely already dead by the time Reeves began performing on the Hayride. See liner notes to *Welcome to My World*, 9.

99. Logan, *Elvis, Hank, and Me*, 118. According to Wolfe, this more microphone-oriented style originated in country music beginning with the Delmore Brothers and other "second generation" country singers. Familiar in pop since Bing Crosby, this carbon microphone-specific style communicated intimacy with listeners. See Wolfe, *A Good-Natured Riot*, 212.

100. Escott, liner notes to *Welcome to My World*, 24–25.

101. On *The Original Louisiana Hayride Archives*, vol. 1.

102. Tucker, "Louisiana Saturday Night," 460–63; Malone, *Country Music, U.S.A.*, 259–61. The phrase "touch of velvet" was used as the title of an album of pop songs that Reeves recorded in the early 1960s.

103. Logan, *Elvis, Hank, and Me*, 121–22.

104. On the Browns, see also Tucker, "Louisiana Saturday Night," 471; Malone, *Country Music, U.S.A.*, 258; McCloud, *Definitive Country*, s.v. "The Browns," by Ivan M. Tribe, 106–7.

105. Logan, *Elvis, Hank, and Me*, 169–71.

106. Jones's early radio announcing experience is reported in Tucker, "Louisiana Saturday Night," 468–69; also see Malone, *Country Music U.S.A.*, 286–88; and McCloud, *Definitive Country*, s.v. "George Jones," 426–29; and Nick Tosches's revealing essay, "George Jones: The Grand Tour." Several biographies exist, including Carlisle, *Ragged But Right*; Allen, *George Jones*; and most recently, Jones with Tom Carter, *I Lived to Tell It All*. (Allen also wrote the Jones entry in Kingsbury, ed., *The Encyclopedia of Country Music*.)

107. On Houston, see Tucker, "Louisiana Saturday Night," 473–75; Malone, *Country Music U.S.A.*, 309, 408; and Logan, *Elvis, Hank, and Me*, 234–35, and 240–41; Logan also reports that Houston appeared in a low-budget Western *King of the Mountain*. Morrison, *Go Cat Go!* 160, describes *Carnival Rock*, produced and directed by Roger Corman (most famous for *Little Shop of Horrors*), as "some of the most wonderful rockabilly film footage in existence."

6. Beyond Country Music

1. Guralnick, *Last Train to Memphis*, 96; two versions of the Rodgers/Hart song from early Sun recording sessions can be heard on Elvis Presley, *Sunrise Elvis Presley*. "Blue Moon" had been a 1949 hit for Billy Eckstine.

2. See Jackson, *Crabgrass Frontier*; Coontz, *The Way We Never Were*, 28–29; and May, *Homeward Bound*, particularly the discussion of "domestic ideology," 10–11.

3. Kincheloe and Kincheloe, "An Interpretative History of Education in Caddo Parish," bound manuscript in Noel Memorial Library Archives and Special Collections, Faculty Collection, Louisiana State University-Shreveport, 77; originally published in the *Shreveport Journal, Sesquicentennial Edition*, 16 September 1985 as "History of Education Marked by Neglect of Black Students." The authors further report that in 1911 almost 2,000 African-American children in Shreveport could not go to school due to a

shortage of classroom space; those who did often attended classrooms with between sixty and eighty students. It would take the Supreme Court fifty-eight years to unanimously enjoin this injustice.

4. These cases are discussed in Bartley, *The New South*, 15, 154–55, 158–60; Goldfield, *Promised Land*, 45, 64–69; Roland, *The Improbable Era*, 33, 35–36; Hurt, ed., *The Rural South since World War II*, 39–40. Another useful source for southern history after World War II is Daniel, *Standing at the Crossroads*.

5. See Guralnick, *Last Train to Memphis*, 132; and the CD *Sunrise Elvis Presley*, which contains five tracks of acetates recorded from *Hayride* broadcasts. These are mainly of historic significance because their audio quality is so poor.

6. Morrison, *Go Cat Go!* 35.

7. Tosches, *Country*, 31–33. Lyricist Max Freedman and composer Jimmy DeKnight wrote "Rock around the Clock." Tosches expounds: "Freedman, born in 1895, had written 'Sioux City Sue,' 'Song of India,' and 'Blue Danube Waltz.' DeKnight was really James Myers of Myers Music." When hired as the movie's technical advisor, Myers "suggested that 'Rock Around the Clock' be used as the film's theme song."

8. See Martin and Segrave, *Anti-Rock*, 59–68; the chapter titled "From the Waist Up," discusses extreme anti-Presley reaction between 1956 and his entry into the military in 1958.

9. See Malone, *Country Music, U.S.A.*, 97.

10. Mailer, "The White Negro," chap. in *Advertisements for Myself*, 340; the essay was originally published in the newspaper *Dissent*, by the City Lights Press in San Francisco.

11. Ibid., 338.

12. Malone, *Country Music, U.S.A.*, 250.

13. Morrison, *Go Cat Go!* 2–3; refers to the 23 June 1956 *Billboard*.

14. Articles from May and September 1955 on Presley's participation in the Jimmie Rodgers Memorial Celebration in Meridian and his *Hayride* contract renewal, respectively, are in Gentry, *The Louisiana Hayride*, vol. 1, 190, 195; articles from March and December 1956 are in vol. 2, 207, 225.

15. Rose Maddox, interview by John Rumble.

16. Malone, *Country Music, U.S.A.*, 217, 248.

17. See Tosches, *Country*, 29–31. Their tune became a 1960 cover hit for the Fendermen.

18. Rose Maddox, interview by John Rumble. Also see Bufwack and Oermann, *Finding Her Voice*, 128–29, regarding the group's "fabulously gaudy, flower-encrusted cowboy/Mexican outfits" that "defined the country music look for a generation to come."

19. Fornatale and Mills, *Radio in the Television Age*, 40.

20. Stan Lewis, "Comments from Stan Lewis," liner notes to *The Jewel/Paula Records Story*.

21. Stan Lewis interview.

22. On the rise of the 45-rpm, see Millard, *America on Record*, 206–8; Barnouw, *The Golden Web*, 245; and Malone, *Country Music, U.S.A.*, on the early 1950s sales of 45s by African-American artists to white audiences.

23. A full account of the events is found in Guralnick, *Last Train to Memphis*, 93–97, and 102–5.

24. Again, the story is recounted in detail in Guralnick, *Last Train to Memphis*, 106–14.

25. Billy Walker interview.

26. Tillman Franks interview.

27. Ibid. Guralnick, *Last Train to Memphis*, also reports the difficulty in gaining a clear picture of how Presley came to the *Hayride*, and concluded "I think the scenario I have presented is as logical a version as one might come up with, but that doesn't mean it happened that way." Franks recalled the Carlsbad gig offering $800; Guralnick, 505, writes that it was $500, still substantial compared to the small fee from the *Hayride*.

28. See Guralnick, *Last Train to Memphis*, 129 (*Opry*) and 213; and Logan, *Elvis, Hank, and Me*, 6, 155–56, and 173.

29. Logan, *Elvis, Hank, and Me*, 179–84. Also see Guralnick, *Last Train to Memphis*, 371; and Pericles Alexander, "The Presley Phenomenon," and "Everybody and His Dog Turns Out for Elvis," Shreveport *Times*, 13 December 1956 and 16 December 1956; Bob Masters, "Mass Hysteria: Frenzied Elvis Fans Rock Youth Center," Shreveport *Times*, 16 December 1956. All three appear in Gentry, *The Louisiana Hayride*, vol. 2, 223, 226–27.

30. This can be heard on Presley, *Good Rockin' Tonight*.

31. Jimmy C. Newman interview.

32. Sonny Harville interview.

33. Hagan, *Grand Ole Opry*, 182; in Carr and Munde, *Prairie Nights to Neon Lights*, 128.

34. Sonny Harville interview. Also Horace Logan, interview by unidentified researcher.

35. See Millar, liner notes to *Bob Luman*. Also Tucker, "Louisiana Saturday Night," 496; Morrison, *Go Cat Go!* 159–61; Logan, *Elvis, Hank, and Me*, 178; McCloud, *Definitive Country*, s.v. "Bob Luman," by James I. Elliott, 489. According to Morrison, Elvis did a series of nine one-nighters in a row in the Kilgore area and Luman attended every one.

36. Dale Hawkins and Fred Carter, Jr., are among other notable musicians who characterize the dynamic; Floyd Cramer is another, with status both as sideman and star soloist and a breadth of stylistic capability.

37. Jerry Kennedy interview.

38. Joe Osborn interview.

39. Quoted in Fishell, "James Burton," 90.

40. D. J. Fontana interview.

41. Ibid.

42. Ibid.

43. Joe Osborn interview.

44. D. J. Fontana interview.

45. Ibid.

46. Jerry Kennedy interview.

47. Joe Osborn interview.

48. D. J. Fontana interview.

49. Ibid.

50. Ibid.

51. See Sanjek "Blue Moon of Kentucky," 38; reprinted in Tichi, ed., *Reading Country Music*, 26.

52. In Morrison, *Go Cat Go!* 67 (italics in source).

53. D. J. Fontana interview.

54. Kienzle, "James Burton," in *Great Guitarists*, 192, 194. Colin Escott includes chapters on Dale Hawkins and James Burton in *Tattooed on Their Tongues*. "Suzie Q" appears, among other places, on the anthology *Rockabilly Essentials*.

55. Stan Lewis interview.

56. Bob Sullivan interview. Both Lewis and Burton recalled the primitive nature of the recording setup, particularly compared to the multitrack technology soon to emerge. See Fishell, "James Burton," 93.

57. Kienzle, "James Burton," 193.

58. Morrison, *Go Cat Go!* 160.

59. Quoted in Fishell, "James Burton," 90.

60. *Carnival Rock* is available on Rhino Video. Luman's group here includes pianist Gene Garr.

61. Fishell, "James Burton," 88, who lists other artists with whom Burton has recorded, among them Nat King Cole, Dean Martin, Frank Sinatra, Johnny Cash, Tom Jones, Henry Mancini, Ray Charles, the Commodores, the Supremes, Johnny Mathis, the Byrds, Waylon Jennings, Kenny Rogers, the Monkees, and so on.

62. Fishell, "James Burton," 90.

63. Joe Osborn interview. Roy Buchanan was another influential session musician who came to Shreveport when Hawkins heard him playing in a club in Oklahoma. Chuck Willis is the Atlanta-born blues singer and songwriter, best known for tunes like "I Feel So Bad" and "It's Too Late."

64. Joe Osborn interview.

65. Ibid.

66. Ibid. Luman's hit was the Felice and Boudleaux Bryant song "Let's Think about Living," which reached No. 7 on pop and No. 9 on country charts in 1960; Luman followed up with the John Loudermilk tune, "The Great Snowman."

67. Ibid. More information on Osborn's career is found in several articles including Gibson, "The Anonymous Kings of Top 40"; Perry, "Joe Osborn," in *Bass Heroes*, 161–63; and Burton, "Legendary Bass Player Has His Day," Shreveport *Times*, 14 June 1991. All are accessible on the website http://www.shreveportcitylights.com/joeosborn/index.htm.

68. Joe Osborn interview.

69. Ibid; also from an advertisement produced by Lakland Basses in Chicago (for the Joe Osborn signature bass).

70. Joe Osborn interview.

71. Ibid.

72. Jerry Kennedy interview.

73. A lively account of Jerry Kennedy's early career is found in Grissim, *Country Music*, 27–34; also useful is Mary Ann Van Osdell, ed., "Music Legends Section" supplement, "Famous Hayriders Return for Glitz and Grits: Kennedy Has Hopes for Industry," Shreveport *Times*, 27 October 1991, 6.

74. Jerry Kennedy interview.

Conclusion

1. See Lhamon, *Deliberate Speed*, for an analysis on the "acceleration" of culture in the postwar era.

2. See Hamm, *Yesterdays*, 407.

Discography

Armstrong, Louis. *Louis "Country Western" Armstrong.* Avco Embassy, 1970.

Cash, Johnny. *Cash.* CD 45520 – 2, American, 1994.

Davis, Jimmie. "Away Out on the Mountain" and "You'd Rather Forget than Forgive." 78 RPM, KWKH Doggone Station, 1928.

———. *Governor Jimmie Davis: Nobody's Darlin' But Mine.* BCD 15943 El, Bear Family, 1998.

———. *Governor Jimmie Davis: You Are My Sunshine.* BCD 16216, Bear Family, 1998.

———. *Rockin' Blues.* LP BFX 15125, reissue on RCA Bear Family Records, 1983.

Dr. John. *Goin' Back to New Orleans.* Cassette 9 26940 – 4, Warner Bros. Records, 1992.

From Where I Stand: The Black Experience in Country Music. CD 9 46428 – 2, Warner Bros. Records, 1998.

Johnnie and Jack (the Tennessee Mountain Boys) with Kitty Wells at KWKH. BCD 15808-AH, Bear Family Records, 1994.

Ledbetter, Huddie "Leadbelly." *The Definitive Leadbelly.* KATCD220, Catfish Records, 2002.

———. *Leadbelly's Last Sessions.* F 2941 – 2942, Folkways, 1953; reissued as SFCD 40068/71. Smithsonian Folkways, 1994.

Newman, Jimmy C. *Folk Songs of the Bayou Country.* DL 74398, Decca, 1963; rereleased in the UK as HAT 3013, Stetson, 1987.

The Original Louisiana Hayride Archives: Classic Country Radio, vol. 1. CDSD 089, TKO Magnum Music Limited/Music Mill Entertainment, 2001.

Pierce, Webb. *The Best of Webb Pierce.* MCA2 – 4087, MCA, 1975.

Presley, Elvis. *Good Rockin' Tonight: The Evolution of Elvis Presley, The Complete Louisiana Hayride Archives.* MME-72628 – 2, Music Mill Entertainment, 2000.

———. *Sunrise Elvis Presley.* CD 67675 – 2, RCA, 1999.

Reeves, Jim. *Welcome to My World.* BCD 15656, Bear Family, 1994.

Rockabilly Essentials. HIPD-40128, Universal Music Special Markets, 1998.

Rodgers, Jimmie. *My Rough and Rowdy Ways: The Legendary Jimmie Rodgers,* RCA ANL1 – 1209 (e), RCA, 1975.

Roots N' Blues: The Retrospective, 1925–1950. CD47912, Sony Music Entertainment, 1982.

Saturday Night—Country Style. "Louisiana Hayride," Armed Forces Radio Transcriptions, Office of Armed Forces Information and Education, Department of Defense, Series End-536, (6 25-min. transcriptions). Copy on file at the Country Music Foundation Library and Media Center, Nashville, Tenn.

Shocked, Michelle. *Arkansas Traveler.* Cassette 314 512 101 – 4, Polygram Records, 1992.

Stars and Guests of the Louisiana Hayride. LP GS 1492, Guest Star Records, n.d. (?).

Thomas, Rufus. *Can't Get Away from This Dog.* CD sxd 038, Stax Records, 1991.

Van Zandt, Townes. *Townes Van Zandt Anthology 1968–79.* CDGR 207 – 2, Charly, 1998.

Waits, Tom. *Nighthawks at the Diner.* 2008 – 2, Elektra/Asylum Records, 1975.

Wells, Kitty. *Kitty Wells: Queen of Country Music (1949–1958).* BCD 15638-DI, Bear Family Records, 1994.

Whitman, Slim. *Vintage Collections.* CD 7243 – 8 – 54321 – 2 – 5, Capitol Vintage, Nashville, 1996.

Films, Videos, and Documentaries

Carnival Rock. Rhino Video, RNVD 2405, 1989; 1958.

Cradle of the Stars. Produced by Rick Smith and Carole Adornetto Leslie. Louisiana Public Broadcasting, 1984.

He Touched Me: The Gospel Music of Elvis Presley. Alexandria, Ind.: Coming Home Music, 1999.

I'll Make Me a World. Produced by Blackside. PBS Video, 1999.

Times Ain't Like They Used To Be: Early American Rural & Popular Music (From Rare Original Film Masters [1928–35]). Shenachie Entertainment, Yazoo 512, 2000.

Bibliography

Interviews

Bailes brothers (Homer, Kyle, Walter, Johnnie). By Ronnie Pugh, 9 June 1983, Nashville, Tenn. Oral History Collection of the Country Music Foundation, Nashville.

Bailes, Homer. By the author, 10 August 1998, Homer, La. Tape recording in author's files.

———. By Rachel Stone, 28 July 1996, *Sunday Stage* radio program, KWKH, Shreveport. Tape recording in author's files.

Bailes, Kyle. By Ronnie Pugh, 19 July 1980, Nashville, Tenn. Transcript in files of the Country Music Foundation.

Bartlett, Ray. By the author, 27 June 2003, Shreveport. Tape recording in author's files.

Brown, Jim Ed, Maxine Brown, and Bonnie Brown. By the author, 27 June 2003, Municipal Auditorium, Shreveport. Tape recording in author's files.

Brown, Thomas E. "Sleepy." By the author, 31 July 1998, Shreveport. Tape recording in author's files.

———. By Rachel Stone, 19 February 1995, *Sunday Stage* radio program, KWKH, Shreveport. Tape recording in author's files.

Douglas, Tony. By the author, 27 June 2003, Municipal Auditorium, Shreveport. Tape recording in author's files.

Fautheree, Jimmy Lee. By the author, 27 June 2003, Municipal Auditorium, Shreveport. Tape recording in author's files.

———. and "Country" Johnny Mathis. By Rachel Stone, 2 July 1995, *Sunday Stage* radio program, KWKH, Shreveport. Tape recording in author's files.

Ferguson, Ernest. By the author, 26 June 2003, Municipal Auditorium, Shreveport. Tape recording in author's files.

Fontana, D. J. By the author, 6 March 1996, Nashville, Tenn. Tape recording in author's files.

Franks, Tillman. By the author, 3 August 1998, Shreveport. Tape recording in author's files.

———. By Ronnie Pugh, 13 August 1980, Nashville, Tenn. Tape recording, Oral History Collection of the Country Music Foundation, Nashville.

———. By Rachel Stone, 9 October 1994, Shreveport. Tape recording.

———. and Murrell Stansell. By Rachel Stone, 17 September 1995, *Hank Williams Special* radio show, KWKH studio, Shreveport. Tape recording in author's files.

Gunning, Stedman. By the author, Summer 1996, Belcher, La. Tape recording lost.

———. By Hubert Humphreys, 18 and 25 June 1981. Transcription. Noel Memorial Library Archives and Special Collections, Louisiana State University in Shreveport.

Harkness, Felton "Preacher," and Jack Green. By Rachel Stone, 16 October 1994, *Sunday Stage* radio program, KWKH, Shreveport. Tape recording in author's files.

Harkness, Jean and Ruth. By the author, 4 August 1998, Vivian, La. Tape recording in author's files.

Harville, Sonny. By the author, 24 July 1999, Shreveport. Tape recording in author's files.

Hendricks, Ray. By the author, 26 June 2003, Municipal Auditorium, Shreveport. Tape recording in author's files.

Kennedy, Jerry. By the author, 7 March 1996, Nashville, Tenn. Tape recording in author's files.

Lewis, Stan. By the author, 18 January 1998, Shreveport. Tape recording in author's files.

Logan, Horace. By Earl Porter, 13 October 1976, Monroe, La. Transcription. Noel Memorial Library Archives and Special Collections, Louisiana State University in Shreveport.

———. By unidentified researcher in Monroe, Louisiana, for 1984 documentary *Cradle of the Stars*. Video in files of the Country Music Foundation, Nashville, Tenn.

Maddox, Rose. By John Rumble, 25 January 1985, Nashville, Tenn. Transcript in files of the Country Music Foundation.

Newman, Jimmy C. By the author, 27 July 1999, by telephone from his home, Christiana, Tenn. Tape recording in author's files.

O'Gwynn, James. By the author, 26 June 2003, Municipal Auditorium, Shreveport. Tape recording in author's files.

Osborn, Joe. By the author, 2 August 1999, Shreveport. Tape recording in author's files.

———. By Rachel Stone, 29 January 1995, *Sunday Stage* radio program, KWKH, Shreveport. Tape recording in author's files.

Page, Frank. By the author, 23 February 1996, Shreveport. Tape recording in author's files.

Sneed, Roy. By the author, 26 June 2003, Municipal Auditorium, Shreveport. Tape recording in author's files.

Sovine, Red. By Douglas B. Green, 3 September 1975, Nashville, Tenn. Oral History Collection of the Country Music Foundation, Nashville.

Stilley, Mallie Ann. By the author, 26 June 2003, Municipal Auditorium, Shreveport. Tape recording in author's files.

Stuckey, Ann. By the author, 27 June 2003, Municipal Auditorium, Shreveport. Tape recording in author's files.

Sullivan, Bob. By the author, 26 June 2003, Bossier City, La. Tape recording in author's files.

Walker, Billy. By the author, 22 July 1999, by telephone to his office, Nashville, Tenn. Tape recording in author's files.

Warwick, Margaret Lewis. By the author, 19 September 2002, by telephone to her home, Shreveport, La. Tape recording in author's files.

Wells, Kitty, and Johnnie Wright. By the author, June 27, 2003, Shreveport. Tape recording in author's files.

Unpublished Sources

Brown, Thomas E. "Sleepy." "Life and Times of T. E. 'Sleepy' Brown." Unpublished memoir, TD [photocopy], 1992, written for the Country Music Foundation, Nashville, Tenn. Photocopy in author's files.

Doran, Shen. Press release. "Immediate News Release of Four Legendary Bailes Bros., Kyle, Johnnie, Walter and Homer." Bailes Brothers File, Country Music Foundation, Nashville, Tenn., n.d. (appears to be from late 1980s).

Edington, John, to his sister, Mrs. Johnson, Shreveport, May 1838. Transcript in files of Noel Memorial Library Archives and Special Collections, Louisiana State University in Shreveport.

Franks, Tillman. "Tillman Franks." TD [one page], n.d. Photocopy in author's files.

Gentry, Robert. *The Louisiana Hayride, "The Glory Years—1948–60: A Compilation of Newspaper Articles, Pictures, and Advertisements.* Vol. 1, *1948–55,* and Vol. 2, *1956–60.* Many, La., 1998.

Harville, Sonny. "The Life and Times of Harland H. 'Sonny' Harville." Unpublished memoir, TD [photocopy], November 21, 1998, written for the declaration of "Sonny Harville Day" in Shreveport and Bossier cities, photocopy in author's files.

Leonard, Albert Harris. Unfinished memoirs, 1917, 1–66. Copy in files of Noel Memorial Library Archives and Special Collections, Louisiana State University in Shreveport.

Logan, Horace. Letter to "All Members of the Hayride from 1948 to 1958." 15 September 1986, Library Archives, Country Music Foundation, Nashville, Tenn.

———. Précis of planned book entitled *The Louisiana Hayride: The Music and the Memoirs.* Library Archives, Country Music Foundation, Nashville, Tenn.

"The Louisiana Hayride." Scrapbook published by KWKH, ca. 1959. Archives, Country Music Foundation, Nashville.

Louisiana Hayride Anniversary Souvenir Album. Published by KWKH Radio Station, 1954 or 1955.

The Louisiana Hayride show logs. 23 June 1956, 14 July 1956, 4 August 1956,11 January 1958. Library Archives, Country Music Foundation, Nashville.

Oermann, Robert K. *Jerry Kennedy Chronicle.* Stouffer Hotel, Nashville. Library Archives, Country Music Foundation, Nashville, Tenn.

Stuck, Goodloe. *Heritage Scrapbook of Northwest Louisiana.* Reprinted from the Shreveport *Times* [daily newspaper]. Shreveport, 1986.

Taylor, Mary, Steamboat Livingston, to Maria H. Marshall, c/o Bennett and Cane, Shreveport, 11 March 1837. Transcript in files of Noel Memorial Library Archives and Special Collections, Louisiana State University in Shreveport.

Woodruff, Lt. E. A. "Removal of the Red River Raft." *Annual Report of the*

Chief of Engineers, 1873–74. Noel Memorial Library Archives, Louisiana State University in Shreveport.

Liner Notes

Bowman, Rob. Liner notes to Rufus Thomas, *Can't Get Away from This Dog.* CD sxd 038, Stax Records, 1991.

Cohn, Lawrence. Liner notes to Leadbelly, *Library of Congress Recordings,* ELK 301/302, Elektra, 1966.

Escott, Colin. Liner notes to Jim Reeves, *Welcome to My World.* BCD 15656, Bear Family, 1994.

Ivey, Bill. "Border Crossing: A Different Way of Listening to American Music." Liner notes to *From Where I Stand: The Black Experience in Country Music.* CD 9 46428–2, Warner Bros. Records, 1998, 8–11.

Kitsinger, Otto. Liner notes to *Johnnie and Jack (The Tennessee Mountain Boys) with Kitty Wells.* BCD 15 808-AH, Bear Family Records, 1994.

———. Liner notes to Webb Pierce, *The Wondering Boy, 1951–1958.* 15522 BCD-DH, Bear Family, 1990.

Lewis, Stan, Diana Haig, and Wayne Jancik. Liner notes to *The Jewel/Paula Records Story: The Blues, Rhythm & Blues and Soul Recordings.* CD 9 42014–2, Capricorn, 1993.

Malone, Bill C. "Charley Pride, American." Liner notes to *From Where I Stand: The Black Experience in Country Music.* CD 9 46428–2, Warner Bros. Records, 1998, 16–17.

Millar, Bill. Liner notes to *Bob Luman: The Rocker.* BFX 15037, Bear Family, 1979.

Mountjoy, Monte. Liner notes to Bob Wills, *The Tiffany Transcriptions,* vol. 6, *Sally Goodin.* Bob Wills and His Texas Playboys, Kaleidoscope Records, C-27, 1987.

Perry, Claudia. "Digging Country's Roots." Liner notes to *From Where I Stand: The Black Experience in Country Music.* CD 9 46428–2, Warner Bros. Records, 1998, 12–15.

Rinzler, Ralph, and Richard Rinzler. Liner notes to *Old-Time Music at Clarence Ashley's,* vol. 1. FA 2355, Folkways, 1961.

Rumble, John. "The Artists and the Songs." Liner notes to *From Where I Stand: The Black Experience in Country Music.* CD 9 46428–2, Warner Bros. Records, 1998, 24–57.

Russell, Tony. Liner notes to Jimmie Davis, *Governor Jimmie Davis: Nobody's Darlin' But Mine.* BCD 15943 El, Bear Family, 1998.

Tricker, Phillip J. Liner notes to *Webb Pierce: The Unavailable Sides, 1950, 1951.* KKCD16, Krazy Kat, 1994.

Wynn, Ron. "This is My Country." Liner notes to *From Where I Stand: The Black Experience in Country Music.* CD 9 46428–2, Warner Bros. Records, 1998, 18–23.

Books and Articles

Albarran, Alan B., and Gregory G. Pitts. *The Radio Broadcasting Industry.* Boston: Allyn & Bacon, 2001.

Allen, Bob. *George Jones: The Saga of an American Singer.* Garden City, N.Y.: Doubleday, 1984.

Allen, William Frances, Charles Pickard Ware, and Lucy McKim Garrison. *Slave Songs of the United States.* New York: A. Simpson, 1867; reprint, New York: Dover, 1995.

Andrews, Raymond. *The Last Radio Baby*. Atlanta: Peachtree Publishers, 1990.

Angoff, Charles. *H. L. Mencken: A Portrait from Memory*. New York: T. Yoseloff, 1956.

Archer, Gleason L. *History of Radio to 1926*. New York: American Historical Society, 1938.

Bargainneer, Earl F. "Tin Pan Alley and Dixie: The South in Popular Song." *Mississippi Quarterly* 30 (Fall 1977): 527–65.

Barnouw, Erik. *A Tower in Babel: A History of Broadcasting in the United States*. Vol. 1, *To 1933*. New York: Oxford University Press, 1966.

———. *The Golden Web: A History of Broadcasting in the United States*. Vol. 2, *1933–1953*. New York: Oxford University Press, 1968.

Bartley, Numan V. *The New South: 1945–1980*. Vol. 11 of *A History of the South*, ed. Wendell Holmes Stephenson and E. Merton Coulter. Baton Rouge: Louisiana State University Press and The Littlefield Fund for Southern History of the University of Texas, 1995.

Becker, Jane S. *Selling Tradition: Appalachia and the Construction of an American Folk, 1930–1940*. Chapel Hill: University of North Carolina Press, 1998.

Benjamin, Louise M. *Freedom of the Air and the Public Interest: First Amendment Rights in Broadcasting to 1935*. Edwardsville: Southern Illinois University Press, 2001.

Biographical and Historical Memoirs of Northwest Louisiana. Nashville: Southern Publishing, 1890; reproduced by the North Louisiana Historical Association, Chicago: Walsworth Publishing, 1976.

Bourgeois, Anna Stong. *Blueswomen: Profiles of 37 Performers, with an Anthology of Lyrics, 1920–1945*. Jefferson, N.C.: McFarland, 1996.

Bradford, Perry. *Born with the Blues*. New York: Oak Publications, 1965.

Brindze, Ruth. *Not to Be Broadcast—The Truth about Radio*. New York: Vanguard Press, 1936.

Broven, John. *South to Louisiana: The Music of the Cajun Bayous*. Gretna, La.: Pelican Publishing, 1987.

Brown, Charles T. *Music U.S.A.: America's Country & Western Tradition*. Englewood Cliffs, N.J.: Prentice-Hall, 1986.

Bufwack, Mary A., and Robert K. Oermann. *Finding Her Voice: The Saga of Women in Country Music*. New York: Crown, 1993 (a later edition appeared through Country Music Foundation and Vanderbilt University Press in 2003; page references are to the original).

Burton, Willie. *On the Black Side of Shreveport: A History/Exploring the Political, Social, Educational, Religious, and Economic Development of Black Citizens in Northwest Louisiana*. n.p., 1983.

Calhoun, Milburn, ed., and Jeanne Frois, asst. ed. *Louisiana Almanac*, 1997–98 edition. Gretna, La.: Pelican Publishing, 1997.

Carlisle, Dolly. *Ragged But Right: The Life and Times of George Jones*. Chicago: Contemporary Books, 1984.

Carney, George O., ed. *The Sound of People and Places: Readings in the Geography of American Folk and Popular Music*. Lanham, Md.: University Press of America, 1987.

Carr, Joe, and Alan Munde. *Prairie Nights to Neon Lights: The Story of Country Music in West Texas*. Lubbock: Texas Tech University Press, 1995.

Carruth, Viola. *Caddo 1000: A History of the Shreveport Area from the Time of the Caddo Indians to the 1970s*. Shreveport: Shreveport Magazine, 1970.

Carson, Gerald. *The Roguish World of Doctor Brinkley*. New York: Holt, Rinehart & Winston, 1960.

Cash, W. J. *The Mind of the South*. New York: Knopf, 1941.

Charters, Samuel. *The Country Blues*. New York: Rinehart, 1959.

Cherry, Hugh. "The Medicine Show: Apprenticeship Avenue for Country Music." *Country Sounds* (September 1986): 41–50.

Cockrell, Dale. *Demons of Disorder: Early Blackface Minstrels and Their World*. Cambridge: Cambridge University Press, 1997.

Cohen, John. "The Folk Music Interchange: Negro and White." *Sing Out!* 14/6 (January 1964): 42–49.

Cohen, Norm. "Early Pioneers." In *Stars of Country Music*, ed. Malone and McCulloh, 3–39.

———, and Anne Cohen. "Folk and Hillbilly Music: Further Thoughts on Their Relation." *JEMF Quarterly* 13/46 (Summer 1977): 50–57.

Coltman, Bob. "Across the Chasm: How the Depression Changed Country Music." *Old Time Music* 23 (Winter 1976–77): 6–12.

Coontz, Stephanie. *The Way We Never Were: American Families and the Nostalgia Trap*. New York: Basic Books, 1992.

Costa, Jean-Charles. "The Country Guitar: The Mysterious Pedal Steel." *Country Music* 1/1 (June 1973): 42–44.

Couch, W. T., ed. *Culture in the South*. Chapel Hill: University of North Carolina Press, 1934; reprint, Westport, Conn: Negro Universities Press and Greenwood Press, 1970.

Craig, Douglas B. *Fireside Politics: Radio and Political Culture in the United States, 1920–1940*. Baltimore, Md.: Johns Hopkins University Press, 2000.

Crawford, Richard. "Notes on Jazz Standards by Black Authors and Composers, 1899–1942." In *New Perspectives on Black Music*, ed. Wright and Floyd, 245–87.

Daniel, Pete. *Standing at the Crossroads: Southern Life since 1900*. New York: Hill and Wang, 1986.

Davis, Edwin Adams. *The Rivers and Bayous of Louisiana*. Baton Rouge: Louisiana Education Research Association, 1968.

Dellar, Fred, and Ray Thompson. *The Illustrated Encyclopedia of Country Music*. New York: Harmony Books, 1977.

Dimick, Howard T. "Visits of Josiah Gregg to Louisiana, 1841–1847." *Louisiana Historical Quarterly* 29/1 (January 1946): 5–13.

Donovan, Frank. *River Boats of America*. New York: Crowell, 1966.

DuBois, W. E. Burghardt. *The Souls of Black Folk*. Chicago: A. C. McClurg & Co., 1903.

Eaken, Sue. "The Plantation System in the Lower Red River Valley." In *Proceedings of the 1985 Red River Symposium*, 21–26.

Escott, Colin. *Hank Williams: The Biography*. Toronto: Little, Brown, 1994, 1995.

———. *Tattooed on Their Tongues: A Journey through the Backrooms of American Music*. New York: Schirmer Books, 1996.

———. with Martin Hawkins. *Good Rockin' Tonight: Sun Records and the Birth of Rock 'n' Roll*. New York: St. Martin's, 1991.

Ewen, David. *All the Years of American Popular Music*. Englewood Cliffs, N.J.: Prentice-Hall, 1977.

Fishell, Steve. "James Burton: First Call for the Royalty of Rockabilly." *Guitar Player* 18 (June 1984): 88–101.

Fitzpatrick, Vincent. *H. L. Mencken*. New York: Continuum, 1989.

Fletcher, Tom. *The Tom Fletcher Story: 100 Years of the Negro in Show Business*. New York: Burdge, 1954.

Flores, Dan L. "Exploration, Ethnography and Archaeology in the Red River Valley." In *Proceedings of the 1988 Red River Symposium*, 5–16.

———. ed. *Jefferson and Southwestern Exploration: The Freeman and Custis Accounts of the Red River Expedition of 1806*. With an introduction and epilogue by Flores. Norman: University of Oklahoma Press, 1984.

———. "A Very Different Story—Exploring the Southwest from Monticello with the Freeman and Custis Expedition of 1806." *Montana: The Magazine of Western History* 50 (Spring 2000): 2–17.

Fornatale, Peter, and Joshua E. Mills. *Radio in the Television Age*. Woodstock, N.Y.: Overlook Press, 1980.

Fowler, Gene, and Bill Crawford. *Border Radio*. Austin: Texas Monthly Press, 1987.

Franks, Tillman. *I Was There When It Happened*. Many, La.: Sweet Dreams Publishers, 2000.

Fricker, Jonathan. "'Cradle of the Stars' and Art Deco Masterpiece: The Shreveport Municipal Auditorium." *Preservation in Print* 24/9 (November 1997): 8–9, 11.

Furia, Philip. *The Poets of Tin Pan Alley: A History of America's Great Lyricists*. New York: Oxford University Press, 1990.

Garvin, Richard M., and Edmond G. Addeo. *The Midnight Special: The Legend of Leadbelly*. New York: Bernard Geis Associates, 1971.

Gelatt, Roland. *The Fabulous Phonograph, 1877–1977*. 2d rev. ed. New York: Macmillan, 1977.

Gentry, Linnell. *A History and Encyclopedia of Country, Western, and Gospel Music*. Nashville: McQuiddy Press, 1961.

George, Nelson. *The Death of Rhythm and Blues*. New York: Pantheon Books, 1988.

Gibble, Kenneth L. *Mr. Songman: The Slim Whitman Story*. Elgin, Ill.: Brethren Press, 1982.

Gibson, Janice Cole. "Doc Tommy Scott's Last Real Medicine Show." *Good Ole Days* (May 1989): 26–29.

Gibson, John. "The Anonymous Kings of Top 40." *Entertainment World*, 16 January 1970.

Gillett, Charlie. *The Sound of the City: The Rise of Rock and Roll*. New York: Outerbridge & Dienstfrey, 1970.

Gilley, B. H., ed. *North Louisiana*. Vol. 1, *To 1865, Essays on the Region and Its History*. Ruston, La.: McGinty Trust Fund Publications, 1984.

Goldfield, David R. *Promised Land: The South since 1945*. Arlington Heights, Ill.: Harlan Davidson, 1987.

Gormanous, Greg, and Chester Williams. "Lead Belly Memorialized." *Lead Belly Letter* 3/1, 2 (Winter/Spring 1993): 1–5.

Graham, Don, James W. Lee, and William T. Pilkington, ed. *The Texas Literary Tradition: Fiction, Folklore History*. Austin: University of Texas at Austin and The Texas State Historical Association, 1983.

Graham, Philip. *Showboats: The History of an American Institution*. Austin: University of Texas Press, 1951.

Green, Archie. "Hillbilly Music, Source and Symbol." *Journal of American Folklore* 78 (July–September 1965): 204–28.

Green, Douglas B. *Country Roots: The Origins of Country Music*. New York: Hawthorne Books, 1976.

―――. "Jimmy C. Newman and His Cajun Country Roots." *Country Music* 7/7 (May 1979): 20, 66, 68.

Grimstead, David. *Melodrama Unveiled: American Theater and Culture, 1800–1850*. Chicago: University of Chicago Press, 1968.

Grissim, John. *Country Music: White Man's Blues*. New York: Paperback Library, 1970.

Grundy, Pamela. "'We Always Tried to Be Good People': Respectability, Crazy Water Crystals, and Hillbilly Music on the Air, 1933–1935." *Journal of American History* 81 (March 1995): 1591–1620.

Guralnick, Peter. *Last Train to Memphis: The Rise of Elvis Presley*. Boston: Little, Brown, 1994.

Gute, Fredricka Doll, and Katherine Brash Jeter. *Historical Profile: Shreveport, 1850*. Shreveport: National Society of the Colonial Dames of America in the State of Louisiana, 1982.

Haden, Walter Darrell. "Vernon Dalhart: Commercial Country Music's First International Star (Concluded)." *John Edwards Memorial Foundation Quarterly* 11/39 (Autumn 1975): 129–36.

Hagan, Chet. *Grand Ole Opry: The Complete Story of a Great American Institution and Its Stars*. New York: Henry Holt, 1989.

Haggard, John. "Bud Isaacs." *Guitar Player* 10/11 (November 1976): 31, 78, 80.

Hall, Lillian Jones. "A Historical Study of Programming Techniques and Practices of Radio Station KWKH, Shreveport, LA, 1922–1950." Ph.D. diss., Louisiana State University, 1959.

―――. "William E. Antony and Paul L. Carriger: Shreveport Broadcast Pioneers." In *Proceedings of the 1985 Red River Symposium*, 27–34.

Hamm, Charles. *Yesterdays: Popular Song in America*. New York: Norton, 1979.

Handy, W. C. *Father of the Blues*. New York: Macmillan, 1941; reprint, Toronto: Collier-Macmillan Canada, Collier Books, 1970.

Hardin, J. Fair. "An Outline of Shreveport and Caddo Parish History." *Louisiana Historical Quarterly* 18 (October 1935): 759–871.

Harkins, Anthony. *Hillbilly: A Cultural History of an American Icon*. New York: Oxford University Press, 2004.

Harlow, Alvin F. *Old Wires and New Waves: The History of the Telegraph, Telephone, and Wireless*. New York: Appleton-Century, 1936; reprint, History of Broadcasting: Radio to Television Series. New York: Arno Press and The New York Times, 1971.

Henrici, Holice H. *Shreveport: The Beginnings*. Lafayette, La.: University of Southwestern Louisiana, Center for Louisiana Studies, 1985.

Herron, Edward A. *Miracle of the Air Waves: A History of Radio*. New York: Julian Messner, 1969.

Hilliard, Robert L., ed. *Radio Broadcasting: An Introduction to the Sound Medium*. 3d ed. New York: Longman, 1985.

Hilmes, Michele. *Radio Voices: American Broadcasting, 1922–1952*. Minneapolis: University of Minnesota Press, 1997.

―――. and Jason Loviglio, eds. *Radio Reader: Essays in the Cultural History of Radio*. New York: Routledge, 2002.

Hirshberg, Charles and Robert Sullivan. "The 100 Most Important People in the History of Country." *Life* (1 September 1994): 24.

Hitchcock, H. Wiley, and Stanley Sadie, eds. *The New Grove Dictionary of American Music*. Vol. 4, *R through Z*. New York: Macmillan, 1986.

Humphreys, Hubert. "The 'Great Raft' of the Red River." In *North Louisiana*, vol. 1, ed. Gilley, 73–91.

Huber, Leonard V. *Advertisements of Lower Mississippi River Steamboats, 1812–1900*. With a Foreword by Frederick Way, Jr. West Barrington, R.I.: Steamship Historical Society of America, 1959.

———. "The Nineteenth Century Struggle to Control Red River." In *Proceedings of the 1985 Red River Symposium*, 76–82.

Hunter, Louis C. *Steamboats on the Western Rivers*. Cambridge, Mass.: Harvard University Press, 1949.

Hurst, Jack. *Nashville's Grand Ole Opry*, with Introduction by Roy Acuff. New York: Harry Abrams, 1975.

Hurt, R. Douglas, ed. *The Rural South since World War II*. Baton Rouge: Louisiana State University Press, 1998.

Ivey, Bill. "The Bottom Line: Business Practices That Shaped Country Music," in *Country: The Music and the Musicians*, ed. Kingsbury, 280–311.

Ivey, William. "Commercialization and Tradition in the Nashville Sound." In *Folk Music and Modern Sound*, ed. William Ferris and Mary L. Hart. Jackson: University of Mississippi Press, 1982, 129–38.

———. "Recordings and the Audience for the Regional and Ethnic Musics of the United States." In *The Phonograph and Our Musical Life: Proceedings of a Centennial Conference, 7–10 December 1977*. ISAM monographs, ed. H. Wiley Hitchcock, no. 14. New York: Institute for Studies in American Music, 1980, 7–13.

Jackson, George Pullen, ed. *Spiritual Folk-Songs of Early America*. New York: Augustin, 1937; reprint, Gloucester, Mass.: Peter Smith, 1975.

Jackson, Kenneth. *Crabgrass Frontier: The Suburbanization of the United States*. New York: Oxford University Press, 1985.

Johnson, E. R. Fenimore. *His Master's Voice Was Eldridge R. Johnson*. Milford, Del.: State Media, 1974.

Johnson, Guy B. "Negro Folk-Songs." In *Culture in the South*, ed. Couch, 547–70.

Jones, George, with Tom Carter. *I Lived to Tell It All*. New York: Villard, 1996.

Jones, LeRoi. *Blues People: Negro Music in White America*. New York: William Morrow and Company, 1963.

Jones, Max, and John Chilton. *Louis: The Louis Armstrong Story*. Boston: Little, Brown, 1971.

Kahn, Ed. "International Relations, Dr. Brinkley, and Hillbilly Music." *John Edwards Memorial Foundation Quarterly* 95/30 (Summer 1973): 47–55.

Kahn, Frank J., ed. *Documents of American Broadcasting*. 2d ed. New York: Appleton-Century-Crofts, 1973.

Keith, Michael C. *Sounds in the Dark: All-Night Radio in American Life*. Ames: Iowa State University Press, 2001.

Kienzle, Rich. *Great Guitarists: The Most Influential Players in Blues, Country Music, Jazz and Rock*. New York: Facts on File, 1985.

Killeen, Sean. "Testimony: Fred Ramsey (1915–1995)." *Lead Belly Letter* 5/1, 2 (Winter/Spring 1995): 9.

———. "Irene, Goodnight." *Lead Belly Letter* 1/1 (Autumn 1990): 3.

Kincheloe, Joe L., and Theresa Scott Kincheloe. "An Interpretative History of Education in Caddo Parish." Bound manuscript in Noel Memorial Library Archives and Special Collections, Faculty Collection, Louisiana State University-Shreveport. Originally published in the *Shreveport Journal, Sesquicentennial Edition*, 16 September 1985 as "History of Education Marked by Neglect of Black Students."

Kingsbury, Paul, ed. *Country: The Music and the Musicians from the Be-*

ginnings to the '90s. 2d ed., Country Music Foundation. New York: Abbeville Publishing Group, 1994.

———. ed. *The Country Reader: 25 Years of the Journal of Country Music.* Nashville: Country Music Foundation and Vanderbilt University Press, 1996.

———. ed. *The Encyclopedia of Country Music.* New York: Oxford University Press, 1998.

Kinkle, Roger D. *The Complete Encyclopedia of Popular Music and Jazz, 1900–1950.* Vol. 1, *Music Year by Year, 1900–1950.* New Rochelle, N.Y.: Arlington House, 1974.

———. *The Complete Encyclopedia of Popular Music and Jazz, 1900–1950.* Vol. 2, *Biographies, A through K.* New Rochelle, N.Y.: Arlington House, 1974.

———. *The Complete Encyclopedia of Popular Music and Jazz, 1900–1950.* Vol. 3, *Biographies, L through Z.* New Rochelle, N.Y.: Arlington House, 1974.

———. *The Complete Encyclopedia of Popular Music and Jazz, 1900–1950.* Vol. 4, *Indexes and Appendices.* New Rochelle, N.Y.: Arlington House, 1974.

Lakoff, George. *Women, Fire, and Dangerous Things: What Categories Reveal about the Mind.* Chicago: University of Chicago Press, 1987.

Lane, Carl D. *American Paddle Steamboats.* New York: Coward-McCann, 1943.

Lee, R. Alton. *The Bizarre Careers of John R. Brinkley.* Lexington: University of Kentucky Press, 2002.

Levine, Lawrence W. *The Unpredictable Past: Explorations in American Cultural History.* New York: Oxford University Press, 1993.

LeVine, Michael. *Johnny Horton: Your Singing Fisherman.* New York: Vantage, 1982.

Lewis, George H. "Duellin' Values: Tension, Conflict and Contradiction in Country Music." *Journal of Popular Culture* 24 (Spring 1991): 103–17.

Lewis, H. M. "The Music in the N. S. Allen Collection: A Look at Musical Life in the Ark-La-Tex during the Last Half of the Nineteenth Century." Paper presented at the Southern chapter of the American Musicological Society meeting at Loyola University, New Orleans, Louisiana, 9 March 1984. Library Archives, LSUS.

Lhamon, W. T., Jr. *Deliberate Speed: The Origins of a Cultural Style in the American 1950s.* Washington, D.C.: Smithsonian Institution Press, 1990.

Lindsey, Henry Carlton. "The History of the Theatre in Shreveport, Louisiana to 1900." M.A. thesis, Louisiana State University, 1951.

———. *Nineteenth Century Theatre in Shreveport, Louisiana (1836–1900).* Brownwood, Tex.: Moore Printing, 1985.

Lipscomb, Mance. *I Say Me for a Parable: The Oral Autobiography of Mance Lipscomb, Texas Bluesman,* compiled and edited by Glen Alyn. New York: Norton, 1993.

Logan, Horace, with Bill Sloan. *Elvis, Hank, and Me: Making Musical History on the Louisiana Hayride.* New York: St. Martin's, 1998.

Lomax, Alan. *The Land Where Blues Began.* New York: Pantheon Books, 1993.

Lott, Eric. *Love and Theft: Blackface Minstrelsy and the American Working Class.* New York: Oxford University Press, 1993.

"Louisiana Hayride." *Shreveport Magazine* (May 1951): 32–33.

Lowery, Walter M. "The Red." In *The Rivers and Bayous of Louisiana,* ed. Davis, 52–73.

MacDonald, J. Fred. *Don't Touch That Dial: Radio Programming in American Life, 1920–1960.* Chicago: Nelson-Hall, 1979; reprint, 1980.

Mailer, Norman. *Advertisements for Myself.* New York: G. P. Putnam's Sons, 1959.

Malone, Bill C., "Country Music, the South, and Americanism." *Mississippi Folklore Register* 10/1 (Spring 1976): 54–66.

———. *Country Music, U.S.A.: A Fifty-Year History.* 2d rev. ed. Austin: University of Texas Press, 1985.

———. *Don't Get above Your Raisin': Country Music and the Southern Working Class.* Urbana: University of Illinois Press, 2002.

———. *Southern Music/American Music.* Lexington: University Press of Kentucky, 1979.

———. and Judith McCulloh, eds. *Stars of Country Music: Uncle Dave Macon to Johnny Rodriguez.* Urbana: University of Illinois Press, 1975.

Marcus, Greil. *Mystery Train: Images of America in Rock 'n' Roll Music.* New York: E. P. Dutton & Co., 1976.

Martin, Linda, and Kerry Segrave. *Anti-Rock: The Opposition to Rock 'n' Roll.* Hamden, Conn.: Archon Books, 1988.

May, Elaine Tyler. *Homeward Bound: American Families in the Cold War Era.* New York: Basic Books, 1988.

May, Margery Land. *Hello World Henderson: The Man behind the Mike.* Shreveport: Press of the Lindsay Co., 1930.

McCall, Edith. *Conquering the Rivers: Henry Miller Shreve and the Navigation of America's Inland Waterways.* Baton Rouge: Louisiana State University Press, 1984.

McChesney, Robert W. *Telecommunications, Mass Media, and Democracy: The Battle for the Control of U.S. Broadcasting, 1928–1935.* New York: Oxford University Press, 1993.

McCloud, Barry. *Definitive Country: The Ultimate Encyclopedia of Country Music and Its Performers.* New York: Berkley Publishing Group, 1995.

McCorkle, Louis W., ed. *1849 Texas Journal of Samuel Wear McCorkle.* Hannibal, Mo.: L.W. McCorkle, 1976.

McLaurin, Ann M., ed. *Glimpses of Shreveport.* Natchitoches, La.: Northwestern State University Press, 1985.

McLuhan, Marshall. *Understanding Media.* New York: McGraw-Hill, 1964.

Meade, Guthrie T., Jr., with Dick Spottswood, and Douglas S. Meade. *Country Music Sources: A Biblio-Discography of Commercially Recorded Traditional Music.* Chapel Hill: Southern Folklife Collection, University of North Carolina at Chapel Hill Libraries in Association with the John Edwards Memorial Forum, 2002.

Mencken, H. L. "The Sahara of the Bozart." In *Prejudices*, Second Series. New York: Knopf, 1920, 136–39.

Mickel, Jere C. *Footlights on the Prairie: The Story of the Repertory Tent Players in the Midwest.* St. Cloud, Minn.: North Star Press, 1974.

Millard, Andre. *America on Record: A History of Recorded Sound.* Cambridge: Cambridge University Press, 1995.

Moore, Jerrold Northrop. *A Matter of Records.* New York: Taplinger Publishing, 1976.

Morley, Patrick. *"This Is the American Forces Network": The Anglo-American Battle of the Air Waves in World War II.* Westport, Conn.: Praeger, 2001.

Morrison, Craig. *Go Cat Go! Rockabilly Music and Its Makers.* Urbana: University of Illinois Press, 1996.

Murray, Albert. *Stomping the Blues*. New York: McGraw-Hill, 1976.

Nachman, Gerald. *Raised on Radio*. New York: Pantheon Books, 1998.

Nathan, Hans. *Dan Emmett and the Rise of Early Negro Minstrelsy*. Norman: University of Oklahoma Press, 1962; reprint, 1977.

National Association of Broadcasters. *The ABC of Radio*. Washington, D.C.: National Association of Broadcasters, 1938.

——. *Standards of Practice for Radio Broadcasters of the United States of America*. Washington, D.C.: National Association of Broadcasters, 1937, 1955.

Nelson, Donald Lee. "The Allen Brothers." *John Edwards Memorial Foundation Quarterly* 7/24 (Winter 1971): 147–50.

Noe, Denise. "Parallel Worlds: The Surprising Similarities (and Differences) of Country-and-Western and Rap." *Humanist* (July/August 1995): 20–22.

Oermann, Robert K. "Honky-Tonk Angels: Kitty Wells and Patsy Cline." In *Country: The Music and the Musicians*, ed. Kingsbury, 212–33.

——. *The Listener's Guide to Country Music*. New York: Facts on File, 1983.

O'Pry, Maude Hearn. *Chronicles of Shreveport*. Shreveport: By the author, 1928; reprint, Shreveport: Martha Serio, 1978.

Owens, William. "Regionalism and Universality." In *The Texas Literary Tradition*, ed. Graham, Lee, and Pilkington, 69–79.

Palmer, Robert. *Deep Blues: A Musical and Cultural History from the Mississippi Delta to Chicago's South Side to the World*. New York: Penguin Books, 1981.

Paper, Lewis J. *Empire: William S. Paley and the Making of CBS*. New York: St. Martin's, 1987.

Penn, Rachel T. "While the Band Discoursed Sweet Airs: A Study of Popular Music in the Social Life of Shreveport, Louisiana, 1875–1900, with Reference to the N. S. Allen Music Collection." M.A. thesis, Louisiana State University, 1987.

Perry, David. "Joe Osborn." In *Bass Heroes: Styles, Stories and Secrets of 30 Great Bass Players, From the Pages of Guitar Player Magazine*, ed. Tom Mulhern. San Francisco: GPI Books, 1993, 161–63 (reprint of article that originally appeared in April 1974).

Peterson, Richard A. "The Dialectic of Hard-Core and Soft-Shell Country Music." *South Atlantic Quarterly* 94/1 (Winter 1995): 273–300.

——. and Paul Di Maggio. "The Early Opry: Its Hillbilly Image in Fact and Fancy." *Journal of Country Music* 4 (Summer 1973): 39–51.

Poindexter, Ray. *Golden Throats and Silver Tongues: The Radio Announcers*. Conway, Ark.: River Road Press, 1978.

Porter, Earl. "The 'Louisiana Hayride': Its Beginning and Early Operation." Unpublished paper, Library Archives, Louisiana State University-Shreveport, 1976.

Porterfield, Nolan. "1,000 Unknown Facts about Country Music." *North American Review* 271 (March 1986): 12–17.

——. *Jimmie Rodgers: The Life and Times of America's Blue Yodeler*. Urbana: University of Illinois Press, 1979.

Price, Robert Bates. "A History of Music in Northwestern Louisiana until 1900." Ph.D. diss., Catholic University of America, 1977.

Proceedings of the 1985 Red River Symposium, by the Red River Regional Studies Center. Shreveport: Louisiana State University-Shreveport, 1986.

Proceedings of the 1988 Red River Symposium, by the Red River Regional Studies Center. Shreveport: Louisiana State University-Shreveport, 1989.

Pusateri, C. Joseph. *Enterprise in Radio: WWL and the Business of Broadcasting in America*. Washington, D.C.: University Press of America, 1980.

———. "Stormy Career of a Radio Maverick, W. K. Henderson of KWKH," *Louisiana Studies* 15 (Winter 1976): 389–407.

Ramsey, Frederic, Jr. *Been Here and Gone*. New Brunswick, N.J.: Rutgers University Press, 1960.

Regatz, Lowell. *The New U.S.: America in the Post-War Era*. Columbus: Ohio State University Press, 1960.

Richards, David, and Tara Zachary. *Guide to Oral History Collections in Louisiana*. Baton Rouge: T. Harry Williams Center for Oral History, Louisiana State University Press, 1996.

Riis, Thomas L. *Just Before Jazz*. Washington, D.C.: Smithsonian, 1989.

Roland, Charles P. *The Improbable Era: The South since World War II*. Lexington: University Press of Kentucky, 1975.

Rosen, Philip T. *The Modern Stentors: Radio Broadcasters and the Federal Government, 1920–1934*. Westport, Conn.: Greenwood Press, 1980.

Rothenbuhler, Eric W., and Tom McCourt. "Radio Redefines Itself, 1947–1962." In *Radio Reader*, ed. Hilmes and Loviglio, 367–387.

Russell, Ross. "Illuminating the Leadbelly Legend." *Downbeat* 37 (1970): 12.

Russell, Tony. *Blacks, Whites, and Blues*. New York: Stein and Day, 1970.

Salassi, Elisabeth. "Hello, World." *Shreveport Magazine* (April 1950): 17.

Sanjek, David. "Blue Moon of Kentucky Rising over the Mystery Train." *South Atlantic Quarterly* 94/1 (Winter 1995): 29–55.

Sanjek, Russell. *American Popular Music and Its Business: The First Four Hundred Years*. Vol. 2, *From 1790 to 1909*. New York: Oxford University Press, 1988.

———. *American Popular Music and Its Business: The First Four Hundred Years*. Vol. 3, *From 1900 to 1984*. New York: Oxford University Press, 1988.

Schafer, William J., with assistance from Richard B. Allen. *Brass Bands and New Orleans Jazz*. Baton Rouge: Louisiana State University Press, 1977.

Schlappi, Elizabeth. *Roy Acuff, the Smoky Mountain Boy*. Gretna, La.: Pelican Publishing, 1978.

Selvin, Joel. *Ricky Nelson: Idol for a Generation*. Chicago: Contemporary Books, 1990.

Shapiro, Henry D. *Appalachia on Our Mind: The Southern Mountains and Mountaineers in the American Consciousness, 1890–1920*. Chapel Hill: University of North Carolina Press, 1978.

Sharp, Cecil. *English Folk Songs from the Southern Appalachians*. London: Oxford University Press, 1917; reprint edition, 1960.

Shestack, Melvin, ed. *The Country Music Encyclopedia*. New York: Crowell, 1974.

Shreveport Centennial: The Story of Shreveport. n.p., 1935; reprint under the auspices of Holiday in Dixie, 1967.

Shreveport Men and Women Builders. Shreveport: J. E. Howe, 1931.

Silvester, Peter J. *A Left Hand Like God: A History of Boogie-Woogie Piano*. New York: Da Capo Press, 1988.

Sindler, Allan P. *Huey Long's Louisiana: State Politics, 1920–1952*. Baltimore: Johns Hopkins University Press, 1956.

Smith, Jessie Carney, and Carrell Peterson Horton, eds. *Historical Statistics of Black America: Media to Vital Statistics*. Detroit: Gale Research, 1995.

Smulyan, Susan. *Selling Radio: The Commercialization of American Broadcasting, 1920–1934*. Washington: Smithsonian Institution Press, 1994.

"Snake Oil Still Rolling Up Sales for Scott's Old Time Medicine Show." *Amusement Business* (25 August 1984): 51.

Southern, Eileen, ed. *Readings in Black American Music*. New York: Norton, 1971.

Stambler, Irwin, and Grelun Landon, eds. *Encyclopedia of Folk, Country, and Western Music*. 2d rev. ed. New York: St. Martin's, 1984.

Stenerson, Douglas C. *Critical Essays on H. L. Mencken*. Boston: G. K. Hall & Co., 1987.

Stribling, Cynthia. "Black and White Elements in the Music of Jimmie Rodgers." *Mississippi Folklore Register* 10/1 (Spring 1976): 41–53.

Stuck, Goodloe. *Annie McCune, Shreveport Madam*. Baton Rouge: Moran, 1981.

Summers, Harrison B., ed. *A Thirty-Year History of Programs Carried on National Radio Networks in the United States, 1925–1956*. Report compiled by the Department of Speech, University of Ohio, 1958; reprint, New York: Arno Press, 1971.

Tarpley, Fred. "Cultural Clash in the Vocabulary of the Red River Valley." In *Proceedings of the 1988 Red River Symposium*, 47–64.

Taylor, Joe Gray. *Louisiana Reconstructed, 1863–1877*. Baton Rouge: Louisiana State University Press, 1974.

Thomas, Rebecca. "There's a Whole Lot O' Color in the 'White Man's' Blues: Country Music's Selective Memory and the Challenge of Identity." *Midwest Quarterly* 38 (Autumn 1996): 73–89.

Thompson, Alan. "Transportation: Riverboats and Railroads of Shreveport." In *Glimpses of Shreveport*, ed. McLaurin, 53–61.

Thomson, Bailey, ed. *Historic Shreveport: A Guide*. Shreveport: Shreveport, Publishing Corporation, 1980.

———. and Patricia Meador. *Shreveport: A Photographic Remembrance: 1873–1949*. Baton Rouge: Louisiana State University Press, 1987.

Tichi, Cecelia. *High Lonesome: The American Culture of Country Music*. Chapel Hill: University of North Carolina, 1994.

———. ed., *Reading Country Music: Steel Guitars, Opry Stars, and Honky-Tonk Bars*. Durham, N.C.: Duke University Press, 1998.

Tindall, George B. *The Emergence of the New South: 1913–1945*. Vol. 10 of *A History of the South.*, ed. Wendell Holmes Stephenson and E. Merton Coulter. Baton Rouge: Louisiana State University Press and The Littlefield Fund for Southern History of the University of Texas, 1967.

Toll, Robert C. *Blacking Up: The Minstrel Show in Nineteenth-Century America*. New York: Oxford University Press, 1974.

Tonachel, Ruth. "Country Music before World War Two; A Selected Bibliography." Washington, D.C.: Library of Congress, Archive of Folk Song, 1978.

Tosches, Nick. *Country: The Biggest Music in America*. New York: Stein and Day, 1977.

———. "George Jones: The Grand Tour." In *The Country Reader*, ed. Kingsbury, 139–73.

———. *Unsung Heroes of Rock 'n' Roll*. Rev. ed. New York: Harmony Books, 1984, 1991.

Townsend, Charles R. *San Antonio Rose: The Life and Music of Bob Wills*. Urbana: University of Illinois Press, 1976.

Tribe, Ivan M. "The Bailes Brothers." *Bluegrass Unlimited* 9/8 (February 1975): 8–13.

Tucker, Steven R. "The Louisiana Hayride, 1948–1954." *North Louisiana Historical Association Journal* 8/5 (Fall 1977): 187–201.

————. "Louisiana Saturday Night: A History of Louisiana Country Music." Ph.D. diss., Tulane University, 1995.

"TV Comes in the Side Door." *Shreveport Magazine* (March 1953): 17, 42.

Tyson, Carl Newton. *The Red River in Southwestern History.* Norman: University of Oklahoma Press, 1981.

Walker, Jesse. *Rebels on the Air: An Alternative History of Radio in America.* New York: New York University Press, 2001.

Weill, Gus. *You Are My Sunshine: The Jimmie Davis Story.* Waco, Tex.: Word, 1977.

Wells, Carol, ed. *War, Reconstruction and Redemption on Red River: The Memoirs of Dosia Williams Moore.* Ruston, La.: McGinty Publications, 1990.

Wheeler, Mary. *Steamboatin' Days: Folk Songs of the River Packet Era.* Baton Rouge: Louisiana State University Press, 1944.

Whisnant, David E. *All That Is Native and Fine: The Politics of Culture in an American Region.* Chapel Hill: University of North Carolina Press, 1983.

White, Llewellyn. *The American Radio: A Report on the Broadcasting Industry in the United States from the Commission on Freedom of the Press.* Chicago: University of Chicago Press, 1947; reprint, New York: Arno Press, 1971.

Wilgus, D. K. *Anglo-American Folksong Scholarship since 1898.* New Brunswick, N.J.: Rutgers University Press, 1959.

Willey, Malcolm M., and Stuart A. Rice. *Communication Agencies and Social Life.* New York: McGraw-Hill, 1933.

Williams, Hank, Jr. *Living Proof: An Autobiography.* New York: G. P. Putnam's Sons, 1979.

Williams, Roger M. "Hank Williams." In *Stars of Country Music,* ed. Malone and McCulloh, 237–54.

————. *Sing a Sad Song: The Life of Hank Williams.* 2d ed. Urbana: University of Illinois Press, 1980.

Winters, John D. "Secession and Civil War in North Louisiana." In *North Louisiana,* vol. 1, ed. Gilley, 159–93.

Wolfe, Charles K. "Black String Bands: A Few Notes on a Lost Cause." *Old-Time Herald* 1/1 (Fall 1987): 15–18.

————. *A Good-Natured Riot: The Birth of the Grand Ole Opry.* Nashville: Country Music Foundation Press and Vanderbilt University Press, 1999.

————. *The Grand Ole Opry: The Early Years, 1925–35.* London: Old Time Music, 1975.

————. *Kentucky Country: Folk and Country Music of Kentucky.* Lexington: University of Kentucky, 1982.

————. "Satchmo Country: Louis Armstrong and Country Music." Paper delivered at the International Country Music Conference, Nashville, May 2003.

————. "The Triumph of the Hills: Country Radio, 1920–50." In *Country: The Music and the Musicians,* ed. Kingsbury, 40–77.

————. "Uncle Dave Macon." In *Stars of Country Music,* ed. Malone and McCulloh, 40–63.

————. "The White Man's Blues, 1922–40." "Profiles in Black & White." *Journal of Country Music* 14/2 (1991): 38–44.

———. and Kip Lornell. *The Life and Legend of Leadbelly.* New York: HarperCollins, 1992.

Woods, Jeff. "Color Me Country: Tales from the Frontlines." "Profiles in Black & White." *Journal of Country Music* 14/2 (1991): 9–12.

Wright, Josephine, with Samuel A. Floyd, Jr. *New Perspectives on Black Music: Essays in Honor of Eileen Southern.* Warren, Mich.: Harmonie Park Press, 1992.

Wright, Richardson. *Hawkers and Walkers in Early America: Strolling Peddlers, Preachers, Lawyers, Doctors, Players and Others, From the Beginning to the Civil War.* Boston: J. B. Lippincott, 1927; paperback reprint, New York: Frederick Ungar, 1965.

Zwigoff, Terry. "Black Country String Bands." *American Visions* 6 (February 1991): 50–52.

Index

Dale, Jeff, 92
Dalhart, Vernon, 51–53, 64,
    164n.44, 166n.27
Dances, nineteenth-century
    Shreveport, 29–31, 159n.23
Davis, Jimmie, 7, 77, 80, 95, 134,
    146
  black-white musical interchange
    and, 25, 38–39, 52–53, 71,
    73, 152
  KWKH and, 8, 59, 71–74, 84,
    150–51
  movies of, 78
  political career of, 63, 73–74, 108
  recordings of, 52, 71–74, 126,
    154n.14, 168n.62
Davis, Norman C., 17–18
"Davis' Salty Dog," 73
"Daydreamin'," 100
Day, Jimmy, 103
"The Death of Floyd Collins," 51
Decca Records, 73
"Deep Elem Blues," 77
Delmore Brothers, 8, 175n.99
Denny, Jim, 129
Department of Commerce, United
    States. See FCC
Dexter, Al, 101, 172n.52
Dey, Roy, 144–45
"Diggy Liggy Lo," 100
Dill, Clarence, 67–68
Disc Jockey, 66, 81–84, 128,
    154–55n.22
"Division point," Shreveport's role
    as, 20, 23
Domino, Fats, 97, 124, 134, 141, 152
"Draggin' Main Street," 115
Driftwood, Jimmie, 113
Dr. John (Mac Rebennack), 25,
    27–28
Duhon, Bessyl, 100–101
Duncan Sisters, 72

"Easy Mr. Tom," 36
Edison, Thomas, 42, 64
Edwards, Larkin, 16
"The Eighth of January," 113
Enloe, James, 72
Everly Brothers, 152
"Everytime I'm Kissing You," 114
Ewing, John D., 9, 65, 75, 82, 90

"Fannin Street," 33
Fannin Street area, 3, 31–34, 39,
    135–36, 159n.34
FCC (Federal Communications
    Commission), 58, 65, 68–70,
    76, 81–84
Ferguson, Ernest, 88
"Five Feet High and Rising," 116
"Flowers On the Wall," 145
Foley, Red, 106
Fontana, D. J., 10, 122, 132–39, 152
  musicians backed in the studio
    by, 138
Fort Towson, 15
Foster, Stephen, 47
Four Deacons, 8
Fox, Curly, 77
Franks, Tillman
  artists managed by, 103, 113–14,
    118, 129, 175n.97
  booking agent, teacher, song-
    writing roles of, 108–9, 138,
    144–45
  Louisiana Hayride stage and live
    radio experiences of, 7, 85–88,
    107, 111
  World War II experiences of,
    79–80, 85
FRC (Federal Radio Commission).
    See Federal Communications
    Commission
Freeman and Custis Expedition,
    the, 14
Friml, Rudolf, 112, 174n.87
Frizzell, Lefty, 104, 116, 133–34, 137
From Where I Stand, 36–38,
    161n.53
"Funny How Time Slips Away," 106

Gibbs, Les, 87
"Giddy-Up Go," 102
Glinn, Lillian, 36
Godfrey, Arthur, 63
"Goin' Steady," 104
"Good Rockin' Tonight," 124
Grand Ole Opry, 45, 76, 91, 106,
    112–13
  Hayride performers coming
    from, 88, 96, 98, 129–30
  Hayride performers leaving for,
    94, 102–4, 107–8, 116, 133

Okeh Records, 43–44, 162n.11
"Old Hen Cackled and the
    Rooster's Going to Crow," 43
"The Old Lamplighter," 116
"Ole Slewfoot," 114
"One & Only," 117
Osborn, Joe
    post–World War II Shreveport as
        musical training ground of,
        10, 133–35, 137, 152
    professional music career of,
        122, 141–44

Page, Frank
    experiences in radio during
        World War II of, 78–79
    "Gatemouth" broadcasts of, 128,
        151, 155n.22
    the *Louisiana Hayride* and,
        90–94, 110, 112, 154n.12
Page, Patti, 134, 138
Paradise Entertainers, 75
Parker, "Colonel" Tom, 108, 113, 130
Parker, Junior, 124
Patterson, W. G., 65
Payne, Leon, 8
Payne, Rufus, 95
Peer, Ralph, 43–44, 48–49, 52,
    118, 152
Perkins, Carl, 124, 133, 152, 161n.53
Perry, Owen, 86
"Phantom 309," 102, 172n.55
Phillips, Sam, 116, 128, 151
Phonograph records, 10–11,
    41–55, 127–28, 146
    commercial categories of, 25,
        36–42, 53–54
    early history of, 42–45, 54, 82,
        162n.7, 165n.50
    impact of, 46
    sales of "hillbilly," 49
    Shreveport and, 41–42
    See also Musical interaction
Piedmont migration, 14, 17–18
Pierce, Webb, 118, 133, 137–38, 145
    the *Louisiana Hayride* and, 8–9,
        103–4, 106–7, 110
    other KWKH broadcasts of, 63,
        86–87
"Pistol Pete's Midnight Special," 38
"Poison Love," 98

Population, nineteenth-century
    Shreveport, 17–19, 156n.20
    African-American, 17–18
    Euro-American, 18–19
"Precious Lord, Take My Hand,"
    40, 161n.61
Presley, Elvis, 108, 110, 165n.2,
    176n.27
    the *Louisiana Hayride* and, 117,
        121–33, 137–40, 145–46,
        149–52
    post–World War II cultural shift
        and, 6, 9–12, 58, 161n.53
"The Prisoner's Song," 51, 64
Pruitt, Felton, 87–88

"Race Music." *See* Commercial
    music categories; Rhythm-
    and-blues
Racism, 26, 39–40, 46–47, 49–50,
    122–25, 149–52
Radio, 10, 57–84
    advertising on, 61–62, 67, 70,
        80–81, 83–84
    formal regulation of, 57–61,
        68–71, 75–76, 82–84,
        167nn.56 and 58
    immediacy of, 7, 62–63, 87, 97,
        133–34
    local, 11, 54–55, 58–69, 81
    phonograph records and, 7, 11,
        54–55, 64–65, 73, 77, 81–82
    and post–World War II culture,
        57–58
    rise of network, 61–63, 75, 80–84
    technology of, 66, 82–83, 94,
        165n.6, 166n.37, 169n.104
    See also Musical interaction;
    KWKH
Radio Digest, 66, 69
Railroads, 6, 21–23, 28, 31, 40
Rains, Hoot, 112
Raney, Wayne, 8
"Red Eyed and Rowdy," 115
"Red Hot," 140
Red-light district. *See* Fannin
    Street area
"Red Nightgown Blues," 38
Red River, 6, 13, 149
    accessibility to New Orleans via,
        15–16